THE CULINARY INSTITUTE OF AMERICA®

IDENTIFICATION · FABRICATION · UTILIZATION

MEAT

Thomas Schneller

KITCHEN PRO SERIES

MEAT

Thomas Schneller

IDENTIFICATION · FABRICATION · UTILIZATION

DELMAR
CENGAGE Learning

Australia • Brazil • Japan • Korea • Mexico • Singapore • Spain • United Kingdom • United States

KITCHEN
PRO
SERIES

KitchenPro Series: Guide to Meat Identification, Fabrication and Utilization
Thomas Schneller

Vice President, Career and Professional Editorial: Dave Garza

Director of Learning Solutions: Sandy Clark

Acquisitions Editor: James Gish

Managing Editor: Larry Main

Product Manager: Nicole Calisi

Editorial Assistant: Sarah Timm

Vice President, Career and Professional Marketing: Jennifer McAvey

Marketing Director: Wendy Mapstone

Marketing Manager: Kristin McNary

Marketing Coordinator: Scott Chrysler

Production Director: Wendy Troeger

Production Manager: Stacy Masucci

Senior Content Project Manager: Glenn Castle

Art Director: Bethany Casey

Technology Project Manager: Christopher Catalina

Production Technology Analyst: Thomas Stover

The Culinary Institute of America

President: Dr. Tim Ryan '77

Vice-President, Continuing Education: Mark Erickson '77

Director of Publishing: Nathalie Fischer

Editorial Project Manager: Lisa Lahey '00

Editorial Assistant: Shelly Malgee '08

Photography:

Keith Ferris, Photographer

Ben Fink, Photographer

For product information and technology assistance, contact us at
Professional & Career Group Customer Support, 1-800-648-7450

For permission to use material from this text or product, submit all requests online at **cengage.com/permissions**
Further permissions questions can be emailed to
permissionrequest@cengage.com

Library of Congress Control Number: 2008931926

ISBN-13: 978-1-4283-1994-3

ISBN-10: 1-4283-1994-8

Delmar
5 Maxwell Drive
Clifton Park, NY 12065-2919
USA

Cengage Learning products are represented in Canada by Nelson Education, Ltd.

For your lifelong learning solutions, visit **delmar.cengage.com**

Visit our corporate website at **www.cengage.com**

Notice to the Reader

Publisher does not warrant or guarantee any of the products described herein or perform any independent analysis in connection with any of the product information contained herein. Publisher does not assume, and expressly disclaims, any obligation to obtain and include information other than that provided to it by the manufacturer. The reader is expressly warned to consider and adopt all safety precautions that might be indicated by the activities described herein and to avoid all potential hazards. By following the instructions contained herein, the reader willingly assumes all risks in connection with such instructions. The publisher makes no representations or warranties of any kind, including but not limited to, the warranties of fitness for particular purpose or merchantability, nor are any such representations implied with respect to the material set forth herein, and the publisher takes no responsibility with respect to such material. The publisher shall not be liable for any special, consequential, or exemplary damages resulting, in whole or part, from the readers' use of, or reliance upon, this material.

Printed in the United States of America
1 2 3 4 5 CRK 10 09

Contents

Recipe Contents

Beef Recipes

Veal Recipes

Pork Recipes

Lamb Recipes

Offal Recipes

ABOUT THE CIA

THE WORLD'S PREMIER CULINARY COLLEGE

The Culinary Institute of America (CIA) is the recognized leader in culinary education for undergraduate students, foodservice and hospitality professionals, and food enthusiasts. The college awards bachelor's and associate degrees, as well as certificates and continuing education units, and is accredited by the prestigious Middle States Commission on Higher Education.

Founded in 1946 in downtown New Haven, CT to provide culinary training for World War II veterans, the college moved to its present location in Hyde Park, NY in 1972. In 1995, the CIA added a branch campus in the heart of California's Napa Valley—The Culinary Institute of America at Greystone. The CIA continued to grow, and in 2008, established a second branch campus, this time in San Antonio, TX. That same year, the CIA at Astor Center opened in New York City.

From its humble beginnings more than 60 years ago with just 50 students, the CIA today enrolls more than 2,700 students in its degree programs, approximately 3,000 in its programs for foodservice and hospitality industry professionals, and more than 4,500 in its courses for food enthusiasts.

LEADING THE WAY

Throughout its history, The Culinary Institute of America has played a pivotal role in shaping the future of foodservice and hospitality. This is due in large part to the caliber of people who make up the CIA community—its faculty, staff, students, and alumni—and their passion for the culinary arts and dedication to the advancement of the profession.

Headed by the visionary leadership of President Tim Ryan '77, the CIA education team has at its core the largest concentration of American Culinary Federation-Certified Master Chefs (including Dr. Ryan) of any college. The Culinary Institute of America faculty, more than 130 members strong, brings a vast breadth and depth of foodservice industry experience and insight to the CIA kitchens, classrooms, and research facilities. They've worked in some of the world's finest establishments, earned industry awards and professional certifications, and emerged victorious from countless international culinary competitions. And they continue to make their mark on the industry, through the students they teach, books they author, and leadership initiatives they champion.

The influence of the CIA in the food world can also be attributed to the efforts and achievements of our more than 37,000 successful alumni. Our graduates are leaders in virtually every segment of the industry and bring the professionalism and commitment to excellence they learned at the CIA to bear in everything they do.

UNPARALLELED EDUCATION

DEGREE PROGRAMS

The CIA's bachelor's and associate degree programs in culinary arts and baking and pastry arts feature more than 1,300 hours of hands-on learning in the college's kitchens, bakeshops, and student-staffed restaurants along with an 18-week externship at one of more than 1,200 top restaurant, hotel, and resort locations around the world. The bachelor's degree programs also include a broad range of liberal arts and business management courses to prepare students for future leadership positions.

CERTIFICATE PROGRAMS

The college's certificate programs in culinary arts and baking and pastry arts are designed both for students interested in an entry-level position in the food world and those already working in the foodservice industry who want to advance their careers. A third offering, the Accelerated Culinary Arts Certificate Program (ACAP), provides graduates of baccalaureate programs in hospitality management, food science, nutrition, and closely related fields with a solid foundation in the culinary arts and the career advancement opportunities that go along with it.

PROFESSIONAL DEVELOPMENT PROGRAMS AND INDUSTRY SERVICES

The CIA offers food and wine professionals a variety of programs to help them keep their skills sharp and stay abreast of industry trends. Courses in cooking, baking, pastry, wine, and management are complemented by stimulating conferences and seminars, online culinary R&D courses, and multimedia training materials. Industry professionals can also deepen their knowledge and earn valuable ProChef® and professional wine certification credentials at several levels of proficiency.

The college's Industry Solutions Group, headed by a seasoned team of Certified Master Chefs, offers foodservice businesses a rich menu of custom programs and consulting services in areas such as R&D, flavor exploration, menu development, and health and wellness.

FOOD ENTHUSIAST PROGRAMS

Food enthusiasts can get a taste of the CIA educational experience during the college's popular Boot Camp intensives in Hyde Park, as well as demonstration and hands-on courses at the new CIA at Astor Center in New York City. At the Greystone campus, CIA Sophisticated Palate™ programs feature hands-on instruction and exclusive, behind-the-scenes excursions to Napa Valley growers and purveyors.

CIA LOCATIONS

MAIN CAMPUS—HYDE PARK, NY

Bachelor's and associate degree programs, professional development programs, food enthusiast programs

The CIA's main campus in New York's scenic Hudson River Valley offers everything an aspiring or professional culinarian could want. Students benefit from truly exceptional facilities that include 41 professionally equipped kitchens and bakeshops; five award-winning, student-staffed restaurants; culinary demonstration theaters; a dedicated wine lecture hall; a center for the study of Italian food and wine; a nutrition center; a 79,000-volume library; and a storeroom filled to brimming with the finest ingredients, including many sourced from the bounty of the Hudson Valley.

THE CIA AT GREYSTONE—ST. HELENA, CA

Associate degree program, professional development programs, certificate programs, food enthusiast programs

Rich with legendary vineyards and renowned restaurants, California's Napa Valley offers students a truly inspiring culinary learning environment. At the center of it all is the CIA at Greystone—a campus like no other, with dedicated centers for flavor development, professional wine studies, and menu research and development; a 15,000-square-foot teaching kitchen space; demonstration theaters; and the Ivy Award-winning Wine Spectator Greystone Restaurant.

THE CIA, SAN ANTONIO—SAN ANTONIO, TX

Certificate program, professional development programs

A new education and research initiative for the college, the CIA, San Antonio is located on the site of the former Pearl Brewery and features a newly renovated 5,500-square-foot facility equipped with a state-of-the-art teaching kitchen. Plans for the 22-acre site include transforming it into an urban village complete with restaurants, shops, art galleries, an open-air *mercado,* an events facility, and expanded CIA facilities, including a demonstration theater and skills kitchen.

THE CIA AT ASTOR CENTER—NEW YORK, NY

Professional development programs, food enthusiast programs

The CIA's newest educational venue is located in the NoHo section of New York's Greenwich Village, convenient for foodservice professionals and foodies alike. At The Culinary Institute of America at Astor Center, students enjoy courses on some of the most popular and important topics in food and wine today, in brand-new facilities that include a 36-seat, state-of-the-art demonstration theater; a professional teaching kitchen for 16 students; and a multipurpose event space.

AUTHOR BIOGRAPHY

Chef Schneller started working with meat at the age of 14 in his family's business. He is by all definitions of the word a "butcher". With over 30 years of meat cutting experience and having taught the meat class at the acclaimed Culinary Institute of America for the past 10 years, Chef Schneller brings a high level of understanding to this book. Chef Schneller also owned and operated his own restaurant and catering business for 11 years, has worked in a variety of restaurant positions including back and front of the house and has an understanding of foodservice. As Chef Schneller continues teaching at the Institute, he is focused on acquiring more knowledge in all aspects of the meat industry.

ACKNOWLEDGEMENTS

When I was little, my dad and I would go to our family's butcher shop on Sunday mornings. We would check the cases and coolers, pick up a bunch of sliced cold cuts, and head over to the local radio station, where he would star in his own show. He would play music, make ads for his shop, and we would enjoy a fine sandwich with mustard. We then would stop by Siller Beef Company and pick out meat from their rails to be delivered to the shop Monday morning. My father was a butcher, but also an entrepreneur and a gourmet. I owe my butchering skill, my knowledge of quality meat, many of my cooking skills, and my general love of food to him. Thanks, Dad!

Over the years, I have experimented with many meat recipes and I would like to thank my wife, Tricia, and my family for always being honest. "What is it?" is a question worth asking sometimes.

Upon coming to The Culinary Institute of America, I embarked on a different journey: Taking my skill and honing it to a higher degree while passing on as much information to my students as possible. The CIA has allowed me to take my dream of publishing a book that keeps this art and craft alive. I would like to thank all of my fellow instructors who inspire me in so many ways, especially Hans Sebald, my co-instructor in the meat class. He is a master butcher and a gentleman.

I would like to thank the CIA's president, Tim Ryan, for allowing us to do great things and facilitating an artisan environment, encouraging creativity and experimentation.

There are many people who helped in the making of this book. My editorial assistant, Shannon Eagan, worked tirelessly on this publication and never once complained about bad jokes and butcher humor. Thanks also to Lisa Lahey for taking a concept and letting it bloom.

Thanks goes to the two photographers, my friend and neighbor, Ben Fink, and the CIA photographer, Keith Ferris. Meat is not photogenic, but they accurately depict things that are not easily done.

The CIA meat storeroom staff, especially Jason Lafalce, contributed by procuring the meats and allowing me to prep them. All of the photo items were kept cold and then used throughout the CIA kitchens.

My teaching assistant during the writing was Carlos Villaneuva, who helped with many of the ideas for photos and props. (The lamb prosciutto was his!) Thanks, Carlos.

Former students helped with the cooking of the recipes, which I would have taken forever to produce alone. Thanks to Adam Cobb, Micheal Igdaloff, Luis Martinez, and Andrea Roshore, who also helped with photos.

I would also like to thank all of the many students that have inspired me over the years. So many great students at the CIA offer ideas and crave the extra knowledge that drives me each day. Butchery may be a lost art for some, but not for those who enter my door.

Thomas K. Schneller

INTRODUCTION

The craft of the butcher dates back to pre-historic times. The term "hunter-gatherer" refers to the earliest humans who separated themselves from the animal world. Through history the butcher was an integral part of many societies. The local butcher was a respected member of the community, a craftsman and artisan. The butcher was a valuable part of the French kitchen brigade system and was responsible for preparing all portions, stocks, roasts, and foundation sauces. Today we find consumers buying more meat products than ever before and knowing less about where their meat is coming from or how it is fabricated. This book is a comprehensive guide for anyone interested in understanding the craft of butchery for the kitchen. Valuable information is presented with clear photos for identifying most meat cuts commonly available to a foodservice operation. Step by step instruction is offered for fabricating a large variety of portion cuts and roasts. Valuable yield information and formulas are included to ensure a proper profit margin. Information on nutritional values in actual portion sizes as opposed to unrealistic small portions gives the user a tool to address calorie counts. Quality grading and information on USDA certified products is included as well as background on animal breeds and how they relate to quality.

In today's meat industry it is often suggested to buy pre-portioned sections to save on labor costs. So why learn the basics? A chef or culinarian that desires to fabricate unique items or understand their options needs a guide that can truly help to decide which way to buy. Also, as the niche market sector of the meat industry grows, more information on fabricating large cuts is necessary in many cases.

Recipes included are designed for the underutilized meat cuts and usable trim from other fabrications to increase profit and diversity.

Purchasing and packaging information is included to enable any chef, purchasing agent, or buyer to better connect with their purveyor. This book uses standards laid out by the North American Meat Processors Association and can be used to enhance the use of their meat buyer's guide.

Beyond a simple technical textbook there are also background and history segments to enable a deeper understanding of the world of meat.

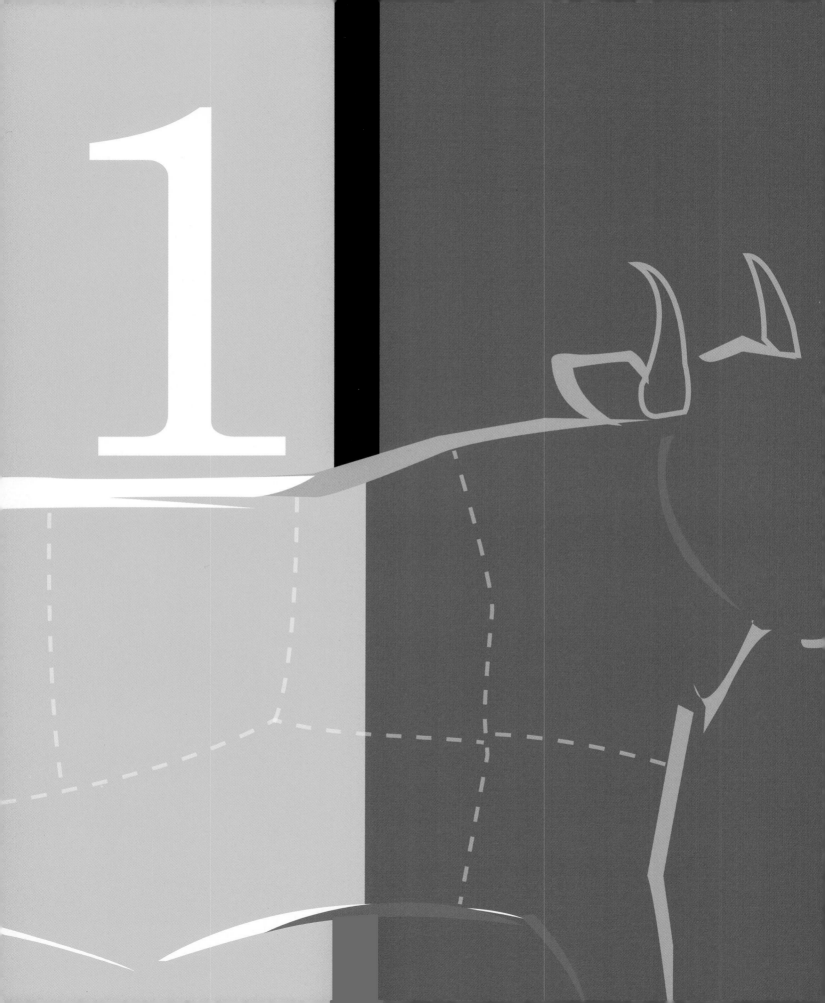

WHAT IS MEAT?

Research tells us that the relatives of *Homo sapiens* scavenged for animal proteins millions of years ago. Earlier hominids hunted eggs and possibly small animals, but were primarily vegetarians. As humans evolved, their ability to hunt with skill allowed them to kill larger animals for meat, tools, and clothing. Techniques for fabricating and preserving meat improved along with hunting skills. As civilizations evolved, so did the artisans of those civilizations. Humans during the late Paleolithic period, around 10,000 to 25,000 years ago, hunted a wide variety of large animals. They had considerable knowledge of all the animals' parts and had a use for many byproducts, such as bones, sinews, hides, and more. Rendering fat for fuel was common and allowed for survival during cold periods and ice ages. Cave drawings found from this period show a variety of large mammals, such as bison, ibex, reindeer, aurochs (early ancestors of oxen), and mammoths.

FIGURE **1.1** A prehistoric cave painting of cattle.

THE BUTCHER

A transition to agriculture occurred around 10,000 years ago. With the advent of agriculture, animals were domesticated rather than hunted and the role of the butcher became necessary to properly fabricate animals into meat that society could use. The craftsman class in early human societies included those who knew the skills to harvest meat from animals. Civilizations grew from small villages and camps to larger centers and cities. Each area developed its own food culture and ways in which it cut and used meats. During the medieval period in Europe, guild systems regulated trade and guaranteed that skills were effectively passed on through generations. The butcher would start as an apprentice at around ten or twelve years of age and, after a few years, became a journeyman. Then, if his or her skill level showed a complete understanding of the craft, a butcher would become a "master." The masters held great political power in a village or city-state and would help regulate trade with the local farmers.

For many years, meat fabrication was done by hand. The advent of higher-quality metals, knives, and tools allowed the butcher to improve his craft. With the coming of the Industrial Revolution in the mid-nineteenth century, meat processing changed. Rather than a small local butcher working with the farmer on a one-to-one basis, modern transportation allowed for meat carcasses to be transported over great distances. By the 1900s, trainloads of animals could be brought to larger packing houses of inner cities. Butchers no longer had to do the entire harvest from slaughter to final product. Assembly-line type fabrication took hold.

Also at this time, farming technologies changed. Farmers could produce more plant food, not only for human consumption, but also for their farm animals. This feeding of animals led to higher-quality products. The use of tractors and farm machinery meant that large animals were no longer needed to pull plows, clear land, or perform any other arduous task they were previously bred for. Now, breeders could concentrate on meat production. Universities developed animal science programs devoted to the "meat breed," whether it was beef, pork, chicken, or lamb.

The growth of the meat industry changed the way meat was fabricated. No longer did a single butcher need to know the entire process of taking the animal from the farmer to the portioned cuts for customers. The practice of having many butchers, each with a specialized skill set, increased the volume of what could be done. Today, modern meat-processing plants fabricate cuts in a huge variety of sizes, quality ranges, trim levels, and styles. This book will help the reader understand the options available to buyers. Having good fabrication skills enables the meat buyer to fully understand the most profitable way to buy. Though it is true that it takes years of butchering experience to become a true master, and that a book cannot possibly teach all the skills necessary, it is also true that having a basic understanding of meat cuts and the options available can directly affect the way you buy.

WHAT IS MEAT?

A basic definition of meat is "the parts of animals fit for human consumption," This broad definition refers to both the edible carcass and offal. The definition of meat varies from species to species. For example, the hide is removed from beef, veal, and lamb, but for pork and poultry, it is considered part of the meat.

The carcass includes the following components: lean muscle tissues, bones, fats, connective tissues, and offal. Offal is not actually part of the carcass, it is the edible byproducts produced in creating the carcass.

Most people consider meat as the steak, roast, or chop, but when considering the whole carcass, we need to consider anatomy. When alive, animals use their muscles to do specific tasks. Certain muscles are used for locomotion and movement. Cattle spend a good portion of their time standing, so they develop thick support muscles.

When considering which meat to use for cooking, we must consider the use of the muscle while the animal was alive. Muscle sections that are used more frequently or perform arduous tasks will be tougher than more sedentary muscle groups. Muscles that are located along the back are used less frequently than muscles that are at the extremities. Certain deep muscles, when isolated and trimmed, have been found to be extremely tender. These muscles may be too small or difficult to fabricate, so may not be considered marketable. The age and method of raising the animal also determine a level of tenderness. What may be considered a quality cut in one species can be quite tough in another.

Motion and Sedentary muscle groups

- Sedentary- along back
- Motion- Located on the front, rear and lower sections of carcass.

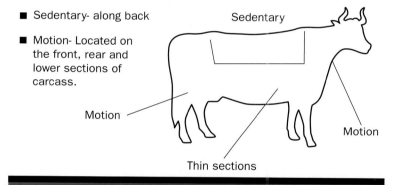

FIGURE **1.2**

MUSCLE FIBERS

There are two basic types of muscle fibers: smooth and skeletal. Smooth muscles are found in the digestive and circulatory systems and are primarily involuntary muscles. These are generally found in offal products, such as tripe.

Skeletal muscles are the more typical meat muscles. They attach to bone to allow the animal to move and perform specific tasks. Skeletal muscles are formed from long, slender muscle cells that form bundles. Muscle bundles are tied together with spring-like myofibrils, which are able to expand and contract in movement. A collagen-protein layer, called perimysium, surrounds these bundles. Acting like a layer of plastic wrap, the perimysium surrounds the bundles. The thicker the perimysium is, the tougher the muscle. The entire larger muscle is enclosed with a layer called the epimysium. Layers become thicker and tougher as the animal matures.

FIGURE **1.3** A beef flank steak with obvious muscle grain.

Muscle fibers are aligned in a directional pattern called the *grain*. When cutting meats, it is important to understand the direction of the grain so as to cut across it to ensure the most tender surface possible. Certain cuts that have an obvious grain can be extremely tough if the cut is made with the grain, as opposed to across it.

The color of muscle fibers depends on the type of muscle and its species. Muscles that receive their energy directly from the bloodstream will be redder in color. The red pigment is due to myoglobin, a protein that holds oxygen to the muscle. Beef, lamb, and venison all have a darker red meat due to the large amount of myoglobin present. Pork, veal, and various types of poultry are a light color because much of the energy for their muscles is achieved anaerobically.

Myoglobin will give meats different color hues depending on length of exposure to oxygen. When meat cuts are in an anaerobic state, such as in a vacuum bag, the myoglobin is a dull purplish red. Once cuts are exposed to oxygen, they "bloom" and become a bright red. This is termed *oxymyoglobin*. After being exposed to oxygen for some time, the oxymyoglobin converts to *metmyoglobin* and turns a brown or gray color. This is usually an indication that the meat is spoiling.

FATS

Different species have different types of lipid combinations. The fat from a hog is chemically different from that of beef, as is that of lamb. The taste and melting points of different fats can reflect different uses in the kitchen. Pork fat is considered more palatable than beef or lamb fat. Lamb fat is very strong in flavor and has a different mouth feel. This is due to the levels of saturated fats, such as stearic or palmitic fatty acids.

The diet of the animal will also affect the flavor of the fat and therefore the taste of the overall meat. Grass-fed or foraged animals will tend to have a stronger or more pronounced flavor than grain-fed animals. Diet also alters the levels of Omega-3 and Omega-6 fatty acids. For example, grass-fed animals will have a higher Omega-3 count. Grain fed animals have an imbalance of Omega 6 to Omega 3 ratio, with Omega 6 being higher. It is important to have a balance of Omega 3 and 6 in the diet.

There are four basic categories used when discussing fat on meat carcasses.

1. Subcutaneous Fat: Fat found directly under the hide or skin of the animal. It is very dense and good for barding or larding. Pork fatback is an example of subcutaneous fat.

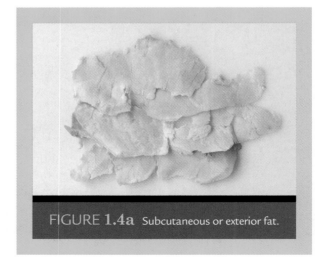

FIGURE **1.4a** Subcutaneous or exterior fat.

2. Lumbar or Kidney Fat: Fat found inside the carcass cavity surrounding the kidney and pelvic region. This fat is very hard and crumbly with little moisture, which makes it very good for rendering and frying.

3. Intermuscular Fat: Fat that is found between muscle groups. It is used to help guide the butcher between muscle cuts.

4. Intramuscular Fat: This is also known as *marbling*. Marbling is fat found within the lean muscle tissues, between muscle bundles. When well-marbled meat is cooked, the fat melts, infusing the cut with flavor and leaving a weakened muscle fiber, which translates into tenderness. Marbling is considered a main indicator of quality. (See Figs 1.4a through 1.4c.)

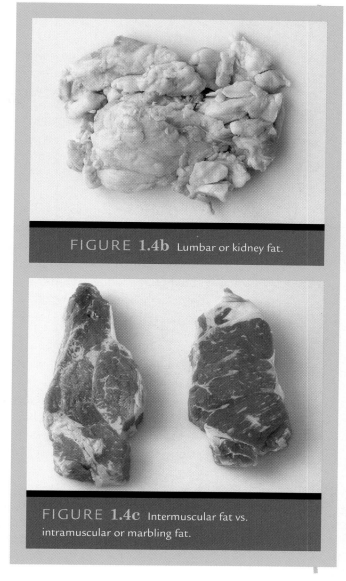

FIGURE **1.4b** Lumbar or kidney fat.

FIGURE **1.4c** Intermuscular fat vs. intramuscular or marbling fat.

CONNECTIVE TISSUES

The most common connective protein in meat is collagen. Collagen is the basic filament that holds together muscle fibers. It is found throughout the carcass and attaches muscle to muscle. Collagen fibers can be described as white, silver, or clear, depending on their thickness or density. Large collagen tendons appear as white, thin bands on muscles or appear silver between muscles; the perimysium covering surrounding tiny muscle bundles is practically clear.

Collagen directly relates to the toughness of a cut of meat. Muscles that are load bearing or are required to do heavy lifting have thicker collagen bands and coarse muscle fibers. If applying a rapid, dry cooking method to these types of motion muscles, the meat will be very tough. A piece of meat from a less-active area will have a much finer fiber and less collagen support material, and will be tender.

Collagen breaks down during a slow, moist cooking application. The fibers unravel and fall apart, dissolving into the liquid. Tougher muscles will become extremely tender if allowed the proper time and heat to do so. Collagen-laden muscles tend to have much more flavor than fine-fibered, tender cuts. When broken down in the sauce of a dish, collagen gives a texture or smoothness to that sauce. In culinary terms, this texture is part of what might be called savory, or *umami*, even though other factors also contribute to this.

Another connective tissue frequently found on meat cuts is the material that connects muscle to bone. This substance, known as periosteum, or bone sheath, is actually part of the bone covering that is pulled away when meat is boned out. On younger animal carcasses, which is the case for most of the meat items we see today, the bones are not ossified or fully hardened. This sheath ends up on the meat item. It can be very tough and does not break down as readily as collagen does. It should be removed, even on moist-cooked meats, unless the meat is cooked for an extremely long time. Bone connectives look similar to collagen but are pinkish in color and can be rough to the touch.

Elastin, another common connective tissue, is found along the back and into the neck of the carcass. It is yellowish and has an elastic feel. It is thick and tough, but is found close to some prized sedentary muscle cuts, so it is necessary to remove it as well.

BONES

Although we do not actually eat the hardened bones of animals, they are an integral part of what is considered meat. Bones end up on the plate as part of a large variety of cuts. The bone-in steak or chop, the barbecued or roasted chicken, spare ribs, and the classic crown roast would not be possible without leaving the bones attached. Bones hold many connective tissues, which dissolve into water when producing stock. These stocks or broths can be reduced to make rich, smooth sauces. The fatty rich marrow found in certain bones is used in some classic dishes.

In the fabrication of meat, bones play an important role for the butcher. Bones are used to identify specific locations on the carcass to make a cut without damaging muscles. Bones act as a roadmap for carcass breakdown. Every typical four-legged mammal used for meat has the same basic bone and muscle structure. Of course, they are not all divided the same, but there are always certain similarities. When deciding to fabricate a cut of meat, whether a full carcass or an individual cut, it is important to understand the bone structure.

OFFAL

Offal can best be described as the edible byproducts of a meat carcass. Examples would be organ meats such as liver, kidney, heart, brain, tripe, certain glands, and intestinal tracts. In addition, the cheeks, tail, and tongue are part of offal. In many cultures, offal is considered a delicacy. Organ meats, such as the liver and kidneys, are high in iron, which translates into a rich flavor. The tail has some meat and a lot of collagen and is typically used for rich braises. Offal is generally inexpensive but requires some skill to cook properly.

Organ meats are composed of fibers that are different from those of lean muscle. Membranes, blood vessels, and connectives need to be removed on livers and kidneys.

Some offal is considered the epitome of high cuisine. An example would be the fattened duck or goose liver known as foie gras. This meat has a consistency that resembles butter and has a rich flavor.

Other delicacies would be the *sweetbread*, or thymus gland, of veal. When properly prepared, this soft-structured gland can be eaten with a fork. This type of offal is an exception to the "inexpensive" nature of offal. They are in high demand and warrant a high cost.

Organ meats tend to be highly perishable and therefore must be used fresh, within a week of slaughter, or purchased frozen. Be sure to keep frozen items below 32° and −4°F/0° and −18°C to ensure the formation of small ice crystals and minimize damage.

QUALITY GRADING

The idea of grading meat for its palatability, or tenderness and taste, has been going on for hundreds of years. Cattle buyers and butchers judged animals for their quality and paid accordingly. The size and age of the animals were assessed and breeds were looked at to determine quality. The breeding of animals for meat quality encouraged importation of animals that improved the quality of the herds.

The United States Department of Agriculture [USDA] began grading beef for quality in 1927. This created standards that established criteria that farmers and processors could try to achieve. Grading for other species followed and modifications to the grading system have been implemented over the decades. The grades helped processors assign value to the meats and allowed the purchaser consistency in product. No longer was an expert butcher required to select meats; a purchaser could simply request a grade and receive a consistent product.

The process of USDA-quality grading is separate from inspection. Grading is not a mandatory function. Unlike inspection, which is paid for by taxpayers, the processor pays for quality grading. What this implies is that, normally, only the higher-grade meats sold for a premium will be quality graded, while lesser meats—meats usually used for processed items—will go ungraded. Many processors have in-house graders and quality assessment teams that perform tasks similar to the USDA, but only the USDA graders can use their specific USDA stamps. Specific grading criteria for beef, veal, and pork are included in this book in the chapter for that meat.

YIELD GRADING

When an animal is slaughtered, a certain amount of the animal is not usable as meat. For example, for beef, 53 to 58 percent is dressed carcass, 14 to 20 percent is edible offal, and 36 to 33 percent is inedible. These amounts may vary on the type of animal and pre-slaughter conditions, but the fact remains that there is a substantial loss during slaughter and evisceration. On the dressed carcass, there may be substantial further loss due to fat content. A *fed,* or fattened, beef animal accumulates extra fat, which reduces the overall yield of the carcass.

The USDA has established a yield-grading system that defines criteria for carcasses. This system defines the *cutability,* the amount of usable meat, in a carcass. It takes into account fat-to-lean ratios and meat-to-bone, or *conformation,* ratios. The weight and size of the carcass is assessed and a number grade is assigned.

Beef and lamb are primarily the only meats that are yield graded. Veal does not have enough fat to degrade its value and pork has a grade system that incorporates yield with its quality grade.

YIELD GRADE	PERCENTAGE OF CLOSELY TRIMMED RETAIL PRODUCT
1	75.5%
2	71.5%
3	67.5%
4	64.9%
5	60.8%

FIGURE **1.5** USDA yield-grade chart.

BASIC BUTCHERY: TOOLS AND EQUIPMENT

In ancient times, stone tools were used to eviscerate an animal and then divide it into its primal cuts. As humans evolved, they developed metal tools to do these tasks. Today, we find tools in the meat industry that enable tasks to be done rapidly and with minimal waste. The list of equipment available and all of their intended uses could fill this book alone; therefore, only the more basic equipment used for basic butchery is included.

KNIVES

What knives do you need to fabricate meat? There are many available knives and some of them are for specific cutting techniques.

Meat fabrication knives:

1. Boning Knife: Available in lengths from five to six inches and a variety of flexes, from completely stiff to very flexible. For general meat cutting, a semi-flexible, six-inch boning knife will perform well. There are strait and angled blades available. The handle of a boning knife needs to fit the user's hand properly and some texture on the handle may be helpful to reduce slippage. Different boning knives are suggested for a variety of tasks; for instance, boning a pork loin requires a knife with some flex to be able to flatten out while boning to increase the surface area covered. If boning a strait-line bone, such as a shank or femur, a non-flexible or stiff boning knife will be more stable.

2. Scimitar: Available in lengths from ten to sixteen inches. This non-flexing knife is curved to allow for smooth trimming of large meat cuts and portion cutting of steaks, cutlets, stew, or cubes. Due to its curved edge, it is not typically used for mincing or chopping.

3. Chef's Knife: A non-flexible, eight- to ten-inch knife that can be used for trimming large cuts, portion cutting, mincing, and chopping. However, it can be a little cumbersome due to its width.

4. Slicer: A twelve-inch knife that is available in flexible, semi-flexible, or stiff models. It is thinner than the chef's knife and, unlike the scimitar, has a straight edge. It is good for trimming large cuts and portion cutting.

5. Clam Knife: A Clam knife may come in handy when Frenching racks of lamb or veal. It is used to scrape the membranes off the bones.

FIGURE **1.6** Top row, from left to right: Clam knife; five-inch curved, flexible boning knife; six-inch curved, flexible boning knife; six-inch stiff boning knife; ten-inch chef's knife; ten-inch scimitar; twelve-inch slicer; cleaver; Bottom row: 25-inch handsaw.

SHARPENING STEEL AND STONES

Sharpening and honing your knife will make it more accurate and reduce the amount of mis-cuts and injuries. A sharp knife is easily maintained with the proper stone and steel. Stones come in various degrees of grit. The higher the grit number, the finer the stone. A typical coarse grit for knives would be 600 and a fine grit 1000. Usually, a knife would be sharpened on the coarse grit first and finished on the fine grit to polish the edge. Some knives made from very hard steel can be sharpened with a higher grit, such as 3000 to 6000. A softer, inexpensive knife would not be able to reap the rewards of these very fine grits.

Some stones are intended for use with mineral or honing oil and others are used with water. Never sharpen a knife on a dry stone. Metal flakes will build up in the stone and render it ineffective.

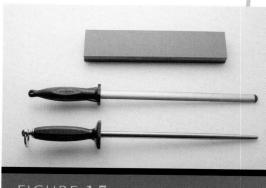

FIGURE **1.7** From top to bottom: Sharpening stone, sharpening or diamond steel, steel.

A sharpening steel is used to hone or correct the knife's edge by sliding the edge of the knife down each side of the steel. It is not a replacement for the stone, and if an edge is lost, it needs to be sharpened, not steeled.

MEAT CLEAVER

Cleavers are available in a variety of weights and sizes. A meat cleaver is used primarily for cutting chops and needs to be relatively heavy to break through chine bones. A meat cleaver can only be used on a butcher block so as not to damage other cutting boards. The butcher block has a natural grain that absorbs the shock of the cleaver. A small cleaver may be used to help fabricate poultry or cooked bone-in roasts.

HANDSAW

Cutting through bone structure can be a challenge and demands nearly as much accuracy as a knife. A quality handsaw can greatly increase the options available to the butcher. Be sure the saw is intended for food use.

BAND SAW

A band saw, although expensive, enables the fabrication of an enormous variety of cuts, such as bone-in steaks, chops, various bone-in roasts, osso buco, stews, and bones for soup. Extreme caution must be used when operating a band saw. Proper cleaning and maintenance is necessary.

MEAT GRINDER

A grinder has a wide range of uses, including in-house burgers, sausages, and forcemeats. Meat grinders are available in a variety of sizes and power ranges. However, rather than buy a separate machine, grinding attachments for other kitchen machinery, such as a mixer or chopper, are an inexpensive alternative. Larger tabletop or floor models offer more horsepower and decrease time required to grind larger quantities.

Proper procedures include chilling grinder parts and meat.

FIGURE **1.8** Diagram of a band saw.

EQUIPMENT INFORMATION AND ASSEMBLY PROCEDURES

STEPS FOR MEAT GRINDER ASSEMBLY (READ FROM RIGHT TO LEFT)

1. Place grinder body on mixer, making sure that the pin fits in the hole on the mixer, tighten finger screw (mixer is not illustrated).

2. Place the worm into the grinder body, making sure that the squared end of the worm fits into the squared hole in the mixer.

3. Place the knife on the thin shaft of the worm, making sure that the flat side faces out.

4. Place the grinder plate on the thin shaft of the worm, line up the pin slot with the pin in the grinder body.

5. Place the face plate on the grinder body, hold the plate with your finger so it does not move, tighten the face plate.

6. Add the feeder tray and grinder is ready for use (feeder tray is not illustrated).

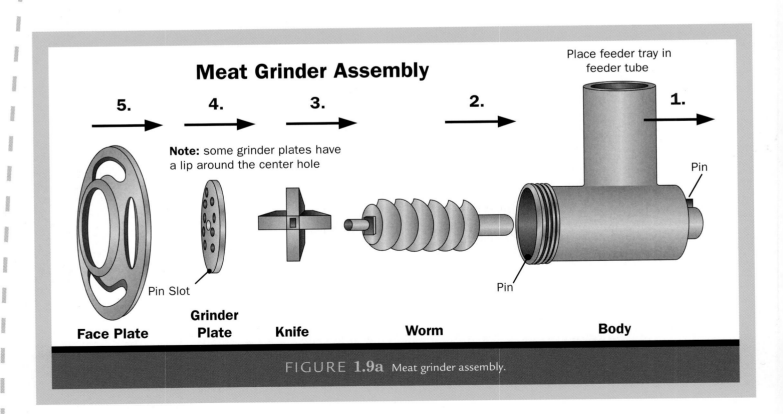

FIGURE **1.9a** Meat grinder assembly.

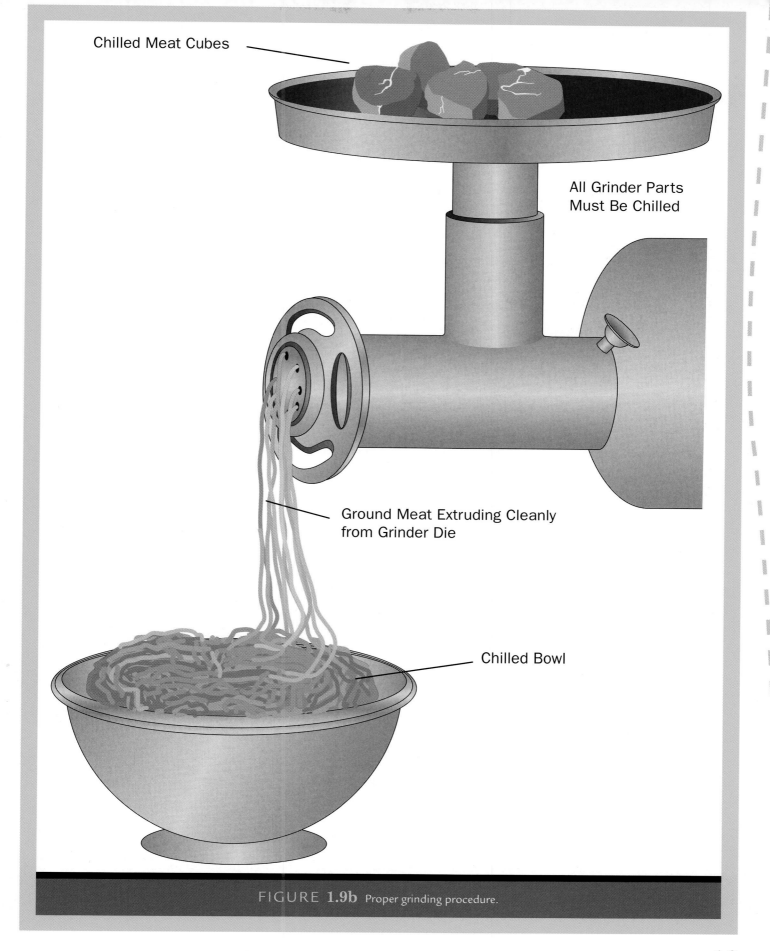

Chilled Meat Cubes

All Grinder Parts
Must Be Chilled

Ground Meat Extruding Cleanly
from Grinder Die

Chilled Bowl

FIGURE **1.9b** Proper grinding procedure.

GRINDER PLATE SIZE

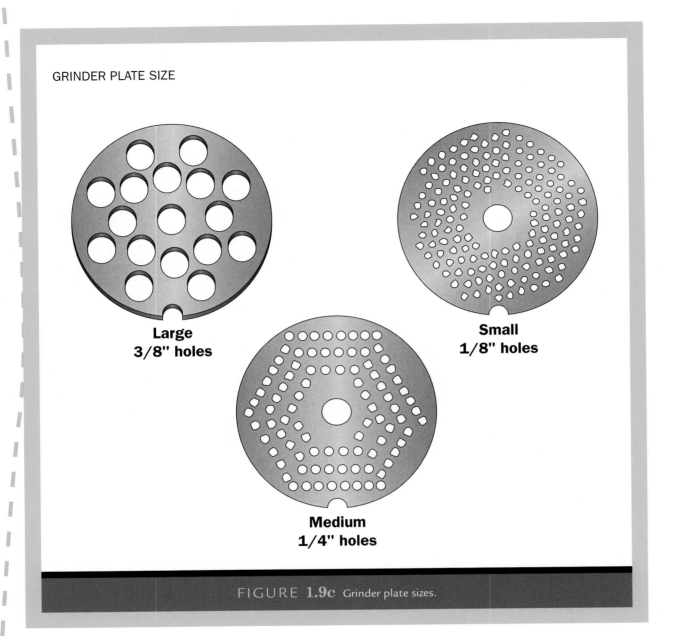

**Large
3/8" holes**

**Small
1/8" holes**

**Medium
1/4" holes**

FIGURE **1.9c** Grinder plate sizes.

PROPER GRINDING PROCEDURES

1. Chill all meat and grinder parts.

2. Set up grinder (see assembly of grinder head).

3. Pass meat through grinder (meat should extrude easily).

4. Rechill meat and grinder.

5. Grind second time.

Note: If meat is not passing through grinder easily, check that grinder parts are assembled correctly.

Hand feed meat into feed tube, use a tamper only when necessary.

HAND HOOK

This simple tool is used instead of using a bare or gloved hand. It allows a good grip on the meat and the ability to create tension between cuts. It can be used for lifting or moving larger pieces of meat.

However, if used incorrectly, the hook can damage the meat. It can be dangerous and should always be used with caution.

SAFETY GLOVES AND EQUIPMENT

Many types of safety gloves are available that can reduce injuries. Kevlar is a typical glove material because it is lightweight, flexible, and washable. Stainless steel mesh guards and aprons may be useful for large-scale cutting.

MEAT FABRICATION TECHNIQUES

TRIMMING

What is meant by the term *trimming*? It could imply removing excess fat off the outside of a meat item. It may mean removing heavy silverskin or collagen bands that surround meat cuts. Some meat cuts may have bone connective tissues, which can be extremely tough and should always be trimmed. Another form of trimming is to shape a piece of meat by trimming off a small section to improve the plate presentation. Whatever the form of trimming, the fabricator needs to understand what the outcome should be.

FIGURE **1.10** Basic trimming technique.

BONING

Boning a meat item can be intimidating and complicated. Understanding the basic bone structure of the meat enables the cutter to fabricate without guessing where the bones are located. The basic bone structure of beef, veal, lamb, pork, and many game meats is basically the same. Certain structures, such as those from the shank, are basic and simple to bone, whereas the bones from the pelvic region, neck, and spine can be difficult.

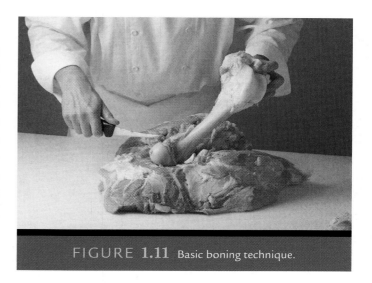

FIGURE **1.11** Basic boning technique.

PORTION CUTTING

Different portions require different techniques. Steaks and medallions should be cut straight up and down, whereas cutlets are often cut on a bias. When portion cutting, be sure to cut across the grain to maximize tenderness. Trim levels can vary with the desired outcome. Leaving some fat is desired on a grilling steak item, whereas a cutlet piece should be completely denuded before cutting.

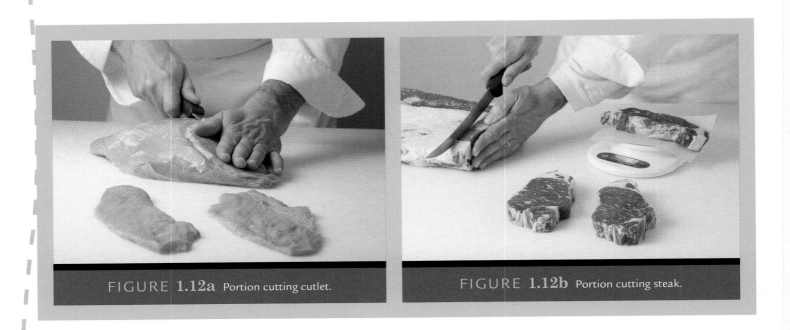

FIGURE **1.12a** Portion cutting cutlet.

FIGURE **1.12b** Portion cutting steak.

BAND SAW

A band saw may not be standard equipment for most kitchens, but it is found in restaurants that fabricate a large number of steaks or chops. Some restaurants dry age their beef cuts and a saw would be required to portion those cuts. It allows a kitchen to change the way things are ordered, where before, many cuts would have to be ordered as portion cuts. With a band saw, the kitchen can custom-cut all the portions. Today, we find small, table-size saws that may make it practical for a restaurant to own a band saw. In any case, the band saw is a very dangerous piece of equipment and should always be used with caution. When using it, be sure there are no distractions and understand the bone structure of the piece being cut. Be sure the blade is tightened correctly, assembled accurately, and is sharp. There are guards that can be used and Kevlar hand protection to ensure safety.

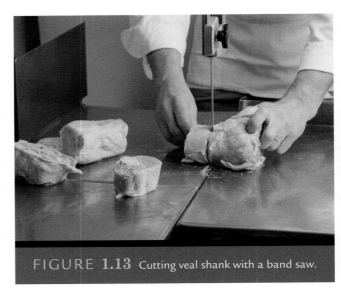

FIGURE **1.13** Cutting veal shank with a band saw.

GRINDING

Unlike a food processor, the grinder gives meat a unique texture. A restaurant may use the grinder to make custom sausages, unique stuffings, and forcemeats, or simply grind meat fresh for a quality burger. Grinding helps utilize any usable trim that occurs when fabricating larger cuts, thereby increasing profitability.

When deciding to grind meat for a burger, sausage, or forcemeat, a proper step-by-step process should be followed.

1. First, decide on the proper fat-to-lean ratio for the grind. A sausage will typically have a ratio of seventy percent lean to thirty percent fat while a burger is generally eighty percent lean to twenty percent fat. However, recipes and fat levels can be customized, depending on the desired outcome.

2. Cut meat into a manageable size for the grinder. If using a small attachment to a mixer, then the pieces should be cut into one to two-inch cubes.

3. Chill all the parts of the grinder and the meat to 32°F. If the meat or machine parts are warm, the fat may separate from the lean tissue and cause an off–texture.

4. Assemble the machine with the knife facing flat against the die and securing with the faceplate, making sure everything is snug.

5. Push meat through the grinder at a rapid pace and do not allow the grinder to run without a steady flow of meat, for it will heat up rapidly. Do not overfill the grinder, which can slow the process. Some processes may require a progressive grind or running the meat through multiple times and changing the die to progressively smaller holes between each grind. This ensures a fat to lean mix and a good texture for certain forcemeats.

6. Clean the grinder immediately after using, and be sure that there is no cross contamination.

ENHANCING AND TENDERIZING

The term *enhanced* meat generally means that the meat has been injected with a solution to increase moisture content. This can be done by simply brining the meat or using an injector. The typical solution for commercially enhanced product would contain water, salt and sodium phosphate. The amount of added ingredients must be placed on the meat packaging. Purveyors often refer to enhanced products as "pumped."

Tenderizing meats can be done either mechanically or chemically. A typical mechanical tenderizer would be a Jaccard knife, which pierces the meat and breaks muscle fibers.

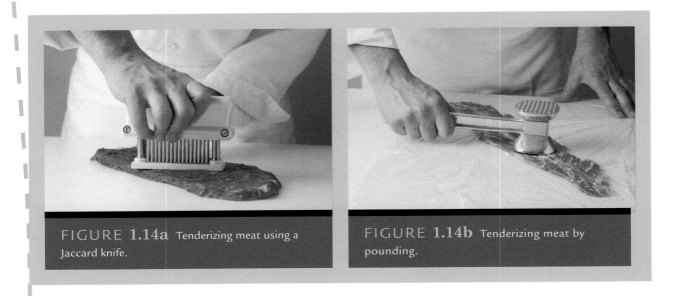

FIGURE **1.14a** Tenderizing meat using a Jaccard knife.

FIGURE **1.14b** Tenderizing meat by pounding.

A typical chemical tenderizer would be Papain, which is derived from Papaya, and contains an enzyme that breaks down protein fibers. Adding acidic ingredients, such as lemon juice, to a marinade also helps break down muscle fiber.

VACUUM PACKAGING

Basic vacuum packaging instructions:

1. Place the item in a bag, allowing two inches of extra space.

2. Position the bag over the chamber so the open end is draped over the sealer bar, but still within the machine.

3. Set the vacuum pressure to the appropriate level for task (most machines can be turned down for fragile items).

4. Close the lid and the machine will automatically equalize pressure, vacuum out air, and seal the bag.

5. Place a label with the product name and pack date on the bag.

FIGURE **1.15** Vacuum packaging machine.

KOSHER AND HALAL MEATS

Kosher (literally "ritually acceptable") meats conform to Jewish dietary laws, whereby an animal is slaughtered according to strict religious guidelines. The Torah describes the procedures.

SHECHITA [THE SLAUGHTER]

The slaughtering process is performed by a trained kosher slaughterer or *shochet*. The trachea and esophagus of the animal are severed with a very sharp knife. The animal is not stunned but this process is very quick and the animal does not experience pain.

BEDIKA

This is the process of special inspection that is done after slaughter. The inspector, or *bodek*, inspects the internal organs to determine whether there is evidence of over seventy different irregularities or growths, which may deem the animal non-kosher, or *treif*. The lungs in particular are carefully inspected.

GLATT KOSHER

"Glatt kosher," although taken to mean "strictly kosher," literally means "smooth" kosher, and refers to meat where the lungs of the animal have no adhesions or scars, thus ensuring that the meat is indeed kosher.

NIKKUR

The process of removing the sciatic nerve, certain fats, and blood vessels from beef, veal, and lamb is called *nikkur*, or deveining. The fact that many of these are deep in muscle tissues in the hind sections of the animal make it impractical. Much of the kosher meat sold in the U.S. is from the fore sections of animals.

KOSHERING

Beyond kosher slaughter, meats can be "koshered." Jewish dietary law bans the consumption of animal blood. The two methods of extracting blood from meat are salting and broiling. The liver must be broiled due to the amount of blood intact. Ground meats cannot be made kosher.

FIGURE **1.16** Kosher stamp.

Kosher meats must be stored "kosher" and cannot come in contact with non-kosher items, such as dairy products, pork, or other non-kosher meats. A stamp is applied to ensure meat is kosher.

HALAL MEATS

Halal is an Arabic term meaning "permissible." When applied to meat, it means that it is deemed fit for consumption according to Islamic law, as referenced in the Qur'an. Under halal, certain meats, such as pork, are outlawed and considered *haraam*, or non-halal.

The slaughter process is similar to the kosher process. Prayers are said at the time of slaughter and strict guidelines are followed.

Halal foods are those that are:

- Free from any component that Muslims are prohibited from consuming.
- Free from anything considered Najis (unclean), according to Shari'ah (law).
- Processed or prepared with equipment free from things considered Najis.
- Free from contamination while prepared or processed with anything considered Najis.

(El-Mouelhy, 1996)

Both kosher and halal meats have stamps applied.

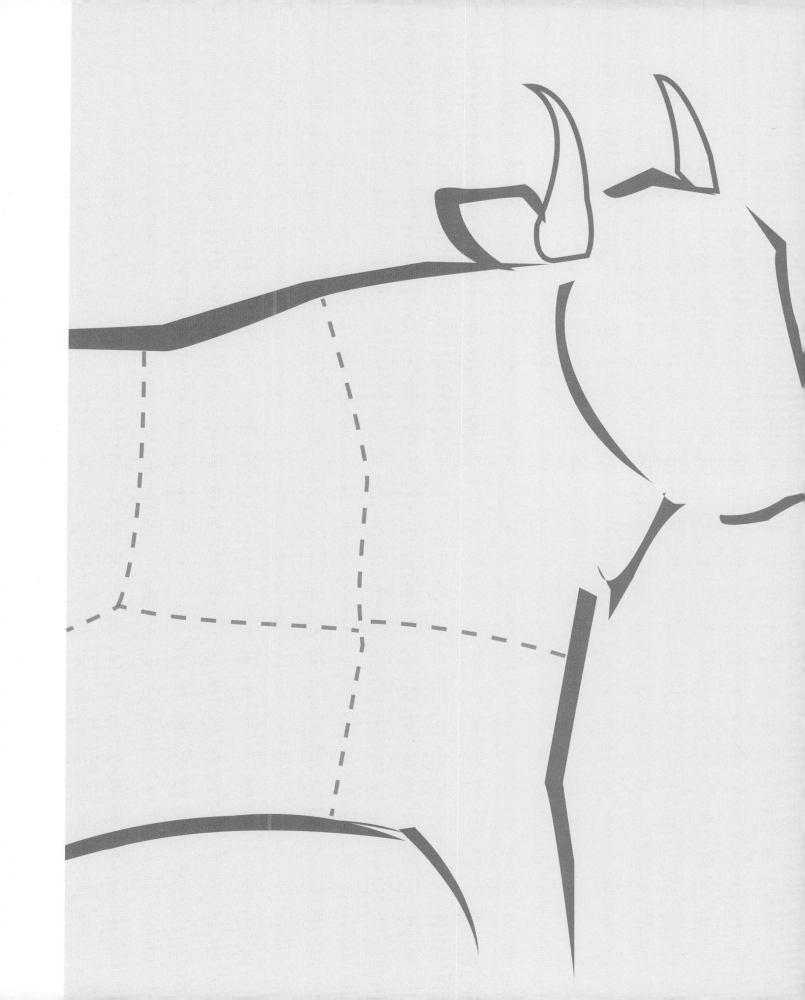

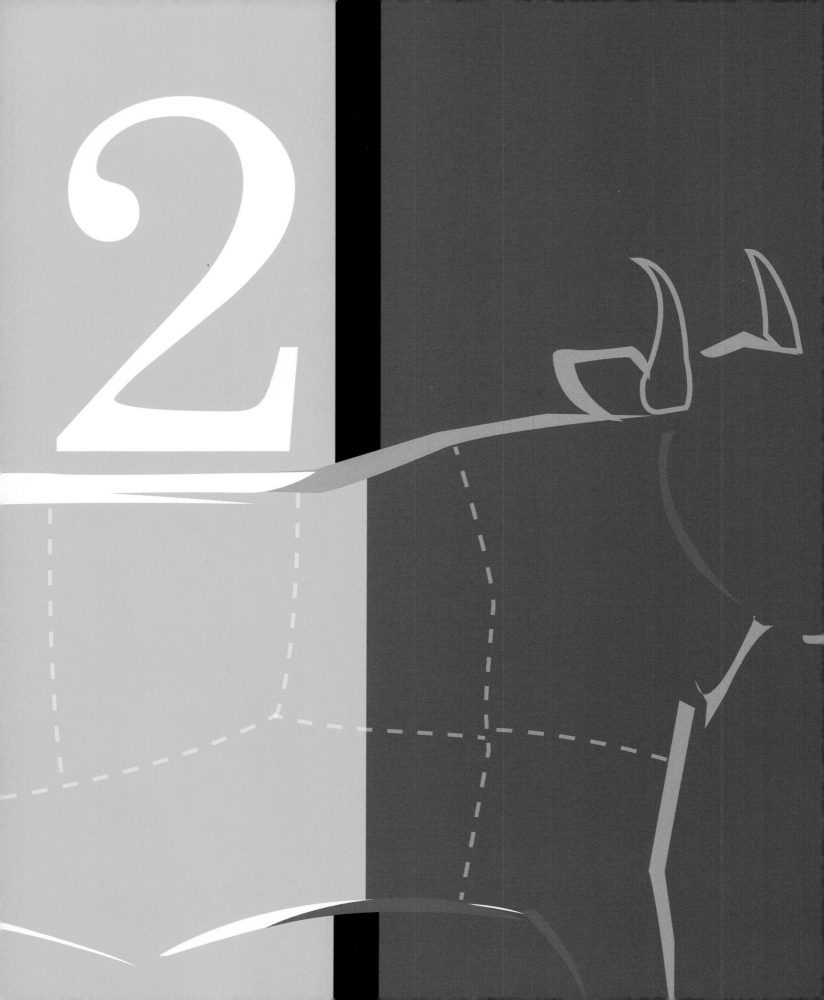

BEEF

Merriam-Webster's Collegiate Dictionary describes beef as "an ox, cow, or bull in a full-grown or nearly full-grown state; especially: a steer or cow fattened for food."

Beef is a versatile meat source with a range from inexpensive hamburgers to the ultimate dry-aged steak. Beef can stand alone, simply grilled or roasted, or be fabricated into a large variety of seasoned products such as sausage and smoked, cured, or marinated items. The hearty flavor of beef makes it a standard favorite on menus.

Beef is divided into two basic types: quality beef from animals specifically raised for meat and meat from animals that were first used in dairy production. Dairy animals are allowed to mature and, because of the toughness and lower meat quality, are often used for processed items, such as ground beef. Quality raised beef is further divided into market cuts. Beef processing plants are divided along these lines as well. "Cow" plants focus on hamburger production, where the entire carcass meat is considered for grinding.

"Fed" quality beef plants process only animals finished on feed to ensure a certain higher quality level. These plants produce the cuts typically seen in restaurants as subprimal, whole-muscle-style cuts with only the trimmings ending up as grind. Many times the fatty trimmings from the fed cattle plants are shipped to the cow plants to mix with the very lean trimmings to make a hamburger formulation. Smaller, niche market "meat-locker"

Beef production in the United States averages twenty-six billion pounds annually, with an average of 120 to 140 thousand head of cattle harvested per day. The average consumption of beef is around sixty-six pounds per person, annually. Beyond U.S. production, beef is raised on a large scale in Brazil, Argentina, Australia, New Zealand, Canada, Uruguay, Mexico, and the European Union. Grazing cattle are found in many countries of Africa and Asia.

operations handle any type of cattle and possibly other species, such as hog, lamb, or bison.

Byproducts of the beef industry include the hides, which are used in a variety of leather products, and fats, which are used to create chemicals such as stearic acid. Other beef byproducts find their way into pet foods, pharmaceutical formulations, fertilizers, and more. In the kitchen, beef bones are used for stock and sauces, adding a full, rich flavor. The fact that beef can be ground and formed into hamburger or sausage allows for the use of much of the trim, adding value to the total carcass.

BEEF BREEDS

All of the world's modern beef breeds descend from the aurochs, an extinct breed of European wild ox. The wild aurochs stood about six feet tall at the shoulder and had large horns, according to depictions found in Neolithic cave dwellings. Domestication of beef began approximately 7000 to 8000 years ago, in what was known as the Fertile Crescent in the Middle East. *Beef*, as we know it today, covers a large number of breeds under the general species of *Bos*.

Many of the modern quality beef breeds originate from the United Kingdom and continental Europe (*Bos taurus*). Other breeds from India (*Bos indicus*) have influenced herds as well. Today, there are over 210 different breeds of cattle, a breed being an animal selected for specific traits that can be passed on to offspring. Much of today's cattle are mixed breeds that may have attributes of the many purebreds they originate from. Some breeds have features that influence cattle in ways that have nothing to do with the actual meat, such as the ability to withstand harsh conditions, including drought or excessive heat. General speed of gain, the ability to grow to market weight rapidly, might be a feature a breeder looks for. Certain breeds are known for their quality meat. Fineness of muscle fibers, ability to develop intramuscular fat or marbling, good yield scores, and size and thickness of the carcass are all genetic features.

TYPICAL BEEF BREEDS

This is a short list of commonly bred beef cattle.

BLACK ANGUS

Origin: Aberdeen, Scotland

Black Angus have black coats, are polled (no horns), have fine muscle fibers, even marbling, and have a high value.

FIGURE **2.1a** Black Angus bull.

FIGURE **2.1b** Black Angus cow.

CHAROLAIS

Origin: France

Charolais have white coats, large carcasses, good muscling scores, and are good for mixing with other breeds.

FIGURE **2.2a** Charolais bull.

FIGURE **2.2b** Charolais cows.

BRAHMAN

Origin: India.

The Brahman is a very hearty breed, adapts to a variety of feeds, and gains weight rapidly from birth.

FIGURE **2.3a** Brahman bull.

FIGURE **2.3b** Brahman cow.

HEREFORD

Origin: England

Hereford have a red coat and a white face. They have good meat quality, a rapid gain to market weight, and were the predominant cattle species in the building of U.S. herds in the seventeenth and eighteenth centuries. They are good foragers and are hearty.

FIGURE **2.4a** Hereford bull.

FIGURE **2.4b** Hereford cattle.

HOLSTEIN

Origin: Europe

The Holstein has a black and white coat and is primarily a dairy cow. They have a small eye muscle, fine fibers, and good marbling; however, they have a lower meat value.

PIEDMONTESE

Origin: Italy

Piedmontese cows have very fine fibers and tender meat without heavy marbling. They have a double muscling trait unique to the breed, which translates to very good yields.

LIMOUSIN

Origin: France

Limousin produce quality meat, have excellent feed efficiency and rapid gain, and are excellent for crossbreeding with fattier breeds.

CHIANINA

Origin: Italy

The Chianina is a large breed known for quality beef. It is the original beef used for the classic *Bistecca alla Fiorentina*, Italian Beefsteak Florentine.

SIMMENTAL
[ALSO, SIMMENTHAL]

Origin: Switzerland

Simmentals are one of the oldest cattle breeds. They have large features, are good for crossbreeding, have widespread genetics, and produce good dairy.

FIGURE **2.5** Holstein cow.

FIGURE **2.6** Limousin steer.

FIGURE **2.7.** Chianina bull.

FIGURE **2.8a** Simmental bull.

FIGURE **2.8b** Simmental cow.

TEXAS LONGHORN

Origin: Spain, but altered over time

These were the first cattle brought to the Americas, about 500 years ago. These cattle adapted to the harsh conditions of the Southwest and thrived without much human influence. As the western landscape changed from open grazing to fenced herds, the need for a self-sufficient, semi-wild beef diminished. The breed was saved from near extinction in the 1920s.

FIGURE **2.9** Texas Longhorn.

WAGYU

Origin: Japan

Wagyu [literally "Japanese Cow"] have extremely high marbling scores and are considered the world's finest beef breed. There are three main bloodlines of Japanese Wagyu: Tajima, Kedaka, and Fujiyoshi; each has certain body types and specific characteristics.

Certain breeds are considered niche-market cattle. Popular niche breeds include Highland, Belgian Blue, Devon, and Belted Galloway. Other breeds have historical value and are protected by societies devoted to continuing the breed. The idea of keeping even relatively obsolete breeds from going extinct is important to ensure a way to mix in desired genetics. Such breeds, although not ideal for present-day meat production, may have traits that ensure disease resistance in beef.

BEEF EVALUATION AND GRADING
QUALITY GRADING

Basic guidelines for evaluating beef were established in 1917, with many changes and improvements following over the years. Grading was established originally to purchase beef for the armed forces during World War I and, later, for steamship lines, restaurants, and railroad dining cars. Grading assigned value to the wide-ranging levels

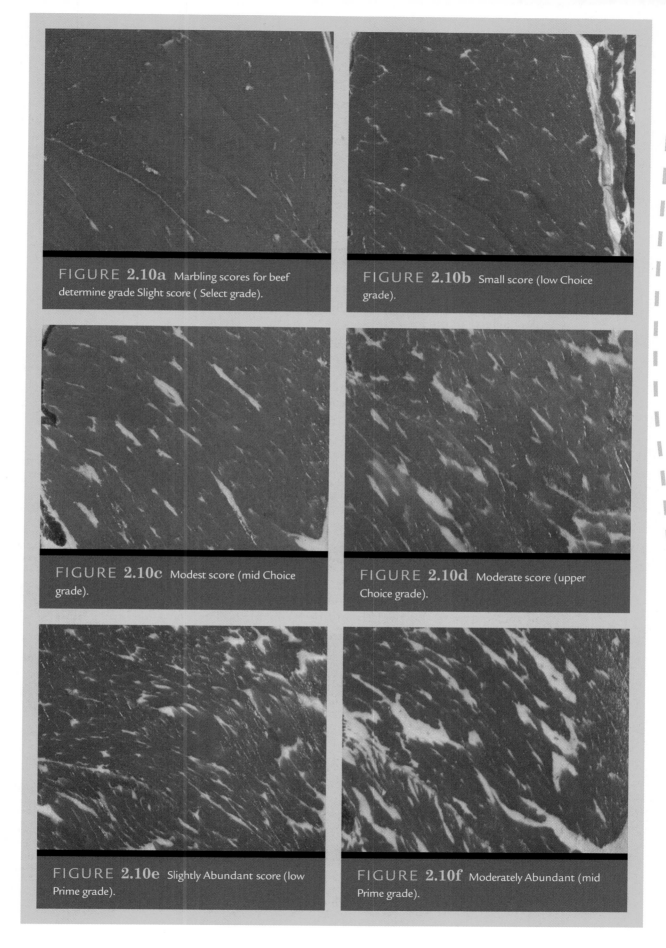

FIGURE **2.10a** Marbling scores for beef determine grade Slight score (Select grade).

FIGURE **2.10b** Small score (low Choice grade).

FIGURE **2.10c** Modest score (mid Choice grade).

FIGURE **2.10d** Moderate score (upper Choice grade).

FIGURE **2.10e** Slightly Abundant score (low Prime grade).

FIGURE **2.10f** Moderately Abundant (mid Prime grade).

of beef available at the time. By 1941, many of the terms now in use were already established, although adjustments to what is required for these grades have been made since that time. Today, beef grading is voluntary and is primarily done to the upper grades of beef to determine value. Grading is paid for by the processor; therefore, all of the lesser-quality beef, although deemed wholesome or fit for consumption, would be excluded from grading.

The USDA has guidelines for grading that include many of the following features:

- Size and weight of the animal
- Age or maturity of the animal
- The weight of the carcass
- Overall fullness or conformation (basic meat-to-bone ratio)
- The color of the lean muscle tissues
- Any defects in the lean muscle tissues
- Marbling scores (intramuscular fat)

Maturity of beef is determined by the bone ossification at points along the vertebrae or by looking at the teeth of the animal. Age categories are used when grading. Maturity is given a letter grade from A to E.

A. 9 to 30 months

B. 30 to 42 months

C. 42 to 72 months

D. 72 to 96 months

E. Above 96 months

High-quality beef would primarily fall into the A maturity range.

Beef is quality graded at what is called the rib eye area, or REA, the spot between the twelfth and thirteenth rib. This location will tell much of what is needed to judge the quality of the entire carcass.

Quality grading defines the "palatability," or taste, tenderness, and mouth feel of the beef. The USDA quality grades include:

- Prime
- Choice
- Select
- Standard
- Commercial
- Utility
- Cutter
- Canner

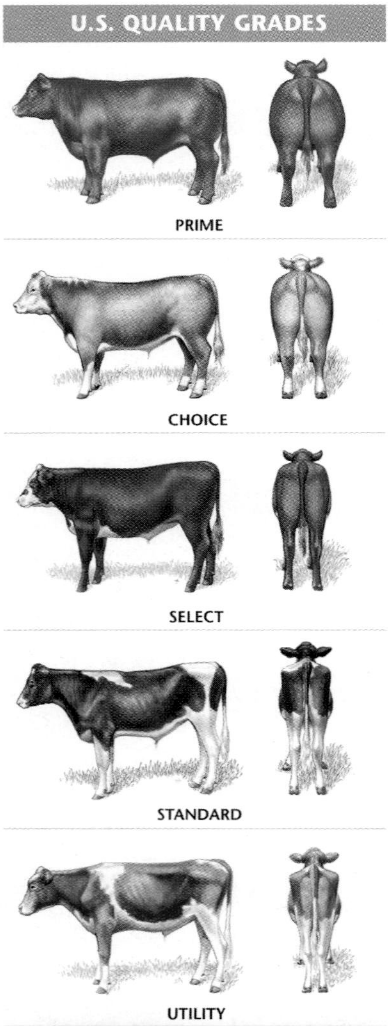

When identifying quality in beef, the buyer must first establish the intended use of the item. Higher-quality beef is typically used in steakhouses, where the flavor and texture are important to the

U.S. QUALITY GRADES

PRIME

CHOICE

SELECT

STANDARD

UTILITY

FIGURE **2.11** U.S. quality grades of slaughter steers.

sale. Choice beef has significant quality and can be used as a quality item; however, the range within choice requires the purchaser to be aware of some lower-end product that could represent a lesser-quality dining experience. Select beef, which has a lower marbling score, usually requires some help to make it more palatable. Select grade cuts may be enhanced or tenderized to aid palatability. Marbling, although not the only factor in quality grading, substantially increases flavor. Without it, beef may be tender, depending on the age and breed, but lacks the flavor of quality beef.

YIELD GRADING

Beef can be yield graded to assign value in a different way. Yield grading of beef judges the cutability of the carcass, which includes the fat-to-lean ratio. Beef yield grades are used when establishing specifics for beef cuts and are determined by the thickness of the exterior fat and the mass of the interior, or lumbar, fat. These, in conjunction with the ratio between the mass of the rib eye area (or muscle score) and the hot carcass weight, are calculated into a yield grade number.

Beef Yield Grades:

- 1 — Leanest (Not typical in beef with much marbling)
- 2
- 3
- 4 — Fat (heavy waste, generally avoided)
- 5 — Fattest (extreme fat, unprofitable and wasteful)

Twos and threes are the most typical grades. Yield grades become less important as restaurants and markets purchase pre-trimmed beef cuts, where the heavy fat is trimmed to predetermined levels by the processor. Over- or undersized items are often deemed "outs," or outsized items, which are often sold at a discount due to their irregularities.

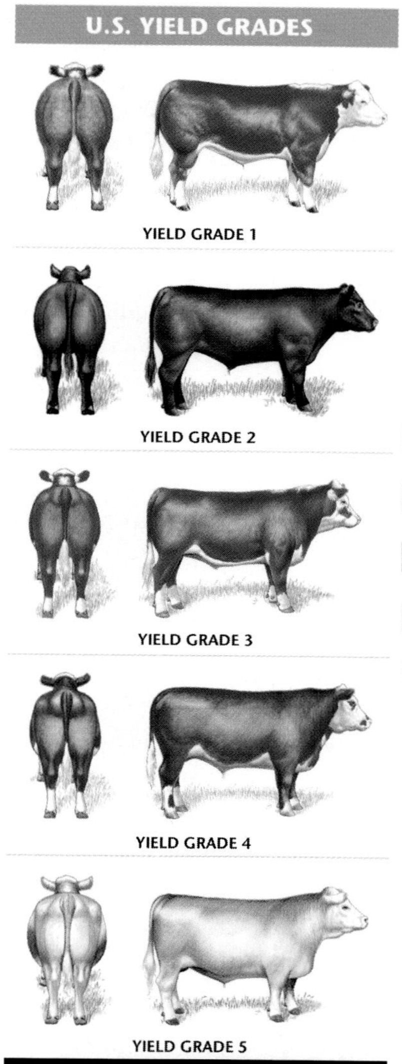

U.S. YIELD GRADES

YIELD GRADE 1

YIELD GRADE 2

YIELD GRADE 3

YIELD GRADE 4

YIELD GRADE 5

FIGURE **2.12** Yield grading.

CERTIFIED AND BRANDED BEEF PRODUCTS

Beyond quality and yield grading, the USDA provides the service of *certifying* a variety of beef products. Certification is generated by beef processors or private entities that want characteristics judged beyond normal quality- and yield-grading standards. The intention is to fine-tune the product and therefore be able to market it more specifically. A typical certified product is "Certified Angus Beef." This item has a live animal requirement that guarantees the cattle will have some Angus characteristics. It also requires a marbling score of *modest*, which eliminates the bottom third of choice; a specific carcass weight of not more than 1000 pounds; and a yield-grade score not more than 3.9.

There are numerous certified beef products available and some will be helpful to ensure a higher level of quality, but the buyer needs to understand the differences between requirements so as not to purchase certain certified items that are no more than clever marketing. The USDA lists all of the requirements for certified products on its

Web site. See http://www.ams.usda.gov/lsg/certprog/certbeef.htm and http://www.ams.usda.gov/lsg/certprog/speccomp.pdf.

Before purchasing a particular product, especially one at a higher price, the consumer needs to compare them to see the actual advantage of one over another.

Processors may also create "branded" products, where beef is selected by in-house graders who can apply certain quality criteria and label the product under a specific company brand name. These products may use the USDA to verify attributes, but also may decide to verify things "in house," which would not be restrained by the agency. A company may use a trim spec as a guideline to ensure a specific yield. Certain companies are separating beef that are achieving marbling scores that are above prime, such as those of the Wagyu cattle or Kobe-style beef. Other companies are identifying feeding practices and branding these traits regardless of marbling scores. *Grass-fed, all-vegetarian diet, antibiotic free*, or *no growth promotants or hormones* are examples of process-verified, branded products. These new market products may have an in-house certification process that guarantees the farmers are adhering to their specific guidelines. The goal of all certified and process-verified products is to differentiate them from standard products, giving the foodservice operator a way to market beef products at a higher cost.

FIGURE **2.13a**
Certified label.

FIGURE **2.13b**
Branded product label.

BEEF CARCASS BREAKDOWN

Beef carcasses are divided into specific sections. The way a carcass is divided depends on the country and culture that is fabricating it. European and English cuts will differ from the standard North American cuts. Countries around the world will differ in the way they cut, depending on the needs and styles of cooking. In this book, all carcasses and cuts will reflect the North American style of fabrication. Meat processors may change cut styles from time to time and subtle changes have occurred over the years to improve products and increase cutability or profit.

Fabricating beef from a whole carcass is a difficult task for an individual. A beef carcass is split down the spine just after slaughter, creating *sides*. A full beef carcass from a decent-quality grade will weigh approximately 600 to 900 pounds; therefore, a beef side is about ten to fourteen feet in length and can weigh upwards of 450 pounds. Buying large cuts of beef and breaking them down requires more than simple skill and accuracy with the knife; there is a necessary amount of physical strength to maneuver such large pieces. For this reason, as well as many other reasons, it is rare to find a restaurant that buys large beef cuts.

Once the beef is split into sides, they are then divided into quarters and then into *primal cuts*. Along with the major primals, there are some minor primal cuts that do not hold as much value. They will be labeled *market forms* in this book. Primals are usually the largest cuts available in beef. They are heavy and difficult to store and fabricate.

Restaurants rarely see the primals and a skilled butcher would be required to fabricate these cuts. If a restaurant wanted to create a custom cut that is not commercially available, a primal may be considered. Fewer and fewer meat purveyors carry primal beef cuts and their value has increased due to the difficulty in transporting them.

After the primals, beef is divided into *subprimals*, which usually represent muscle separations of the primal. Subprimals may be trimmed to a specific level or divided further. In the foodservice industry, subprimals and their trimmed versions are known as hotel restaurant and institution (HRI) cuts. There are a multitude of trim levels and specifics for these cuts and it is important to recognize those differences and be able to make decisions based on yield percentages and labor. Many restaurants will fabricate their own portions from HRI cuts and utilize the trim that may result. HRI cuts require some extra skill. This book will focus on fabrication of HRI cuts into portions.

Portion cuts, *portion-control cuts*, or *value-added cuts* all refer to items that are generally ready to cook. These cuts are simple to use and require no skill level. The initial price may be higher than HRI cuts, however, and portion cuts are inflexible. Your menu item would need to stay within the portion size ordered. An advantage of portion cuts is the ease of inventory control.

Another subcategory of the portion cut would be the *reformulated* cut. These cuts refer to those that take pieces and meld them together by a chemical bonding process to create a "new" portion.

PRIMALS

- Round
- Loin
- Rib
- Chuck

MINOR PRIMALS

- Plate
- Brisket
- Foreshank

The North American Beef Processors Association [NAMP] has developed a number system that identifies most of the beef cuts available today. Meat processors develop their own code numbers that may or may not incorporate the NAMP numbers, but meat purveyor salesmen are familiar with them. This book uses the NAMP numbers as a guide, but be sure to identify individual processors' codes to receive the exact specs you require. Some cuts may have multiple names; listed below are the most typical.

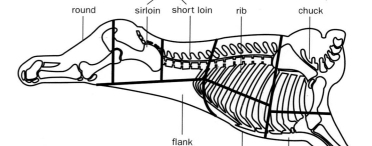

Beef skeletal structure

FIGURE **2.14** Beef skeletal structure with primal divisions.

ROUND

The beef round or back leg is generally the largest primal. It consists of large, lean muscles that have a high yield percentage. The cuts vary in quality and size. The largest and most tender is the *top round*. In foodservice, the top round is used most

FIGURE **2.15** Beef primal round.

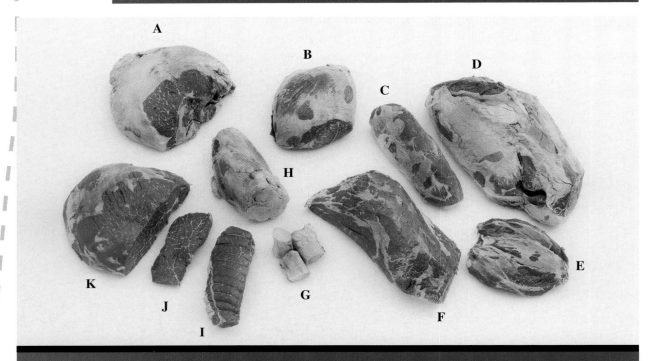

FIGURE **2.16** A. Top round or inside round; B. knuckle; C. eye round; D. gooseneck round; E. heel; F. bottom round or outside round; G. marrow bones; H. shank; I. top round roast, tied; J. top round London Broil; K. top round, cap off.

often as roasts, steaks, and various thin-sliced items. Other round cuts are lean and do not have much connective tissue, but their muscle fibers tend to be slightly thick and therefore can be tough. Retail stores embrace the round cuts, selling them as roast for reasonable prices, but foodservice operations often struggle to create high-value cuts from most of the round. The classic buffet presentation of the *steamship roast* includes the entire round with its shank bone Frenched and trimmed to specific levels. This large (sometimes upwards of sixty-five pounds) roast can be an awe-inspiring carving station at large functions and weddings.

Subprimal Cuts
- Top / inside round
- Eye round
- Knuckle
- Shank
- Bottom / outside round flat
- Heel

ITEM AND NAMP NUMBER	DESCRIPTION/ FABRICATION	SUGGESTED COOKING METHOD/APPLICATION	AVERAGE SUGGESTED WEIGHT IN POUNDS	TYPICAL PACKAGE SPECS
158 Round, primal	Large, full primal	Round cuts tend to be large, full muscle cuts that can be slow roasted; some dry cooked as steaks, braised, or ground	70–100	Sold individually
166B Steamship round with handle	Full primal, trimmed for large roasting	Slow roasting, 8 or more hours; be sure to check temperature. Used for carving station, catering	60–70	Sold individually
167 Knuckle	Untrimmed, requires fabrication; also known as *sirloin tip*	Roast, steak, braise, can be split; *tip side* is tender	10–14	4 per box
167A Knuckle, peeled	Trimmed, may need some fabrication	Roast, steak, braise, can be split; *tip side* is tender	8–12	
168 Top / inside round	Untrimmed, needs fabrication; sold with various levels of fat trim	Roast beef, slicing steak, *London Broil*, sliced thin for stuffing and rolling (roulade, braciole) thinner for quick cook	17–23	3 per box
169A Top round, cap off	Trimmed, roast ready; can be purchased split	Same as above	16–19	4 per box
170 Bottom round (gooseneck)	Large, three sections: outside, eye, and heel	Braise, roast, some sections for stew or grind	24–30	2 per case
171B Outside round flat	Trimmed or untrimmed	Braise, pot roast, sauerbraten; can be roasted and sliced thin; excellent for jerky	12–16	4 per case
171C Eye round	Trimmed	Braise, pot roast, oven roast (sliced thin), inexpensive carpaccio or fondue (well trimmed)	3–6	12 per case
Heel (no NAMP number)	trimmed	Braise, stew, grind, consumé, goulash, ragout (good flavor)	2–3	varies
Hind shank (no NAMP number)	Sold bone in or boneless	Braise, stew, grind, consumé, goulash, ragout (good flavor)	7–9	2 per bag, 4 bags per case

FIGURE **2.17** NAMP HRI chart for beef round.

FIGURE **2.18a** Trimmed beef loin (outside view).

FIGURE **2.18b** Trimmed beef loin (inside view).

LOIN

The beef loin holds more value than any other section. The HRI cuts are some of the most tender and expensive on the carcass and are generally dry cooked as quality steaks and roasts. The loin is fabricated in two ways. First, the loin can be cut in a way to fabricate for large steaks, such as the porterhouse and t-bone. These two steaks are standards on many steakhouse menus.

Second, the loin can be fabricated into individual subprimals, creating the beef tenderloin and striploin separately; these are often the marquee steaks on the menu, demanding the highest prices. Beyond the exclusive cuts, the loin also holds a few cuts of lesser quality that are also very popular menu items. The top sirloin is a large section of the loin and offers a reasonable steak or roast with many options when cutting. It is typically sold as a large steak for slicing or broken into its *eyes,* or sections, and individual portion cut. It is used in some classic dishes such as *churasco*, where it is cut into large chunks and grilled on skewers. Bistro-style steaks from the tri tip, flank, and sirloin flap are flavorful and have unique textures that, if cut correctly, can offer a very satisfying dining experience.

Subprimal Cuts
- Striploin
- Tenderloin
- Shortloin
- Sirloin
- Flank

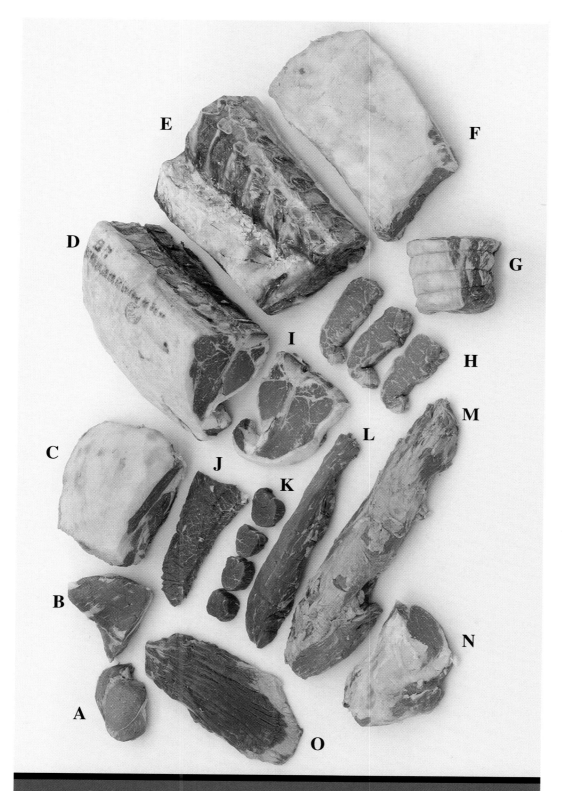

FIGURE **2.19** A. beef ball tip; B. beef tri tip; C. top sirloin butt; D. beef shortloin; E. bone-in beef striploin; F. boneless beef striploin; G. striploin roast; H. striploin steaks; I. porterhouse steaks; J. sirloin flap; K. beef tenderloin medallions; L. beef tenderloin, denuded; M. beef tenderloin, PSMO; N. beef tenderloin butt; O. beef flank steak.

FIGURE **2.20** NAMP HRI cuts chart for beef loin.

ITEM AND NAMP NUMBER	DESCRIPTION/ FABRICATION	SUGGESTED COOKING METHOD/APPLICATION	AVERAGE SUGGESTED WEIGHT IN POUNDS	TYPICAL PACKAGE SPECS
172 Loin (primal)	Full loin, trimmed, requires fabrication	Cuts from the loin are generally dry cooked as steaks or roasts; many options exist from the many cuts created from the loin	55–80	Sold individually as hanging beef
174 Shortloin trim specs—0 × 1, 1 × 1, 2 × 3	Only purchased for cutting porterhouse and t-bone steaks; requires band saw	Grill, chargrill, broil; high heat preferred; can be dry aged	22–28 (varies with trim specs)	3 per box; can also be purchased as hanging beef for dry aging
1174 Porterhouse / t-bone portion cuts	Porterhouse has larger tenderloin eye	Grill, chargrill, broil; high heat preferred	Customer specified	Varies with processor
175 Striploin, bone in trim specs—1 × 1, 2 × 3 tail measurements	Requires band saw; cut for portions	Grill, chargrill, broil as bone-in steak, shell steak, top loin steak, New York strip or Kansas City strip steak; can be dry aged	18–20	4 per box; can also be purchased as hanging beef for dry aging
1179 Striploin portion cut	Trimmed	See above	Customer specified	Varies
180 Striploin, boneless trim specs—0 × 1, 1 × 1, 2 × 3	Trim levels vary, requires some fabrication	Grill, chargrill, broil as boneless steak, pan sear, sauté, New York strip steak; can be divided into medallions	8–14, depending on trim level; be sure to order within a 21-pound range for consistent portion sizing	6 per box
1180 / 1180A Striploin portion cut	Trimmed, "A" is missing the vein steaks	See above	Customer specified	Varies
181 Sirloin	Large bone-in item, requires extensive fabrication	Very large bone-in steaks if crosscut on band saw, grill, broil	19–28	Sold individually
184 Top sirloin butt, boneless	Requires some fabrication; sold with varying amounts of trim	Grill, broil, pan sear, sauté, large slicing steaks, divided into portion steaks	12–15	6 per box

(Continues)

ITEM AND NAMP NUMBER	DESCRIPTION/ FABRICATION	SUGGESTED COOKING METHOD/APPLICATION	AVERAGE SUGGESTED WEIGHT IN POUNDS	TYPICAL PACKAGE SPECS
1184 Top sirloin portion cut	Trimmed; a variety of specs available	Grill, broil, pan sear, sauté	Customer specified	Varies
185A Sirloin flap	Trimmed	Slicing steak, barbecue, grill, broil, excellent for marinating, may need tenderizing	3–4	6 per bag, 2 per box; Packaging varies with processor
185B Ball tip	Trimmed, may need trimming of collagen bands	Slicing steak, grill, broil	2–3	6 per bag, 3 per box
185D Tri tip	Defatted, trimmed	Slicing steak, barbecue, grill, broil, excellent for marinating, may need tenderizing, carne asada	2–3	6 per bag, 3 per box
189 Tenderloin, full	Untrimmed, poor yield	For roasting whole if fat is desired	8–10	8 per case
189A Tenderloin, PSMO (peeled, side muscle on)	Most typical purchase; requires trimming	Roasting whole, grill, broil, sauté, filet mignon, medallions, tournedoes, served raw as carpaccio, steak tartare, brochette, kebab;	4.5–6.5	12 per case
190 Tenderloin, side muscle off	Requires some trimming	See above	4–5	12 per case
190A Tenderloin, skinned, denuded	Trimmed	See above	3–4	12–14 per case
1190 A / B Tenderloin portion cuts	Trimmed, "B" considered *barrel* cut without any gaps	Grill, broil, sauté, filet mignon, medallions, tournedoes,	Varies	Varies with processor
191 Tenderloin butt	Thick side or head of tenderloin; sold with varying trim levels	Can be used for all tenderloin applications; also for the classic roast chateaubriand	2–4	2 per bag, 18 per box; Packaging varies with processor
193 Flank steak	Trimmed	Grill, broil, London Broil, slicing steak, stuff and braise	1–3	6 per bag, 4 per box; Packaging varies with processor

FIGURE **2.21a** Beef rib primal.

FIGURE **2.21b**

FIGURE **2.21c** Beef rib breakdown: A. Beef export rib, B. Boneless beef ribeye lip on, C. Beef back ribs, D. Beef short ribs Korean style short cut, E. Beef short ribs, F. Beef rib cap, G. Beef rib steak boneless, H. Beef rib steak bone-in.

RIB

The rib is the smallest of all the primals, averaging only thirty to forty pounds. The rib has one main section, the *rib eye*. Other than the rib eye, there are only a few short ribs and a cap of blade meat. The rib of beef is known for popular steak cuts, such as the Delmonico and the cowboy steak. It is best known for the roast fabricated from the eye. The terms *standing rib* and *prime rib roast* are commonly seen on buffet menus, and the roast has been a customer favorite for many years. Even a lower-quality grade of rib eye can present fairly well, because the eye muscle has sections and layers of fat, infusing the cut with extra flavor. Some chefs today are separating the rib eye into its individual layers. The top layer, sometimes known as the inner *deckle*, is highly marbleized and considered one of the most flavorful cuts on the entire carcass.

Subprimal Cuts
- Rib eye (bone in or boneless)
- Short ribs
- Blade meat

FIGURE **2.22** NAMP HRI cuts for beef rib.

ITEM AND NAMP NUMBER	DESCRIPTION/ FABRICATION	SUGGESTED COOKING METHOD/APPLICATION	AVERAGE SUGGESTED WEIGHT IN POUNDS	TYPICAL PACKAGE SPECS
103 Rib	Full primal	Multiple uses, purchased to dry age "Tomahawk Chop" portion cut	35–40	Sold as individual item
109 Rib, roast-ready	Large rib bone-in item with feather bones and thick cap fat included; poor yield	For roasting only; standing rib roast, prime rib	18–26	3 per case
109D Export style 109E	Rib bones in, fat cover off, short-cut, two-inch lip included	Standing rib roast, prime rib, bone-in rib eye steak, cowboy steak, Frenched bones	16–20	4 per case
1103 Rib steak portion cut, bone in	Trimmed	Bone-in rib eye steak, cowboy steak	Customer specified	Varies
112A Rib eye, lip on	Boneless, no cap, two-inch lip of fat included	Boneless rib roast, prime rib, boneless rib steak, Delmonico steak	11–14	6 per case
112 Rib eye roll	Boneless, well trimmed	Well trimmed boneless rib roast, boneless rib steak, Delmonico steak	8–10	6–8 per case
1112 / 1112A Rib steak, portion cut, boneless	Trimmed, "A" has lip of fat on	Boneless rib steak, Delmonico steak	Customer specified	Varies
1103 Rib steak, portion cut, bone in	Has curved rib bone in	Bone-in rib steak, cowboy steak if Frenched	Customer specified	varies
123B Short ribs	Three bone sections, can be cut into Korean or flanken style	Braising, slow roasting, barbecue style	3–4	4 per bag, 4 bags per case
124 Beef back ribs	Not as meaty as short ribs	Braising, slow roasting, barbecue	As specified	

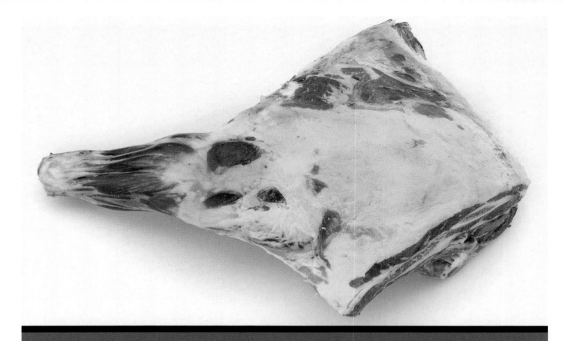

FIGURE **2.23** Beef arm chuck.

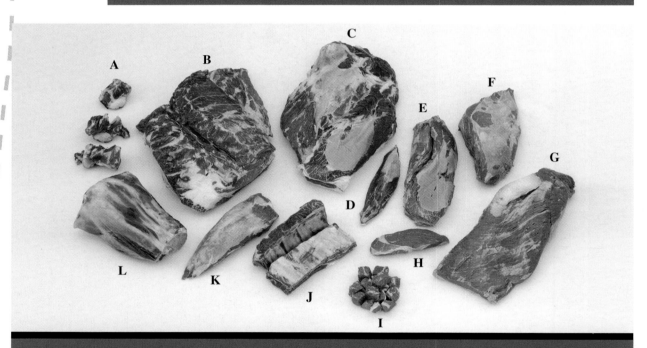

FIGURE **2.24** A. Beef neck bones; B. beef chuck roll; C. beef shoulder clod; D. beef *teres major*/shoulder tender; E. beef top blade; F. trimmed beef shoulder clod heart; G. beef brisket; H. beef shoulder London Broil; I. beef chuck stew; J. beef short ribs/Korean or flanken style; K. beef scotch tender; L. beef foreshank.

CHUCK

The beef chuck contains muscles that experience more movement and range of motion than any of the other primal cuts do, resulting in some cuts being very tough and many cuts containing multiple muscle groups with connective tissues. These cuts have great flavor and are excellent for braising, stews, and grind. For years, the chuck was simply cut across all the muscle groups on the band saw, creating the *chuck steak*. Today, we see the chuck also being separated into individual muscle cuts. This has allowed for the discovery of some tender, deep-shoulder muscles that can be dry cooked and are excellent

ITEM AND NAMP NUMBER	DESCRIPTION/ FABRICATION	SUGGESTED COOKING METHOD/APPLICATION	AVERAGE SUGGESTED WEIGHT IN POUNDS	TYPICAL PACKAGE SPECS
		FIGURE 2.25 NAMP HRI cuts for beef chuck.		
113 Chuck	square-cut (primal)	Chuck cuts are flavorful but tend to be tougher; excellent for stewing, goulash, grinding, large braises, barbecue, slow roasting	79–106	1 per case
114 Shoulder clod	Large, untrimmed, requires some fabrication	Braising, pot roast, stew, slow cooking, grind; can be dry cooked if trimmed correctly	15–21	3 per case
114C Shoulder clod, trimmed	Large trimmed, requires some fabrication	Braising, pot roast, stew, slow cooking; can be dry cooked if trimmed correctly	13–18	3 per case
114D Top blade/ flatiron	Defatted, silverskin and connective tissues on	Braising roast or steak; dry cook as flatiron steak if trimmed	5–6	1 per bag, 10 per case
114E Shoulder roast/ heart of clod	Trimmed center section of clod	Braising roast; dry cook as "shoulder London Broil" if well trimmed	8–10	6 per case
Teres Major / Shoulder tender	Small / very tender	Grill, broil, cut as medallions	1–2	6 per bag, 8 bag per case
116A Chuck roll	Trimmed / tied	Slow roast, grill, barbeque, braise	15–21	3 per case
116D Chuck eye roll	Centercut portion cut of chuck roll, very flavorful	Slow roast, grill, barbeque, braise, chuck eye steak	5–7	
116B Chuck tender	Small, tough	Braise, stew, goulash, ragout, grind	2–3	

as steak items. The bone structure of the chuck is the most complex and requires a high skill level to fabricate it. The bones themselves, especially those from the neck, make a superior stock. They contain a lot of connective tissue and usually a fair amount of meat.

Subprimal Cuts
- Shoulder clod
  (Includes the top blade, *teres major*, heart of the clod)
- Chuck roll
  (Includes the chuck eye roll, under blade)
- Chuck tender
- Short ribs

PLATE, BRISKET, AND FORESHANK

These cuts in their rough form, as cut from the whole carcass, contain a lot of bone and waste fat. Being lower on the carcass, they tend to be tough but very flavorful. The brisket has multiple uses. It is a mainstay of beef barbecue, being smoke roasted for hours. Brisket, cured and seasoned, is used for corned beef and pastrami. It is a favorite as pot roast as well.

The plate contains short ribs and the skirt steak. The skirt is the original *fajita* and is actually the diaphragm of the animal. The two sides of the diaphragm are connected in the middle of the carcass at the *hanger*. The hanger is considered a high-flavor, quality steak known as the *Anglaise* in French cooking.

The foreshank contains some of the toughest muscles on the carcass. It is primarily used for grind and can make a quality broth or stock.

Subprimals
Plate:

- Short ribs
- Skirt steak
- Hanger steak

Brisket:

- Fresh, cured
- Whole or split

Foreshank:

- Whole or boneless

FIGURE **2.26** NAMP HRI cuts for beef plate, brisket, and foreshank.

ITEM AND NAMP NUMBER	DESCRIPTION/ FABRICATION	SUGGESTED COOKING METHOD/APPLICATION	AVERAGE SUGGESTED WEIGHT IN POUNDS	TYPICAL PACKAGE SPECS
120 Brisket 120 A / B (also purchased as corned beef if cured)	Boneless, deckle off Flat section (leaner) Point section (fatty)	Braise, barbecue, slow cooking, can be purchased as corned beef and simmered	10–12	6 per case
121c Plate, skirt steak (diaphragm), outside	Higher quality than inside skirt, needs to be peeled and defatted	Grill, broil, *fajita*, pan sear, cut across grain	2–3	4 per pack, 12 packs per case (packaging varies
121d Plate, skirt steak, inside	Lesser quality, requires fabrication	Grill, broil, pan sear (may require tenderization before cooking), cut across grain	3–4	4 per pack
Hanger steak	Also known as the *steak anglaise*. Requires peeling and removal of large collagen band	Very flavorful steak; grill, broil, sauté; may require marinade or tenderizing		2 per bag, 6 per case

BEEF OFFAL

- Beef liver
- Tripe
- Oxtail
- Tongue
- Cheeks

Beef offal are, generally, reasonably priced and can offer some unique flavors and textures. Braised oxtail creates a rich full flavor; the cheeks also are presented as a very flavorful braise; the tripe is used in many classic dishes and needs a long cooking time. Beef tongue is often cured and smoked, which gives it a ham-like flavor.

FIGURE 2.27 NAMP HRI cuts for beef offal.				
ITEM AND NAMP NUMBER	DESCRIPTION/ FABRICATION	SUGGESTED COOKING METHOD/APPLICATION	AVERAGE SUGGESTED WEIGHT IN POUNDS	TYPICAL PACKAGE SPECS
Beef offal		Beef offal tend to be strong in flavor; prices tend to be very reasonable		
Beef oxtail	Sold singular or portion cut into sections	Slow braise, soups, stews, ragout	2–4	6 per box
Beef tripe	Honey comb tripe is best; sold frozen in blocks	Slow braise, stew, used as ingredient in other dishes	Varies	Sold by box weight; frozen
Beef tongue	Fresh or smoked; requires peeling	Slow cooked, simmered, boiled	3–4	Varies
Beef cheeks	May require some fabrication, trimming, washing	Very flavorful, slow braised	.5–1	Sold as large frozen block, 60 pounds; packaging can vary
Beef liver	Requires peeling and blood vessel removal; requires slicing into portions	Strong flavor; sautéed, pan seared	8–10	1–2 per box
Beef kidney	Requires removal of blood vessels in center	Strong flavor; steak and kidney pie, slow cooked	2—2.5	Varies
Beef blood	Liquid	Used for coagulation sausages; Boudin Noire, blood sausage or pudding, kishka, blutwurst	1 gallon	1-gallon container

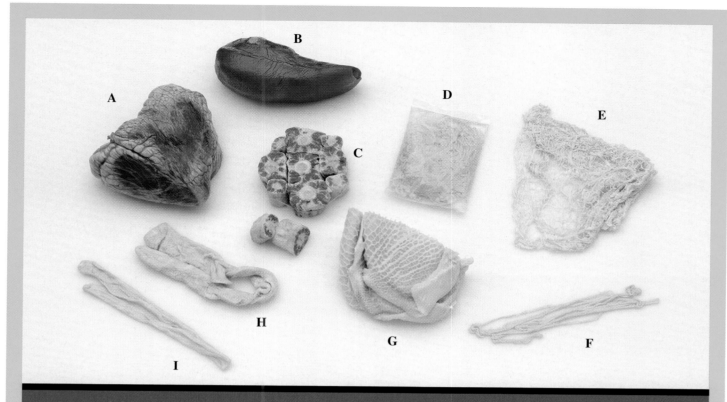

FIGURE 2.28 Offal: A. Beef heart; B. smoked beef tongue; C. beef oxtail, portion cut; D. sheep casings; E. pork caul fat; F. hog casings; G. beef tripe; H. beef middle casings; I. beef round casings.

FABRICATION OF BEEF CUTS

BEEF ROUND

The beef round is the largest of the primal cuts of beef. It contains the subprimal cuts top round, knuckle, eye round, heel, bottom round flat, and the shank. Each section varies in tenderness, with top round being the best. The shank and heel are the two toughest sections. The round is sold whole and is most often broken down into the subprimals. The round is sometimes sold as a *steamship*, which has the shank Frenched and the aitch bone removed. It is slow roasted and used as a carving station item.

TOP ROUND

The top round is most often cooked as a large roast. It is excellent for slicing roast beef, due to its large collagen-free muscle structure. It can be used for large slicing steaks, but is better if marinated or pinned (mechanically tenderized). The top round is also excellent for thin slicing as a stuffed and rolled

FIGURE 2.29 Beef top round (NAMP 168/169).

FIGURE **2.30a** The top round can be fabricated into roasts or steaks. Trim the exterior cap fat to 1/8 inch thickness.

braising cut (roulade, bracciole, paupiette) or even thinner as a quick sauté or stir-fry.

Fabrication of a Beef Top Round to a Large Roast

Trim cap fat to 1/8 inch thickness

Trim *soft side* muscle and remove blood vessels and connectives

Trim connectives and membranes from underside

Split roast if desired

Tie using a butchers knot

FIGURE **2.30b** Cut away fatty tail section about two inches from end.

FIGURE **2.30d** Top round can be roasted whole or divided into smaller roasts. Divide with natural grain. A top round yields three, four- to five-pound roasts.

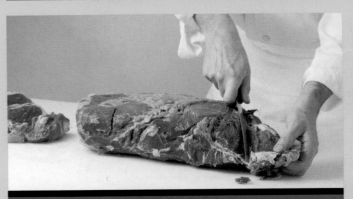

FIGURE **2.30c** Turn over and remove soft side muscle. Soft side contains blood vessels and tougher fibers(169C).

FIGURE **2.30e** Tie roasts using butchers twine. Space knots evenly for presentation and even cooking.

Alternatives — Remove cap for super-trimmed roast
Cut into large London Broil type steaks.
Slice into 1/4-inch cutlets for stuffing and rolling.
Slice very thin for quick cooking, such as fondue, wok cook, cheese steak.

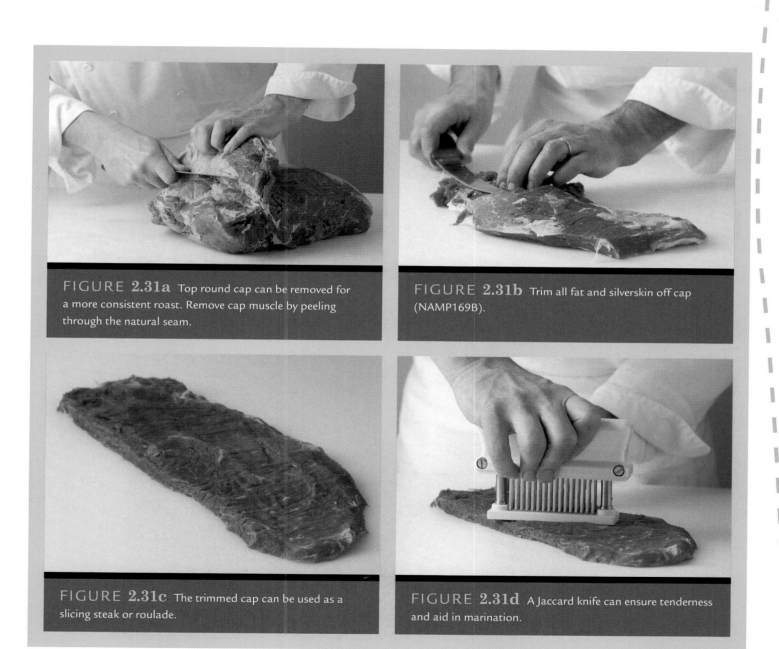

FIGURE **2.31a** Top round cap can be removed for a more consistent roast. Remove cap muscle by peeling through the natural seam.

FIGURE **2.31b** Trim all fat and silverskin off cap (NAMP169B).

FIGURE **2.31c** The trimmed cap can be used as a slicing steak or roulade.

FIGURE **2.31d** A Jaccard knife can ensure tenderness and aid in marination.

FIGURE **2.32** Rather than tying the top round into roasts, cut large London Broil steaks. Top round yields six or seven large one-inch steaks (NAMP 1169).

FIGURE **2.33** Slicing a portion of beef top round to use for a roulade.

Hint from the butcher: Slightly freezing the top round will allow for very thin slicing.

BEEF GOOSENECK ROUND

The gooseneck is a section of the round containing the bottom round flat, eye round, and heel. These three cuts are very lean, but tough. The gooseneck remains the most reasonably priced of all the cuts in the round.

FIGURE **2.34** Beef gooseneck round (NAMP 170).

FIGURE **2.35a** The gooseneck is comprised of three sections: the eye round, the bottom round flat, and the heel (NAMP 171B, 171C, 171F).

FIGURE **2.35b** To divide into sections, start by dividing away the eye round through the natural seam.

FIGURE **2.35c** Separate heel and thick fat from back end.

FIGURE **2.35d** The bottom round flat can be trimmed for roasting or braising. Trim heavy silverskin off side. Trim fat to 1/8-inch thickness.

FIGURE **2.35e** Tie roast using slipknot to shape.

FIGURE **2.35f** Knots lined up for easy removal.

FIGURE **2.35g** The heel section is tougher and can be used for stewing or braising.

FIGURE **2.35h** Cut into strips and crosscut for cubes. Heel meat also has great flavor when ground as burger.

BEEF SHANK

The beef shank is one of the toughest muscles on the carcass but also one of the most flavorful. It is loaded with collagen, which adds a lot of flavor and protein to the dish. It is used for a superior stew or a flavorful grind.

Beef Shank and Cut Beef Stew Cubes

- Trim exterior fat.
- Find "bone side," where the bone is near the surface.
- Run knife down one side of the bone, then the other, angling into the bone. Loosen meat from the base of the shank.

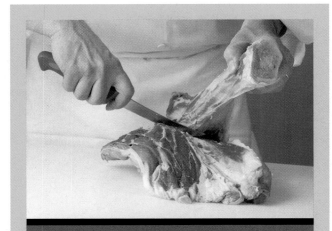

FIGURE **2.36c** Once both sides are loosened, cut underneath towards the base.

FIGURE **2.36a** Beef Shank; peel exterior membrane.

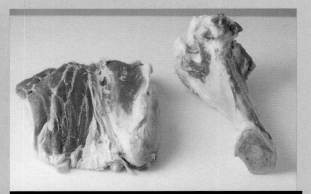

FIGURE **2.36d** Boneless shank meat and "marrow" bone.

FIGURE **2.36b** Find the bone near the surface. Outline bone on either side, cutting from the thinner side towards the thicker base of the shank.

FIGURE **2.36e** Trim the shank and cut into cubes for stewing.

- Trim exterior fat.
- Cut into strips and crosscut into stew cubes.

BEEF LOIN

The loin contains the four subprimals: striploin, tenderloin, sirloin, and flank. The striploin and part of the tenderloin form the shortloin. All of these cuts are popular menu items and therefore cost more, on average. These are sold bonein or boneless, with varying trim levels, or as portion-control cuts.

BEEF STRIPLOIN

The striploin is one of the best-known and most readily identifiable cuts of beef. It is typically fabricated into quality steaks, such as the New York strip or shell steak. It can also be used for a quality roast, giving a very consistent slice. Today, we see some chefs splitting the striploin the long way to cut into medallions or thin slicing for carpaccio.

FIGURE **2.37** Beef striploin, bonein (NAMP 175).

Beef Striploin for Roast or Steaks

Trim exterior to desired thickness.

Remove large collagen band approximately two inches across top of eye muscle.

Remove bone connective tissues from underside.

Cut off "vein" steak from sirloin side (if roasting, tie with two-inch spacing).

Portion cut with palm flat against steak, making an even portion; weigh steak for accuracy.

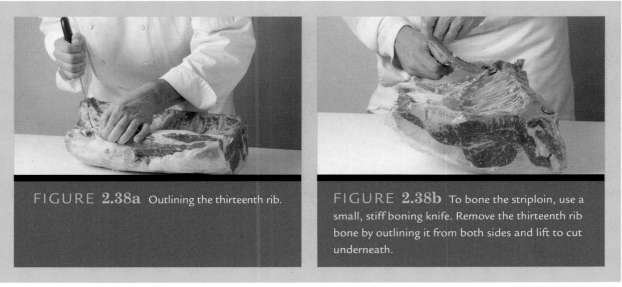

FIGURE **2.38a** Outlining the thirteenth rib.

FIGURE **2.38b** To bone the striploin, use a small, stiff boning knife. Remove the thirteenth rib bone by outlining it from both sides and lift to cut underneath.

(Continues)

FIGURE **2.38c** Cut through the chine bone area flat across all bones at about a 45-degree angle.

FIGURE **2.38d** Peel away the feather bones by keeping the knife flat and cutting downward.

FIGURE **2.38e** Remove finger bones by hooking knife underneath thick section and peeling towards the flat part of each bone. There are typically five or six flat finger bones.

FIGURE **2.38f** Remove the thick tail fat trimming to desired thickness. A typical measurement is to leave one inch of fat on the rib end and trimming to zero inches on the sirloin end. This creates a (NAMP 180) 0x1 striploin, a typical foodservice spec.

FIGURE **2.38g** To fabricate striploin into roast or steaks, start by trimming cap fat to 1/8-inch thickness. Use a larger knife such as a scimitar or slicer.

FIGURE **2.38h** Remove the heavy collagen band located along the top side of the striploin. Typically, it is two inches wide. Remove all bone connectives from underside, also.

FIGURE **2.38i** Tie roast at about two-inch intervals to maintain shape. Some chefs are splitting the striploin lengthwise to create two smaller roasts.

FIGURE **2.38j** When cutting portions of striploin steaks, use a scimitar or slicing knife. Be sure to hold steaks flat with palm when cutting and weigh each for accuracy.

(*Continues*)

(Continued)

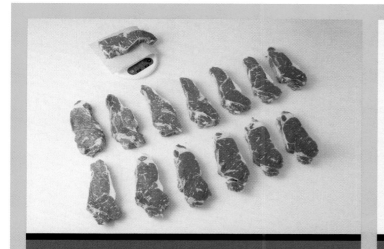

FIGURE **2.38k** A typical yield from a ten- to twelve-pound 0x1 striploin will be about fourteen to sixteen, eight-ounce steaks.

FIGURE **2.38l** On the sirloin side of the striploin is the vein end steak. Note the difference between the two steaks. The one on the left is the tougher vein steak, with a collagen band running through the middle. For portion steaks (NAMP 1180), the vein steak may be included. The center cut (NAMP 1180A) eliminates the vein steak.

BEEF TENDERLOIN

The beef tenderloin has the finest fibers of any cut in the carcass and, therefore, is very tender, highly prized, and the most expensive. The tenderloin is very popular on many menus and is served as many different dishes. Filet mignon, tournedoes, and chateaubriand are just a few of the classics that are made from the tenderloin.

FIGURE **2.39** Beef tenderloin PSMO (NAMP 189a).

Beef Tenderloin Fabricated into Roast or Steaks

Remove long side muscle (also known as chain).

Remove membranes from top side.

Peel collagen silverskin from the tail or thin side towards the head or thick side. Be sure to eliminate collagen between the large side muscle.

Remove large fat deposits on bottom side by scraping them loose.

Remove any bone tissues and collagen bands from head end.

Tuck tail and tie for roast *or*

Remove large side muscle at angle and portion cut for steaks or medallions.

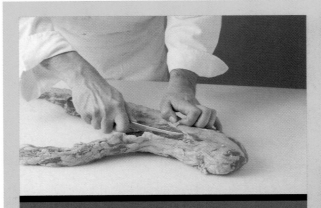

FIGURE **2.40a** The tenderloin is typically cleaned for roasting whole or cutting for portions. Pull away the long side muscle, or chain, and thin membranes. Most of this can be done by hand or with minimal use of a knife.

FIGURE **2.40b** Peel away collagen silverskin by placing the tip of the knife under the tail end and working the knife towards the head end. Peeling a tenderloin is always directional, so as not to work against the grain.

FIGURE **2.40c** Turn over the tenderloin and remove any connectives and fat chunks. Fat can be removed by scraping the underside towards the tail. Be careful not to over trim.

FIGURE **2.40d** Cleaned or denuded tenderloin (NAMP 190A).

FIGURE **2.40e** To roast the tenderloin, tuck the tail about two inches.

FIGURE **2.40f** Tie the roast from the tail to the head at about two-inch intervals. Do not over-tighten knots.

FIGURE **2.40g** To cut portion steaks, remove the large side muscle or head section, angling slightly to open the natural seam.

(*Continues*)

FIGURE **2.40h** Cut even portions using a scimitar or slicing knife. Hold the portion steady and be sure to keep the thickness even. Weigh each portion and be as accurate as possible.

FIGURE **2.40i** Smaller end sections can be butterflied to improve shape. Larger cuts to be cooked well done are often butterflied to ensure quicker cooking.

FIGURE **2.40j** Tenderloin steaks can be shaped by wrapping in plastic or cheesecloth.

FIGURE **2.40k** Typical yield of a six-pound tenderloin at four- to five-ounce portions (NAMP 1190A).

FIGURE **2.40l** Barding a tenderloin medallion with bacon or lard to increase moisture.

FIGURE **2.40m** The chain, or long side muscle, can be trimmed of fat and silverskin. Place flat, cover with plastic wrap, and pound to 1/4-inch thickness. The chain can be grilled as a fajita-type steak.

FIGURE **2.40n** The cleaned chain can be stuffed and rolled and tied or skewered as a roulade, pinwheel, or involtini.

BEEF SHORTLOIN

The beef shortloin is purchased primarily for cutting steaks, specifically the *porterhouse* and *t-bone* steaks. Cutting these steaks requires the use of a saw, preferably a band saw.

FIGURE **2.41** Beef shortloin (NAMP 174).

Hint from the butcher: The band saw is an extremely dangerous piece of equipment. Be sure the band saw is in good working order and has a sharp blade. It is advisable to practice cutting some less-valuable cuts and gain confidence before cutting the shortloin. Be sure there are no distractions while using the band saw and observe an experienced butcher before attempting such use.

Portion Cutting T-Bone Steaks

Pre-trim shortloin to reduce individual trimming of steaks.

Place the shortloin tenderloin side down.

Adjust saw so guide is at desired thickness.

Run shortloin through blade and hold steak as it passes blade.

Trim steaks to desired level.

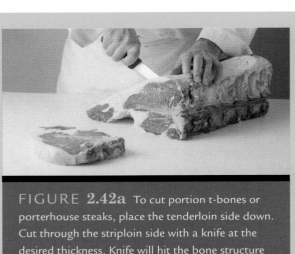

FIGURE **2.42a** To cut portion t-bones or porterhouse steaks, place the tenderloin side down. Cut through the striploin side with a knife at the desired thickness. Knife will hit the bone structure about halfway through.

FIGURE **2.42b** Cut through bones with hand saw and finish cut with knife. Avoid cutting the entire steak with the saw. This can slightly damage the steak's surface. Porterhouse are typically cut with a band saw.

FIGURE **2.42c** Trim edges of steak. Some chefs choose to remove the tail section, which is somewhat tougher.

FIGURE **2.42d** Cutting short ribs with a band saw.

BEEF TOP SIRLOIN BUTT

The top sirloin is a tender steak or roast cut and is widely used in the foodservice industry. It is a flexible cut that can be used as a roast, large slicing steak, small portion cut, or cubed for skewers such as brochette, churasco, or kebob. It can also be cut thin for quick grilling, for example, in a cheesesteak or Satay. It is sold whole or sectioned.

FIGURE 2.43 Top sirloin butt (NAMP 184).

Beef Top Sirloin Butt to Portion Steaks

Trim fat top to desired thickness.

Remove cap section.

Divide through natural seam and eliminate collagen band.

Portion cap at slight angle across grain.

Portion main sections, cutting perpendicular to cutting board.

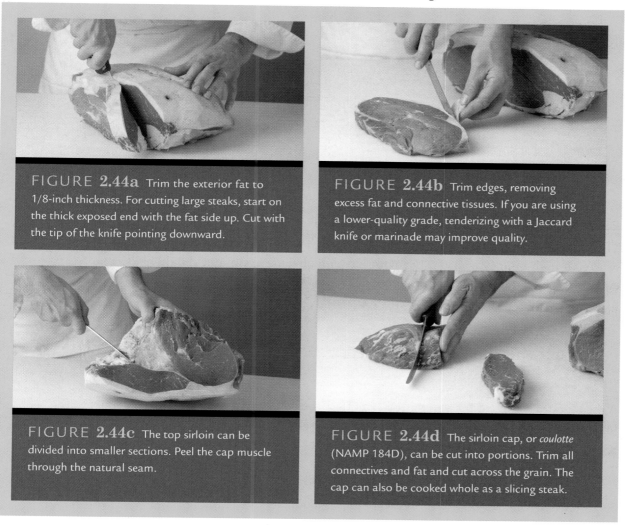

FIGURE 2.44a Trim the exterior fat to 1/8-inch thickness. For cutting large steaks, start on the thick exposed end with the fat side up. Cut with the tip of the knife pointing downward.

FIGURE 2.44b Trim edges, removing excess fat and connective tissues. If you are using a lower-quality grade, tenderizing with a Jaccard knife or marinade may improve quality.

FIGURE 2.44c The top sirloin can be divided into smaller sections. Peel the cap muscle through the natural seam.

FIGURE 2.44d The sirloin cap, or *coulotte* (NAMP 184D), can be cut into portions. Trim all connectives and fat and cut across the grain. The cap can also be cooked whole as a slicing steak.

(Continues)

(*Continued*)

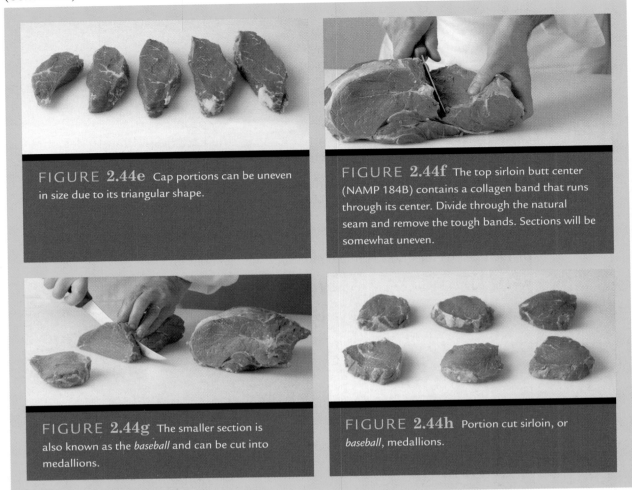

FIGURE **2.44e** Cap portions can be uneven in size due to its triangular shape.

FIGURE **2.44f** The top sirloin butt center (NAMP 184B) contains a collagen band that runs through its center. Divide through the natural seam and remove the tough bands. Sections will be somewhat uneven.

FIGURE **2.44g** The smaller section is also known as the *baseball* and can be cut into medallions.

FIGURE **2.44h** Portion cut sirloin, or *baseball*, medallions.

BEEF BOTTOM SIRLOIN TRI TIP AND FLAP

These cuts are popular, inexpensive steaks, used in a quick sauté or stir-fry, barbecue, or even a high-quality braise. They both have an obvious grain and should always be cut across the fibers to ensure tenderness.

Sirloin Flap, Tri Tip to Steak

Trim any excess fat and silverskin.

Cut across grain on a slight bias.

BEEF FLANK

A steak cut often used for marinated London Broil, quick grilling steaks, stir-fry, or fajita. The flank can be butterflied and opened for stuffing.

Butterflied Flank Steak

Trim off excess fat.

Slice along entire length with palm flat. Use a thin blade, such as a slicer, to minimize friction.

BEEF RIB

BONING OUT BEEF RIB

The beef rib eye is fabricated into steaks or roasts. It is often purchased pre-trimmed and almost oven ready. To fabricate it into portion steaks requires some minor trimming and can be completed in minutes. More complicated fabrication, such as frenching the bones for cutting cowboy steaks, may take a little longer.

FIGURE **2.45** Primal beef rib (NAMP 103).

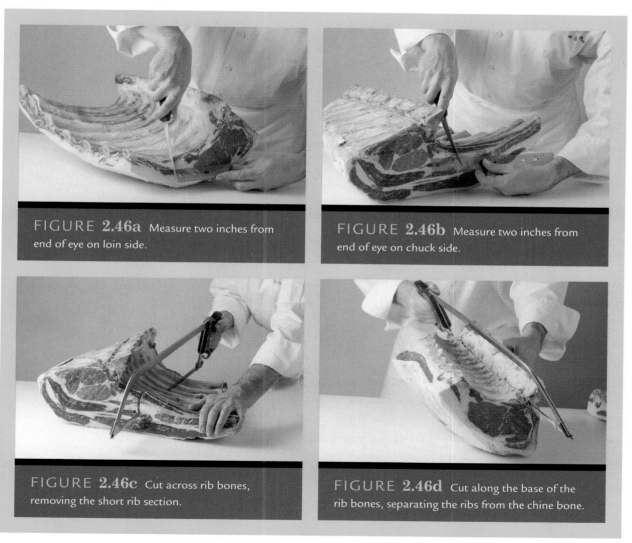

FIGURE **2.46a** Measure two inches from end of eye on loin side.

FIGURE **2.46b** Measure two inches from end of eye on chuck side.

FIGURE **2.46c** Cut across rib bones, removing the short rib section.

FIGURE **2.46d** Cut along the base of the rib bones, separating the ribs from the chine bone.

(Continues)

(Continued)

FIGURE **2.46e** Peel away the feather bones with a semi-flexible boning knife.

FIGURE **2.46f** Remove the cap or deckle by cutting through the natural seam.

FIGURE **2.46g** Peel away the yellow elastin band that runs along the top of the eye muscle.

FIGURE **2.46h** To fabricate the roast ready rib (NAMP 109), remove the meat from the fat cap and tie it and the feather bones back on the rib eye.

FIGURE **2.46i** The roast ready was intended to roast slowly with all of the covering to protect the eye muscle.

BONELESS BEEF RIB EYE PORTION CUT

Trim excess fat on cap.

Remove fat along lip.

Slice portion with palm flat against steak, cutting with tip pointing down.

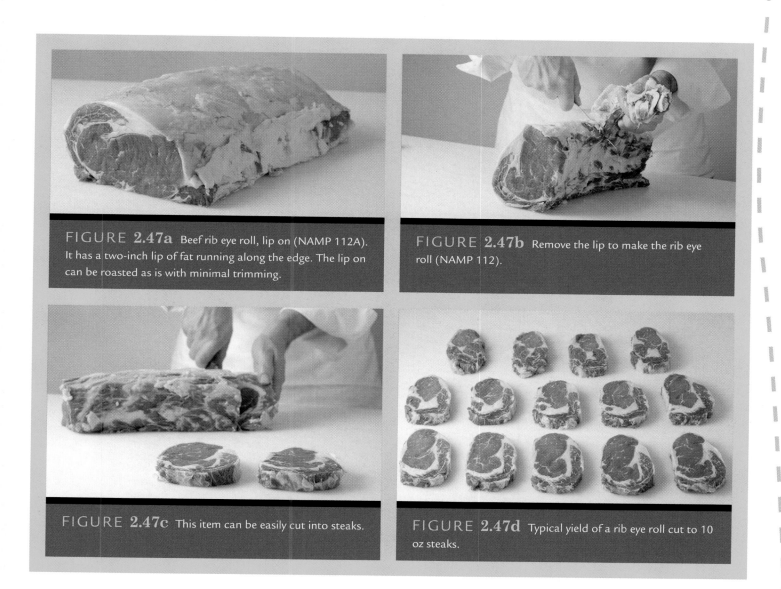

FIGURE **2.47a** Beef rib eye roll, lip on (NAMP 112A). It has a two-inch lip of fat running along the edge. The lip on can be roasted as is with minimal trimming.

FIGURE **2.47b** Remove the lip to make the rib eye roll (NAMP 112).

FIGURE **2.47c** This item can be easily cut into steaks.

FIGURE **2.47d** Typical yield of a rib eye roll cut to 10 oz steaks.

MAKING SHORT RIBS

FIGURE **2.48a** To make short ribs, trim away the fatty side of the ribs.

FIGURE **2.48b** Crosscut the short ribs into two-inch portions for braising.

FIGURE **2.48c** The cap meat, or deckle, from the top of the rib makes an excellent stew cut. Trim away excess fat.

FRENCHING BONE-IN BEEF RIB

- Score across bones at edge of lip.
- Score on each individual bone to loosen membrane.
- Pull lip with membrane off bones and scrape each bone to remove debris.

FIGURE **2.49a** Beef roast ready, cover off, or export style rib (NAMP 109D or 109E).

FIGURE **2.49b** Frenching the rib will enhance presentation. After piercing between each rib, score down along the bones.

FIGURE **2.49c** Peel away the membranes and meat from the bones.

FIGURE **2.49d** Frenched rib roast.

FIGURE **2.49e** To cut large bone-in rib eye or cowboy steaks (NAMP 1103B), cut between each bone. Be sure to cut the eye muscle evenly.

BEEF SHOULDER CLOD

Beef shoulder clod can be used as braising roasts or portion cut into steaks. The clod contains four basic sections: the top blade (also known as the flat iron), the heart of the clod, the shoulder tender (*teres major*), and a no-name trim section. Due to its current popularity, the shoulder tender is often removed from the clod and sold separately. The top blade is often split lengthwise to create the flat iron grilling steak. The heart of the clod can be cut for an inexpensive London Broil-type steak.

FIGURE **2.50** Beef shoulder clod (NAMP 114) untrimmed or trimmed (NAMP 114 C), pictured.

Beef Shoulder Clod Divided into Roasts

• Trim excess fat from exterior.
• Follow natural seams to remove top blade section.
• Remove no-name trim section.
• Divide heart of clod into two or three roasts.

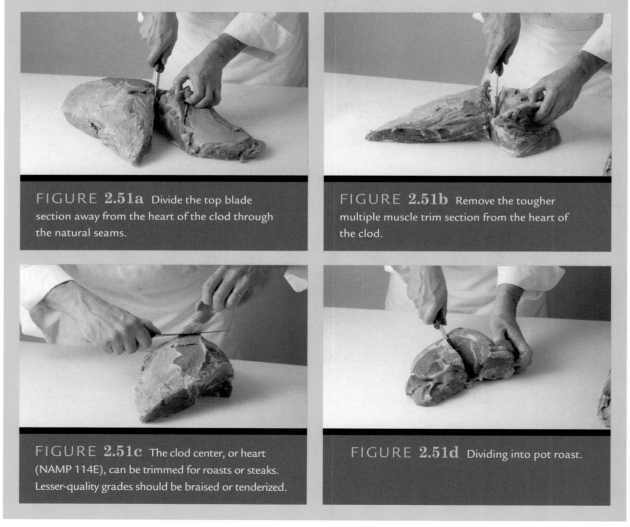

FIGURE **2.51a** Divide the top blade section away from the heart of the clod through the natural seams.

FIGURE **2.51b** Remove the tougher multiple muscle trim section from the heart of the clod.

FIGURE **2.51c** The clod center, or heart (NAMP 114E), can be trimmed for roasts or steaks. Lesser-quality grades should be braised or tenderized.

FIGURE **2.51d** Dividing into pot roast.

(Continues)

(Continued)

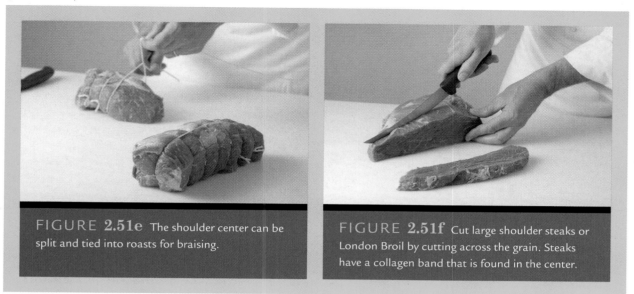

FIGURE **2.51e** The shoulder center can be split and tied into roasts for braising.

FIGURE **2.51f** Cut large shoulder steaks or London Broil by cutting across the grain. Steaks have a collagen band that is found in the center.

Heart of Clod Portion Cut for Steaks
- Trim excess collagen bands and fat.
- Determine grain direction.
- Cut across grain with palm flat against steak.

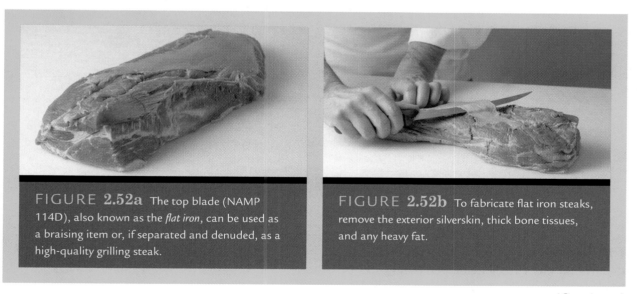

FIGURE **2.52a** The top blade (NAMP 114D), also known as the *flat iron*, can be used as a braising item or, if separated and denuded, as a high-quality grilling steak.

FIGURE **2.52b** To fabricate flat iron steaks, remove the exterior silverskin, thick bone tissues, and any heavy fat.

(Continues)

(*Continued*)

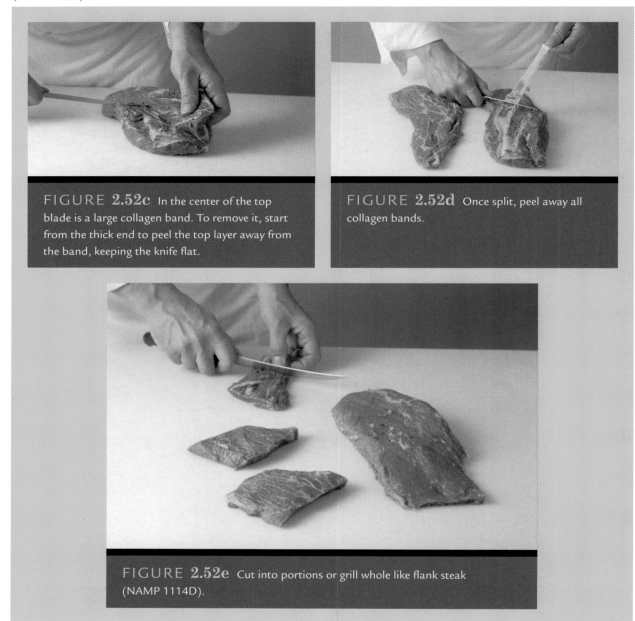

FIGURE **2.52c** In the center of the top blade is a large collagen band. To remove it, start from the thick end to peel the top layer away from the band, keeping the knife flat.

FIGURE **2.52d** Once split, peel away all collagen bands.

FIGURE **2.52e** Cut into portions or grill whole like flank steak (NAMP 1114D).

Top Blade into Portion Flat Iron Steak

Remove fat and exterior collagen bands.

Find thick flat silver collagen band on large end.

Peel back top layer.

Remove collagen band from inside.

BEEF CHUCK ROLL

The beef chuck roll is a large section containing many muscle pieces. It would be very time consuming and unprofitable to isolate every single muscle. Some divisions can be done easily and can create some interesting, very flavorful dishes. The middle of the chuck roll contains the *chuck eye roll*, which is an extension of the rib eye. While not as tender, the chuck eye roll offers a flavorful roast. The other main section is known as the *chuck flat*, which is tougher, but is excellent for stewing and braising. Its meat is similar to short ribs.

FIGURE **2.53** Beef chuck roll (NAMP 116A).

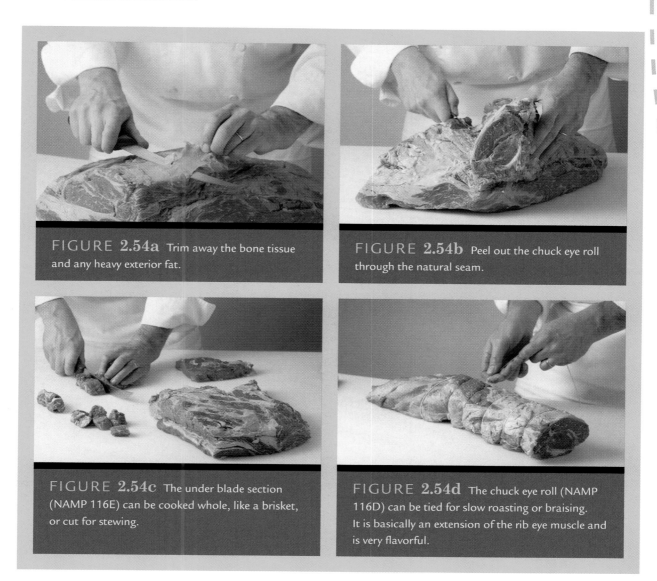

FIGURE **2.54a** Trim away the bone tissue and any heavy exterior fat.

FIGURE **2.54b** Peel out the chuck eye roll through the natural seam.

FIGURE **2.54c** The under blade section (NAMP 116E) can be cooked whole, like a brisket, or cut for stewing.

FIGURE **2.54d** The chuck eye roll (NAMP 116D) can be tied for slow roasting or braising. It is basically an extension of the rib eye muscle and is very flavorful.

Chuck Roll Separation

- Find natural seam between the chuck eye roll and the chuck flat.
- Trim excess collagen from cuts.
- Tie into roasts or cut for stew.

Hint from the butcher: The hanger steak is similar to the skirt steak in that it is peeled the same way, but it has a thick collagen band that must be removed.

SKIRT STEAK

The skirt steak can be purchased pre-trimmed but it is often cost effective to trim this item in the kitchen.

Skirt Steak Trim

- Loosen membrane from thick end.
- Place palm on exposed steak, pulling off membrane in short sections.
- Turn over and trim underside.
- Trim off collagen edges and extra fat.

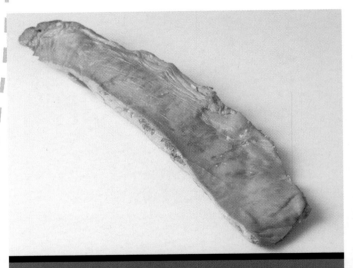

FIGURE **2.55** Beef outside skirt (NAMP 121 C). The skirt is typically used as a grilling steak.

FIGURE **2.56a** The skirt needs to be peeled. First cut along the edges to release membrane.

FIGURE **2.56b** Pull up membrane while holding steak flat. Most of the membrane will pull away by hand but may require a knife.

FIGURE **2.56c** Trim collagen bands away from edges with large knife.

(Continues)

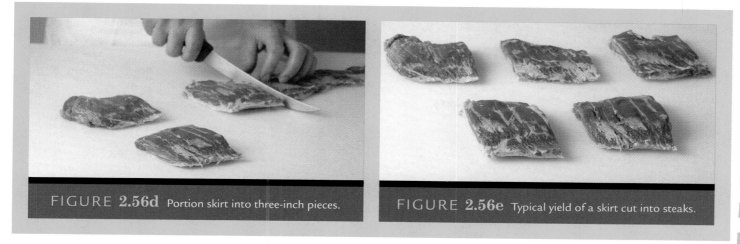

FIGURE **2.56d** Portion skirt into three-inch pieces.

FIGURE **2.56e** Typical yield of a skirt cut into steaks.

BEEF BRISKET

The brisket can be divided and trimmed to minimize the fat rendered into the dish being made from it. The brisket can also be left whole, but trimming it improves the dish being created. Follow natural seam to separate.

FIGURE **2.57a** Beef brisket (NAMP 120). The brisket needs to be trimmed of its nose fat before braising or barbecuing.

FIGURE **2.57b** Trim the back fat from the brisket before braising or barbecuing.

FIGURE **2.57c** The brisket can be separated for more consistent slicing (NAMP 120A).

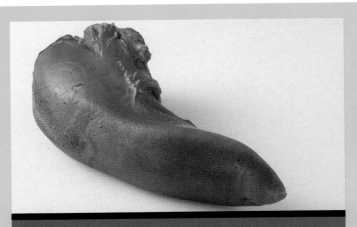

FIGURE **2.58a** Smoked beef tongue.

FIGURE **2.58b** After cooking the tongue, remove the thick membrane from the exterior. Score along the bottom.

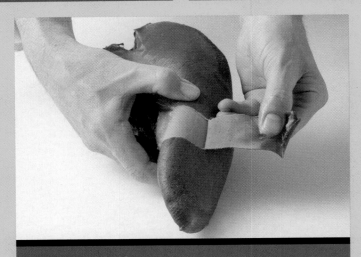

FIGURE **2.58c** Peel the exterior membrane. Remove any excess fat or connectives.

FIGURE **2.59a** Beef marrow bones.

FIGURE **2.59b** Push the marrow through with the thumb.

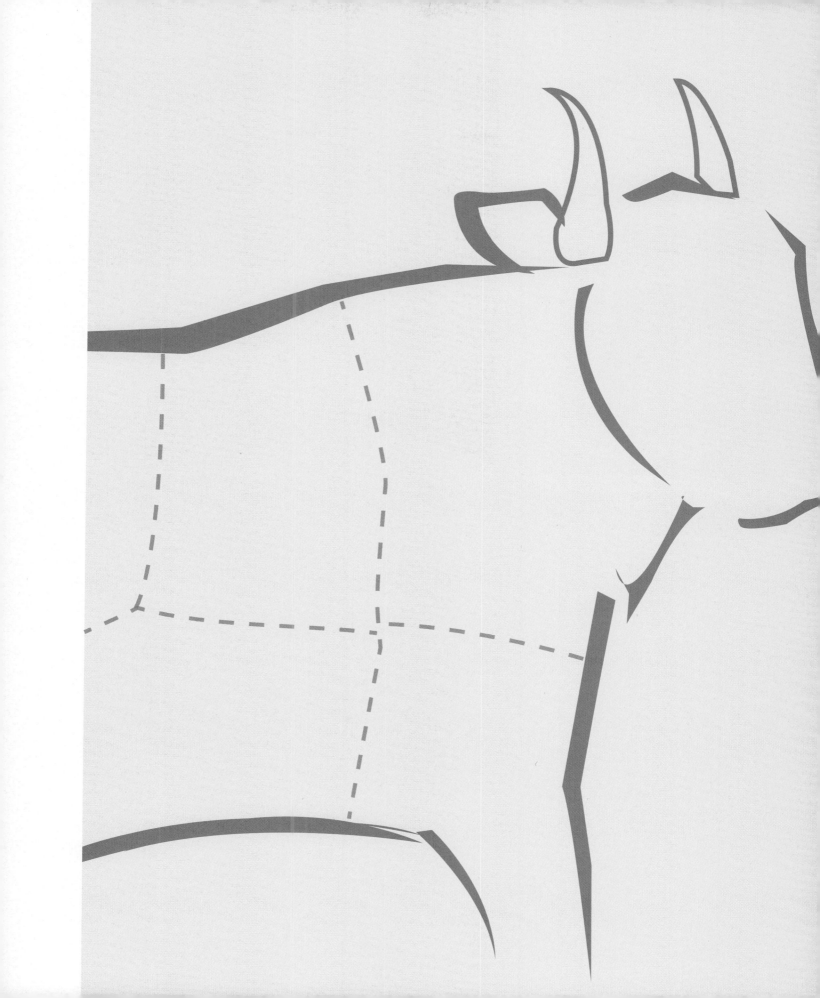

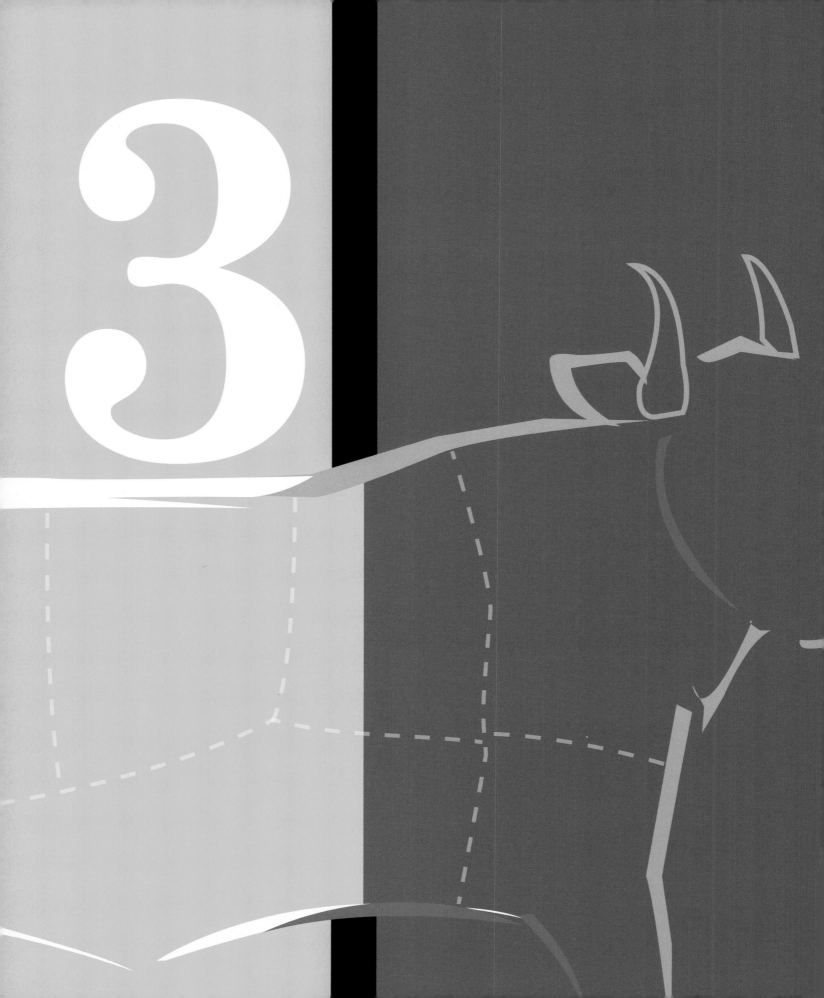

VEAL

The renowned French chef, culinary writer, and restauranteur Auguste Escoffier used veal bones for sauces and stocks. The fine flavor of veal was a mainstay in many of his recipes. His *selle de veau*, veal saddle roasted and served with a sauce made from the reduction of a browned veal stock, is a classic.

Veal is the meat derived from young calves not yet weaned off milk. A veal calf does not have a fully developed rumen, or paunch. The rumen is the largest compartment of the stomach in ruminant animals, and it is where food, particularly grass, is broken down by microorganisms or returned to the mouth as cud for the animal to chew.

Most veal is produced from the male offspring of dairy animals. Dairy farmers focus on milk production; therefore, they generally will keep the females to become milkers. The male offspring do not have the best genetics for beef production and are sold off to become veal. The primary veal breed is Holstein, which is not as well suited for beef due to the muscle scores that it typically achieves. The rib eye tends to be small, even though it will marble well.

Dairies and related industries also supply milk by-products for feeding veal. The dairy industry annually receives approximately $250 million from the veal producers for the calves and by-products.

Most veal available is considered "special fed," or raised on a feed high in nutrients, enabling the animal to grow rapidly. Feeds are formulated to keep iron levels relatively low, which ensures the color of the veal will be lighter than that of a grazing animal. Color is used in grading and contributes to the assigned value of the meat; color is considered when veal processors categorize carcasses.

VEAL GRADING AND EVALUATION

The USDA quality grades for veal depend on the size and conformation (meat to bone ratio) of the veal and color and quality of the lean muscle tissue.

USDA Quality Grades

- Prime
- Choice
- Good
- Standard
- Utility

Veal has become a specialized meat and growers are able to achieve very specific quality scores. This lack of diversity means that veal grading has narrowed. In 1977, 29.1 percent of veal graded as prime, 44.7 percent as choice, 22.8 percent as good, and 3.4 percent as standard. By 2006, only 3.7 percent graded prime, 94.9 percent choice, and 1.4 percent good. Choice graded veal has become the standard and growers are consistently hitting the choice mark. As a result, some veal processing companies have opted not to USDA grade and simply apply a company name brand to their products. In these cases, the company stamp or name brand is used to establish a quality standard. There are also veal products that are not graded because they are under- or oversized and therefore would achieve a low grade. Be sure to establish your color and weight specs with the purveyor or simply use the USDA grade as a guide when purchasing veal.

Veal animals will reach 400 to 500 pounds in around eighteen to twenty weeks. These weights and ages exceed what was once considered normal for veal in the past. Traditionally, veal was under three months of age, but due to modern feeding practices, animals are allowed to grow larger and still be considered high quality.

VEAL CLASSIFICATIONS AND CATEGORIES

Veal is grouped according to age. These classifications help decide whether the processor will accept or decline an animal.

BOB VEAL

Bob veal calves are less than three weeks old and are tender but have an underdeveloped size and flavor. Since they are inexpensive, they can be used for processed items, such as grind. Some chefs are using the Bob veal racks for a smaller plate presentation or appetizer.

SPECIAL-FED VEAL

This is the typical high-quality veal that is most prevalent and is considered today's standard. This veal is fed a specific formula that enables the animal to grow quickly with the ideal color for veal. It is normally a light pink color and tender.

SUBCATEGORIES

Stall Raised

Stall-raised veal is grown indoors in its own specific stall under a climate-controlled environment. These calves can also be raised outdoors and tethered to a veal shed, which resembles a large dog house. This control enables the farmer to monitor feeding and growth.

Group Raised

Group-raised veal are raised in groups of six or more and allowed freedom to roam within a large indoor stall. New transponder technologies enable the farmer to monitor growth in a group by observing the amount of feed each animal drinks daily. Growth is recorded and data can be used to see which animals are gaining fastest.

PASTURE RAISED / FREE RANGE

The animal is allowed to roam free, drinking mother's milk. Generally, the meat is a rosy pink color with a more pronounced flavor. Because the animal is allowed more movement, the meat can be slightly tougher than special-fed veal. Most processors prefer pasture-raised veal to be younger and smaller than the special-fed veal. This guarantees a higher level of tenderness and a lighter color. Most pasture-raised veal is grown without antibiotics, but this is not a requirement.

CALVES

Although any young beef animal can be called a calf, the classification *calf* implies an animal that weighs less than 750 pounds and has not yet reached puberty. The meat from this animal, which is usually weaned, is red; it is similar to beef but without marbling. Although the meat can be tender, it does not resemble the color of quality veal. This product should be inexpensive and is not extensively available.

YIELD GRADING

Because veal does not have a significant amount of fat, there is no USDA yield grading for veal.

VEAL CARCASS BREAKDOWN

The veal carcass is not broken down in the same way that beef is. A beef carcass is split immediately after slaughter, whereas the veal carcass is not. Veal is divided into hind and fore *saddles*, traditionally between the eleventh and twelfth rib bones. The hind and fore saddles are divided further into the primal cuts. The primals can be purchased unsplit or untrimmed but, in most cases, restaurants do not buy these primals in this unprocessed form. Cuts are normally split and trimmed into typical HRI or portion cuts.

Beyond the major primals, there are two minor primals, or *market forms*, that are not included in the major primal cuts.

PRIMALS

- Legs
- Loin
- Hotel rack
- Square cut chuck or shoulder

MARKET FORMS

- Breast
- Foreshank

Veal cuts fabricated from these primals are offered according to the NAMP Buyer's Guide using the number system aforementioned in this book. Many veal processors go outside the NAMP guidelines and customize cuts. Processors have created their own product code numbers and will sometimes custom fabricate cuts for large customers.

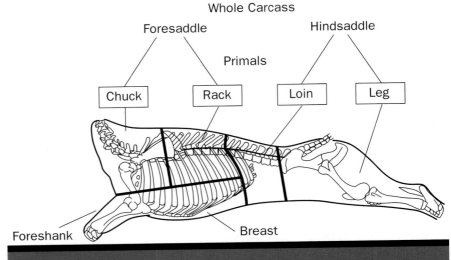

Veal Carcass Breakdown

FIGURE **3.1** Veal skeletal structure with primal divisions.

LEGS

Veal legs can be purchased in pairs, but this is unlikely in today's market. The leg can be purchased whole and then fabricated in the restaurant. This requires a fair amount of skill and time. Once boned, the leg is divided into subprimals. Each subprimal can then be trimmed completely and is typically cut for cutlets. Subprimals vary in tenderness and it may be difficult for a restaurant to utilize all of the subprimals equally, therefore it is common to buy each subprimal individually. Subprimals are often portion cut into exacting ounce portions and many restaurants choose to purchase veal cutlets prefabricated. Some catering services use the leg of veal as a steamship roast similar to that of beef. This impressive presentation requires the leg to be roasted whole and carved on a buffet line.

A whole leg of veal will also yield a fair amount of usable trim for grinding, stewing, or fortifying a stock. There is also a shank that is best known as a portion cut, osso buco. The entire veal leg will only yield three or four portions of osso buco. The bones from the veal leg are a good quality for stock.

SUBPRIMALS / HRI CUTS

- Hind shank
- Top / Inside round
- Bottom / Outside round
- Eye round
- Heel
- Knuckle
- Sirloin / Rump
- Tenderloin Butt
- Flank

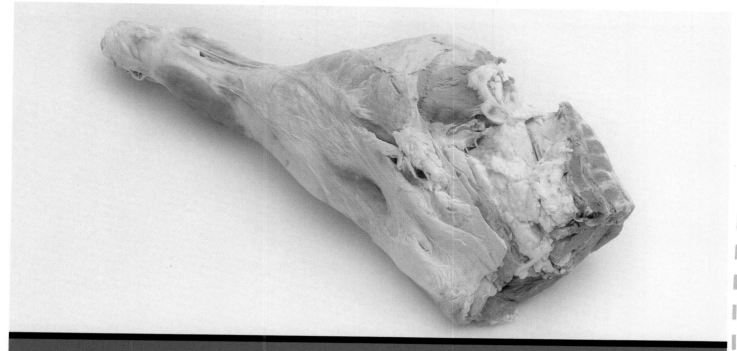

FIGURE **3.2** Leg of veal.

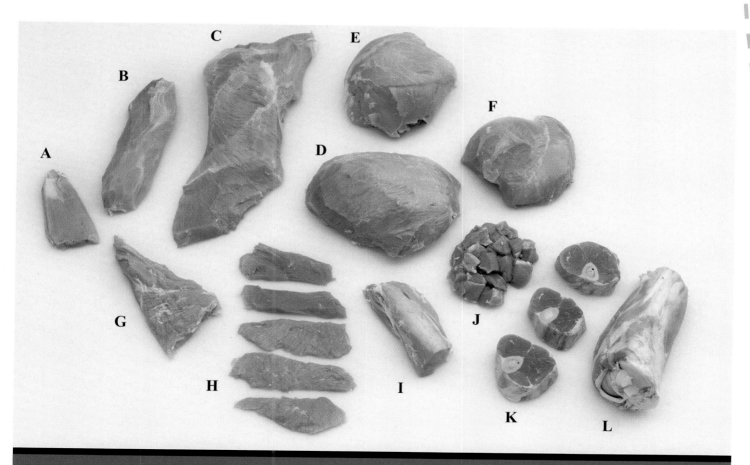

FIGURE **3.3** A: Veal Flank, B: Veal eye round, C: Veal bottom round, D: Veal top round cap off, E: Veal knuckle, F: Veal sirloin, G: Veal tri tip, H: Veal portion cut leg cutlets, I: Veal tenderloin butt, J: Veal leg stew, K: Veal osso buco, L: Veal hind shank.

FIGURE **3.4** Veal leg HRI cuts.

ITEM AND NAMP NUMBER	DESCRIPTION/ FABRICATION	SUGGESTED COOKING METHOD/APPLICATION	AVERAGE SUGGESTED WEIGHT IN POUNDS	TYPICAL PACKAGE SPECS
334 Veal leg primal / split	Whole primal leg; requires major fabrication and a high skill level; shank is typically cut off and packaged separately	Cutlets, roasts, usable trim for grind or stew, bones for stock	45–50	1 per box
Veal leg / steamship	Shank bone exposed and cut as handle, pelvic bone removed, trimmed	Roast whole	30–35	1 per box
Veal leg TBS (top, bottom, sirloin)	Sectioned leg trimmed and divided into subprimals	Cutlets, roast	18–20	3 different sections per box
349 Top round	Whole subprimal; requires fabrication; cap muscle removal	Large high-quality cutlets, cap for usable trim, emincé	7–9	3 per box
349a Top round, cap off	Trimmed, ready to cut for cutlets	Large high-quality cutlets, sauté	6–8	3 per box
1349a Top round cutlets	Ready to cook, large high-quality cutlets	Sauté	4–6 ounce cutlets	Varies
350 Bottom round (gooseneck)	Sold as the entire gooseneck with bottom round flat, eye round, and heel; requires some sectioning	Lesser-quality cutlets, roast, braise	8–10	3 per box
Eye round	Trimmed and ready to roast or cut into cutlets	Roast whole, cutlets, medallions	2	2 per bag, 6 per box

(Continues)

ITEM AND NAMP NUMBER	DESCRIPTION/ FABRICATION	SUGGESTED COOKING METHOD/APPLICATION	AVERAGE SUGGESTED WEIGHT IN POUNDS	TYPICAL PACKAGE SPECS
351 Knuckle	Requires some fabrication; separate through natural seams	Cutlets, some trim for usable trim	3–4 each	3 per box
352 Sirloin hip (top sirloin butt)	Trim for cutlets	High-quality cutlets, medallions, sauté	4–5 lbs each	3 per box
Flank steak (no NAMP number)	Minor trim required	Grilling, slice across grain; marinating	.5	Varies
337 Hindshank	Sold whole or blocked	Braising whole or cut for osso buco	3–4	2 per bag, 6 bags per case
1337 Hindshank, osso buco, portion cut	Ready to cook	Braised	2-inch typical; thickness specified by customer	6 per bag, 4 bags per case
1336 Veal leg cutlets	Ready to cook; full muscle cuts; not knitted together	Sauté	2- to 6-ounce portions, specified by customer	Varies; typically 12 per bag
1302 Veal slices	Ready to cook; tougher sections mechanically tenderized; some fat or connectives may be present	Sauté	2–6 ounces	Varies

LOIN

The loin, or *saddle*, consists of the *longissimus* and *psoas major* muscles (strip-loin / tenderloin respectively). It has the distinctive t-bone structure and the cuts from it are very tender and flavorful. It can be sold as an entire saddle, which is unsplit and connected at the spine. This purchase would require a band saw, so is not typical for most restaurants. More often, it is sold as a trimmed and split loin, otherwise known as a *shortloin*. Even this item presents problems for a restaurant that cannot cut its own portions because it does not have a band saw. It is common to purchase the loin pre-cut as chops. It can also be purchased as a boneless strip-loin with a variety of trim levels available.

SUBPRIMAL / HRI CUTS

- Full loin / Saddle, unsplit
- Trimmed loin / Split (Shortloin)
- Striploin (Bone in loin)
- Striploin boneless (Boneless loin)
- Tenderloin

VEAL HOTEL RACK

The veal hotel rack is often considered the finest cut for chops or roasting. It has a distinctive bone structure that adds to the look of the plate. It is often Frenched or trimmed and exposing the ends of the rib bones guarantees attention to the

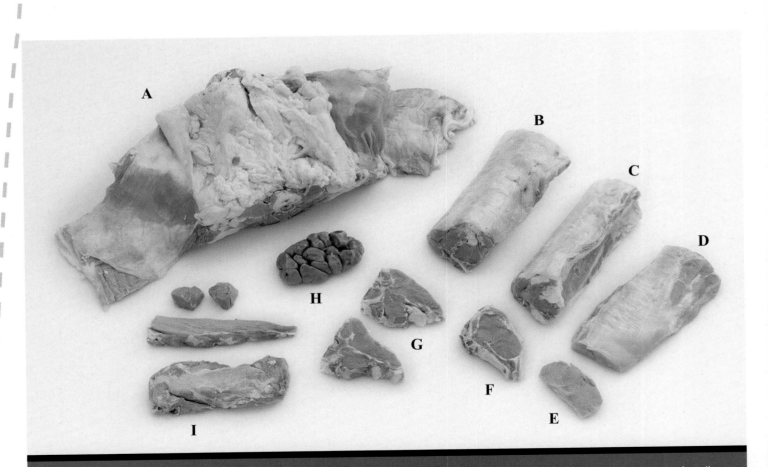

FIGURE **3.5** A: Veal loin primal/saddle, B: Veal loin trimmed, C: Veal loin trimmed, block ready, D: Boneless veal loin trimmed to silver, E: Veal loin medallion, F: Veal loin chop rib end, G: Veal porterhouse, H: Veal kidney, I: Veal tenderloin and medallions.

FIGURE **3.6** Veal loin HRI cuts.

ITEM AND NAMP NUMBER	DESCRIPTION/FABRICATION	SUGGESTED COOKING METHOD/ APPLICATION	AVERAGE SUGGESTED WEIGHT IN POUNDS	TYPICAL PACKAGE SPECS
331 Veal loin (full saddle) primal	Full loin un-split; requires a bandsaw and trimming; may contain all of the kidney fat	High-quality, dry cook items	20–30	1 per box
332 Loin trimmed / split (shortloin)	Trimmed to a 4" × 4" flank tail length; requires fabrication; band saw for chops	Roast whole, cut for chops	4–5 each; typically sold as pairs	2 per box
332a Loin trimmed / split / block ready (shortloin)	Trimmed to 1x0 tail length; requires band saw to cut chops	Roast whole, cut for chops	3–4 each; typically sold as pairs	4 per box
344 Loin striploin / boneless 1 × 1, 0 × 0, denuded	Sold partially or fully trimmed	Medallions, boneless chops, cutlets, roast whole	2–3	6 per box
346 / 347d Tenderloin	Sold as butt end or whole 9 (psmo); may require trimming and silverskin removal	Medallions, roast whole	1–3 pounds each (varies)	2 per bag, 6 bags per box; Can also be sold individually packaged

center of the plate. In its primal form, it is also unsplit, attached at the spine. The rack, also known as the *rib of veal*, is often sold in a variety of trim levels, enabling the purchaser to consider which is most logical and/or profitable. Although often expensive to purchase, this cut can command a high price on menus. Traditionally, the rack contains seven ribs but can be purchased as a six-rib rack. A few producers have defied traditional cutting and are now selling eight and even nine-rib racks.

SUBPRIMALS / HRI CUTS
- Veal hotel rack, unsplit
- Veal hotel rack, split and chined
- Veal hotel rack, chop or roast ready
- Veal rack, Frenched
- Boneless veal rib eye

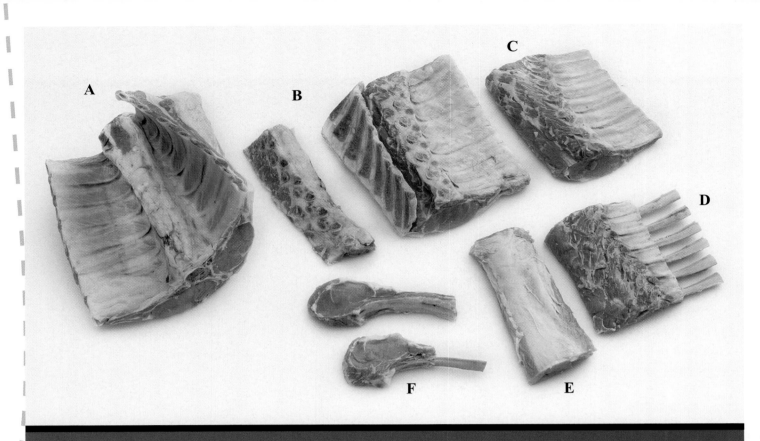

FIGURE 3.7 A: Veal hotel rack, B: Veal hotel rack split and chined, with chine bone, C: Veal rack chop ready, D: Veal rack frenched, E: Boneless veal rib eye, F: Veal rack chops.

VEAL SQUARE CUT SHOULDER

The veal shoulder, otherwise known as the *chuck*, is comprised of a multitude of muscles that are all relatively active and therefore tend to be tough but flavorful. The shoulder has a complicated bone structure; therefore, it is typically purchased boneless. Bone-in cuts are still fabricated but are difficult to present as a portion. The cuts from the shoulder tend to be less expensive than other cuts and are affordable for a larger scope of foodservice operations. The cuts from the shoulder typically require a slow cook method such as braise, stew, or slow roasting.

As with beef, these complicated muscles can be separated and all of the connective tissues removed for use as dry-cook items. The veal industry is currently contemplating separating the shoulder into untraditional cuts to achieve higher values and give chefs more dry-cook options. As previously stated, the veal shoulder is purchased boneless, but the neck bones, which can be purchased separately, are prized for their flavor when used in stocks.

SUBPRIMALS / HRI CUTS

- Veal square cut shoulder, boneless
- Veal shoulder clod, trimmed and untrimmed
- Veal neck roast
- Veal chuck eye roll
- Veal chuck / scotch tender

ITEM AND NAMP NUMBER	DESCRIPTION/FABRICATION	SUGGESTED COOKING METHOD/ APPLICATION	AVERAGE SUGGESTED WEIGHT IN POUNDS	TYPICAL PACKAGE SPECS
306 Veal hotel rack, split and chined, 6 or 7 ribs (Some producers are now fabricating 8-rib racks)	Sold whole or split and chined; requires trimming and some bone removal, Frenching the bone ends for presentation	Roasted whole, grill, broil, pan sear as chops	6–7 pounds single; 12–14 pounds pair	6 per box
306b Veal rack, chop or roast ready (Sold as 6- or 7-rib rack)	Sold split and well trimmed, 4" × 4" trim level; may require some minor fabrication, Frenching the bone ends for presentation	Roasted whole, grill, broil, pan sear as chops	7-rib rack, 5-pound average; 6-rib rack, 4–5 pound average	4 per case
306c Veal Rack, Frenched (6- or 7-rib rack)	Trimmed and Frenched; may require cleaning of the Frenched bones.	Roast whole or chops	3–4	6 per case
307 Veal ribeye	Boneless; Sold with a variety of trim levels; tie as roast or cut into medallions / steaks	Roast whole, grill, broil, sauté medallions or steaks	2–3	6 per case
1306b Veal rack chops	Chine off / cap off trimmed	Grill, broil, sauté	10–16 ounces, as specified	12 per box; Packaging can vary
1306e Veal rack chops, Frenched	Cleaned, Frenched	Grill, broil, sauté	10–14 oz as specified	12 per box; Packaging can vary

FIGURE **3.8** Veal hotel rack HRI cuts.

FIGURE 3.9 A: Veal chuck outside arm, B: Veal foreshank, C: Veal shoulder clod trimmed, D: Veal short ribs, E: Veal Brisket, trimmed, F: Boneless veal breast, G: Bone-in veal breast.

VEAL BREAST, VEAL FORESHANK

The veal breast represents the plate and brisket combined. It has thin layers of meat and fat on a rib bone structure. It is normally reasonably priced and can have a remarkable profit margin. The breast can be opened and stuffed and roasted, braised, or poached. Some processors are now fabricating veal short ribs from the breast, which are sold as individual portion cuts. The breast can be boned, yielding a good quality stew, usable trim for grinding, and quality bones for stock. Curing and smoking the boneless breast and serving it as veal bacon, sliced and crisped like regular pork bacon, provides an interesting alternative.

ITEM AND NAMP NUMBER	DESCRIPTION/FABRICATION	SUGGESTED COOKING METHOD/ APPLICATION	AVERAGE SUGGESTED WEIGHT IN POUNDS	TYPICAL PACKAGE SPECS
309 Veal chuck, square cut	Whole primal cut, requires major fabrication and high skill level	Braise, grind, stew, slow roast	25–30	1 per box
309b Veal chuck, square cut, boneless	Whole primal, boneless; contains many sections; requires a large amount of fabrication	Braise, grind, stew, slow roast	15–20	1 per box
310 Outside shoulder	Large section includes clod, top blade, and chuck tender; requires trimming and fabrication	Braise, stew, slow roast	6–8	2 per box
310 A or B shoulder clod	Includes the top blade and main section of the clod. Sold untrimmed and trimmed, lean	Braise, stew, slow roast	5–6	3 per box
310c Chuck tender	May need silverskin / collagen removed	Small braise, stew	1–3	12 per box
311 Blade roast, neck off	Containing the chuck eye and flat underblade section; has some fat and may need trimming	Braise, stew, slow roast	12–14	2 per box
Veal neck meat (no NAMP number)	Some heavy connective tissues	Very flavorful braise; long, slow cooking	3–5	3 per box

FIGURE **3.10** Veal square cut shoulder.

FIGURE **3.11** Veal breast, foreshank HRI cuts.				
ITEM AND NAMP NUMBER	DESCRIPTION/ FABRICATION	SUGGESTED COOKING METHOD/ APPLICATION	AVERAGE SUGGESTED WEIGHT IN POUNDS	TYPICAL PACKAGE SPECS
312 Foreshank, whole	May require ends to be cut, trimming	Braise whole	3–4	3 per pack, 4 per case
1312 Foreshank, osso buco portion cut	Ready to cook; may be tied to keep shape	Braise	Specify width	12 per pack, packaging varies
313 Breast of veal (also sold with pocket)	Requires trimming and partial or full bone removal; generally inexpensive	Stuff and roast or braise; can be boned for stew, grind, or stock	15–18	4 per box
Veal breast, boned rolled tied	Trimmed, ready to roast	Braise or roast slow	8–10	6 per box
Veal brisket	Trimmed, may require minor fabrication, cut for stew	Braise, roast slow, stew	3–4	Varies
Veal stew	Ready to cook; sold in various sizes, 1–2 inch cubes	Stew	Specify size	Varies

The veal foreshank is cut for portioned osso buco. The quality of the foreshank is not equal to the hindshank, and, therefore, should be more reasonably priced. The foreshank has more connective tissues and the bone structure has less marrow; it also tends to fall apart when braised. It may make sense to tie the osso buco to maintain shape.

VEAL OFFAL

Veal offal hold more value than most other species. Classic dishes include sautéed calves liver, poached sweetbreads, braised veal cheeks, and sautéed veal kidneys with

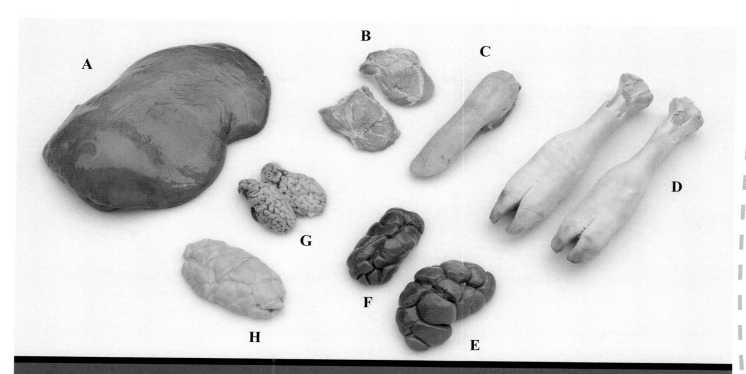

FIGURE **3.12** A: Veal liver, B: Veal cheeks, C: Veal tongue, D: Calves Feet, E: Beef kidney, F: Veal kidney, G: Veal brains, H: Veal thymus or Sweet breads.

FIGURE **3.13** Veal offal.				
ITEM AND NAMP NUMBER	DESCRIPTION/ FABRICATION	SUGGESTED COOKING METHOD/APPLICATION	AVERAGE SUGGESTED WEIGHT IN POUNDS	TYPICAL PACKAGE SPECS
Veal cheeks	May require some trim	Very tender braise	.5	5-pound bags
3710 Veal tongue	Peel	Braise, terrines	1–2	4 per bag
3772 Veal sweetbread/ thymus gland	Sold as sets or two pieces; should be peeled	Poach, peel, and then sauté	.5	Varies
3724 Veal liver	Requires peeling and slicing	Sauté, pan sear	6–8	2 per box
3728 Veal kidney	Center fat and blood vessels require trimming	Sauté	1–2	Varies

cognac. The veal feet are used to make a stock that is very high in protein and can be clarified to make aspic.

- Veal liver
- Veal sweetbread / Thymus gland
- Veal kidneys
- Veal cheeks
- Veal brains
- Veal feet

VEAL FABRICATION

BONING LEG OF VEAL

Many chefs no longer consider boning the leg of veal an absolute necessity because processors are fabricating the leg into its subprimals or portion cuts. It may make sense to bone the leg if the foodservice operation can justify use of all of its components, including usable trim and bones. Boning and fabricating an entire leg of veal into cutlets requires a high level of skill but can be profitable.

Fabricating the leg of veal requires a series of steps.

1. Remove shank through knee joint. (If the leg comes vacuum packed, the shank may be removed already.)

2. Remove flank and exterior membrane.

3. Loosen and remove veal tenderloin butt.

4. Remove pelvic bone, including tailbone, by cutting through the ball and socket joint.

5. Follow natural seam to remove femur bone.

6. Remove patella (knee cap).

7. Follow natural seams to separate subprimals.

8. Completely trim the subprimals and remove all connective tissues.

FIGURE **3.14a** Veal Leg Primal (NAMP 334).

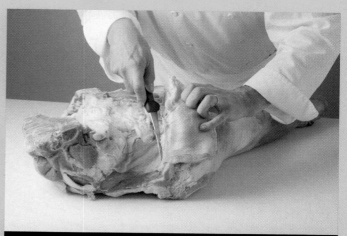

FIGURE **3.14b** To bone the leg of veal for cutlets, start by removing the flank steak and thick fat surrounding it.

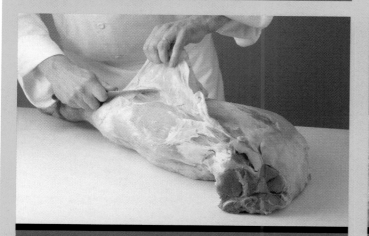

FIGURE **3.14c** Remove the exterior membrane by pulling up and creating tension. It is easier to remove the membrane while the leg is whole.

FIGURE **3.14d** Remove the shank by cutting through the knee or stifle joint. The shank can be cut for osso buco, roasted whole, or boned and cut for stewing. Use a non-flexing boning knife to bone the leg of veal.

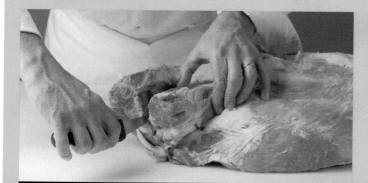

FIGURE **3.14e** The leg contains a small piece of the tenderloin. Peel away the tenderloin butt by scooping it away from the chine and hipbones.

FIGURE **3.14f** Begin removing the pelvic bone by cutting along the top round section, exposing the ball and socket joint.

(Continues)

(*Continued*)

FIGURE **3.14g** Cut through the socket and work the knife underneath the pelvic bone. Be sure to stay close to the bones and not scar the sirloin underneath it.

FIGURE **3.14h** Remove femur bone by cutting through natural seam next to top round section. Be sure to stay close to the bones, working down both sides evenly.

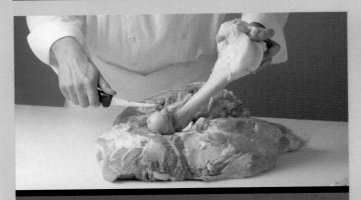

FIGURE **3.14i** Lift the femur up by one end, scraping the meat down, and release it.

FIGURE **3.14j** Remove the kneecap bone.

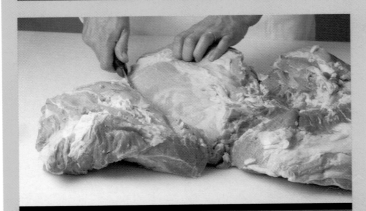

FIGURE **3.14k** To separate the leg into subprimals, start by seaming away the top round section. Follow all natural seams, trying to stay as accurate as possible.

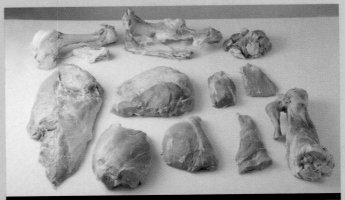

FIGURE **3.14l** The leg yields the top round, bottom /gooseneck round, knuckle, sirloin hip, shank, tenderloin butt, flank steak, and tritip. It also yields about six pounds of bones and five to seven pounds of usable trim if completely trimming all subprimals. All sections can be purchased separately or in combinations, as well as a variety of trim specs.

PORTION CUTTING VEAL CUTLETS

Veal cutlets can be easily fabricated from trimmed subprimals, whether you buy the subprimals prefabricated or bone the whole leg. Cutting cutlets requires an understanding of the final intended use. A quick sautéed cutlet needs to be tender. Consistent size is important for plate presentation. The subprimals of veal all have a specific grain and, when cutting, care must be taken to cut across the grain. Cutlets should be cut on a bias to increase surface area. Be sure to use a portion scale to accurately cost the cutlets.

Pounding cutlets may be necessary to achieve a uniform thickness, slightly tenderize the veal, and increase the surface area.

1. Establish the grain direction.
2. Place palm over area to be cut.
3. Set knife at top of cutlet and pinch the meat into the knife.
4. Cut cutlets using smooth, even cuts.
5. Place plastic wrap over the cutlet and pound lightly.
6. Thick or odd-shaped cuts can be butterflied.

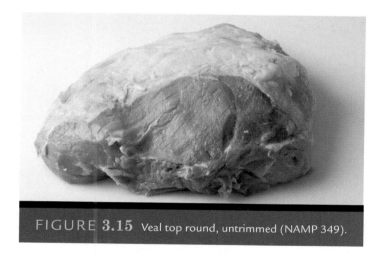

FIGURE **3.15** Veal top round, untrimmed (NAMP 349).

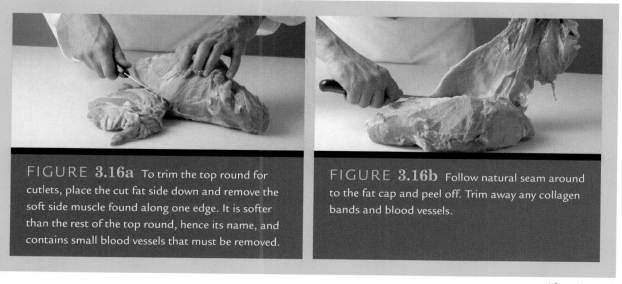

FIGURE **3.16a** To trim the top round for cutlets, place the cut fat side down and remove the soft side muscle found along one edge. It is softer than the rest of the top round, hence its name, and contains small blood vessels that must be removed.

FIGURE **3.16b** Follow natural seam around to the fat cap and peel off. Trim away any collagen bands and blood vessels.

(Continues)

FIGURE **3.16c** Veal top round, cap off (NAMP 349A) and cap trim.

FIGURE **3.16d** The top round can be cut into large cutlets or divided into smaller sections. To cut, place hand flat against the thick side of the round. Using a slicer or scimitar, cut directly under the palm to about 1/4-inch thickness at a 45-degree angle.

FIGURE **3.16e** Cutlets should be pounded slightly to increase size and uniformity. Be sure not to over pound.

FIGURE **3.16f** The typical yield from a veal top round is twelve to fifteen, six-ounce cutlets.

FIGURE **3.16g** The cap can be cleaned and cut into thin strips for a quick sauté. Be sure to cut across the grain.

PORTION CUTTING VEAL OSSO BUCO

Cutting osso buco requires a band saw. Each shank yields only three or four portions from the center. The end bones can be used for stock or sauces.

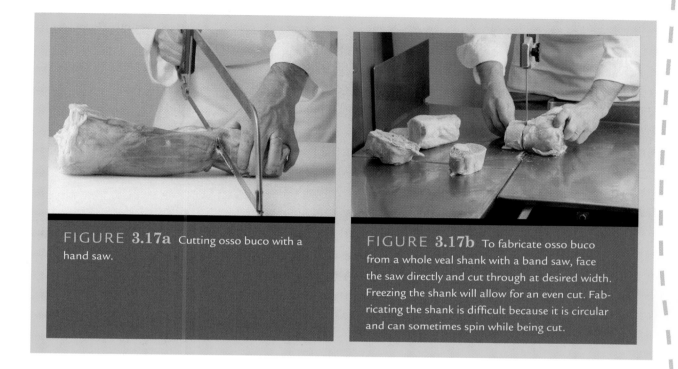

FIGURE **3.17a** Cutting osso buco with a hand saw.

FIGURE **3.17b** To fabricate osso buco from a whole veal shank with a band saw, face the saw directly and cut through at desired width. Freezing the shank will allow for an even cut. Fabricating the shank is difficult because it is circular and can sometimes spin while being cut.

VEAL GOOSENECK

The veal gooseneck contains three subprimal cuts: the bottom round, the eye round, and the heel. Each can be purchased separately or in combination. These cuts have coarser muscle fibers, which can relate to toughness. Be sure to cut across the grain to ensure tenderness. The heel, in particular, is best used as a braise or stew item.

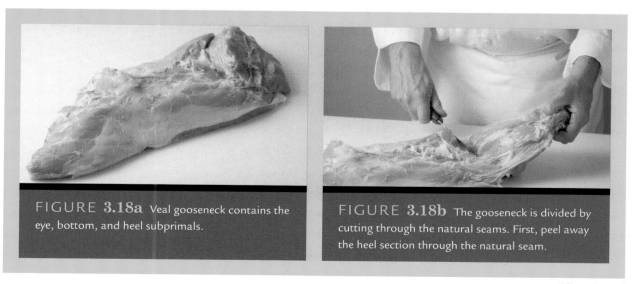

FIGURE **3.18a** Veal gooseneck contains the eye, bottom, and heel subprimals.

FIGURE **3.18b** The gooseneck is divided by cutting through the natural seams. First, peel away the heel section through the natural seam.

(Continues)

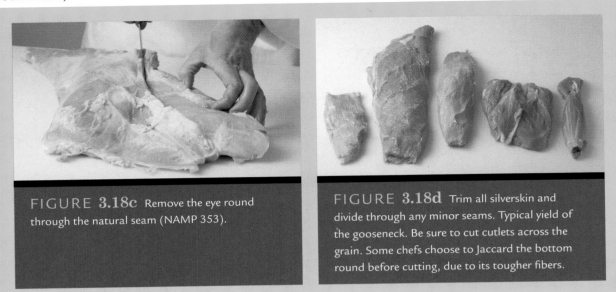

FIGURE **3.18c** Remove the eye round through the natural seam (NAMP 353).

FIGURE **3.18d** Trim all silverskin and divide through any minor seams. Typical yield of the gooseneck. Be sure to cut cutlets across the grain. Some chefs choose to Jaccard the bottom round before cutting, due to its tougher fibers.

VEAL SIRLOIN BUTT

The sirloin, also known as the hip, is a high-quality subprimal that makes an excellent cutlet or medallion. It has one collagen band that runs through the middle. Once this is removed, it is one of the tenderest of all veal cuts.

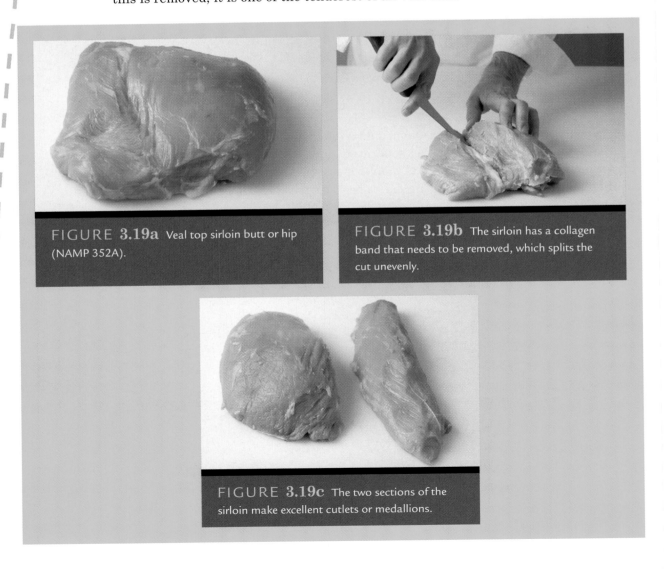

FIGURE **3.19a** Veal top sirloin butt or hip (NAMP 352A).

FIGURE **3.19b** The sirloin has a collagen band that needs to be removed, which splits the cut unevenly.

FIGURE **3.19c** The two sections of the sirloin make excellent cutlets or medallions.

FABRICATING VEAL LOIN

PORTION CUTTING VEAL LOIN CHOPS

The veal loin is typically cut into bone-in chops. Veal loin chops are usually cut with a band saw but can be cut by hand with a cleaver. Many foodservice operations opt to purchase precut loin chops.

Boneless chops, medallions, or cutlets can easily be fabricated from a boneless loin.

VEAL TENDERLOIN INTO PORTION MEDALLIONS

The veal tenderloin can be fabricated as delicate portion medallions. Trim the silver-skin connective tissues and wrap the tenderloin in plastic wrap or cheesecloth to shape it. Cut into portion cuts.

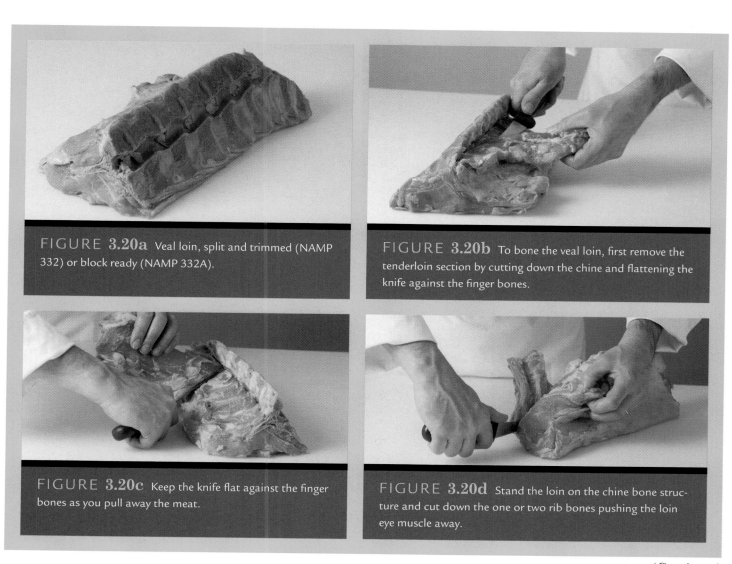

FIGURE **3.20a** Veal loin, split and trimmed (NAMP 332) or block ready (NAMP 332A).

FIGURE **3.20b** To bone the veal loin, first remove the tenderloin section by cutting down the chine and flattening the knife against the finger bones.

FIGURE **3.20c** Keep the knife flat against the finger bones as you pull away the meat.

FIGURE **3.20d** Stand the loin on the chine bone structure and cut down the one or two rib bones pushing the loin eye muscle away.

(Continues)

(Continued)

FIGURE **3.20e** Cut down the finger bones, pressing the knife flat against them.

FIGURE **3.20f** Cut around the "step" of the chine bone and release the loin eye from the feather bones.

FIGURE **3.20g** Remove the membrane that lies on top of the loin.

FIGURE **3.20h** Remove all the fat and silverskin bands to completely denude the loin.

FIGURE **3.20i** Veal loin, boned and denuded (NAMP 344A).

FIGURE **3.20j** The boneless loin is cut into medallions using a scimitar or slicer. Slight angle can increase surface area. Be sure to cut across the grain.

(Continues)

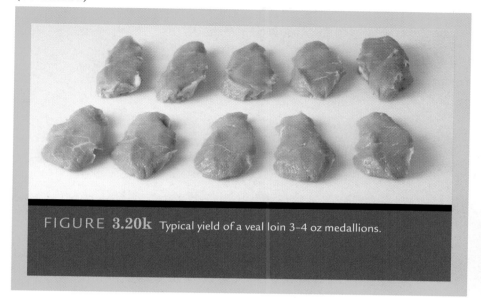

FIGURE **3.20k** Typical yield of a veal loin 3–4 oz medallions.

FIGURE **3.21** The veal loin can also be cut into bone-in chops. Cut through loin eye muscle with knife and then chop through the chine bone with a meat cleaver or saw.

FIGURE **3.22a** Veal tenderloin butt (NAMP 346 or 346A).

FIGURE **3.22b** To cut into medallions, denude the tenderloin and wrap tightly in plastic.

FIGURE **3.22c** Twist the plastic wrap, forming a sausage-like shape.

FIGURE **3.22d** Cut portions and weigh for accuracy.

FABRICATING VEAL HOTEL RACK

The veal rack can be fabricated into various high-value dishes. Chops, roasts, and boneless medallions can all be fabricated in the kitchen with relative ease. The hotel rack can be sold unsplit, but most companies sell it split and chined or further fabricated into various trim levels, portion cuts, or into boneless rib eye.

FIGURE **3.23** Veal hotel rack (NAMP 306).

VEAL RACK, SPLIT AND CHINED, CAP REMOVAL

Removing the chine bone and peeling off the tougher cap with a small blade bone enables the rack to be easily cut into portions. Once fabricated, this cut can be called *chop* or *Roast Ready*.

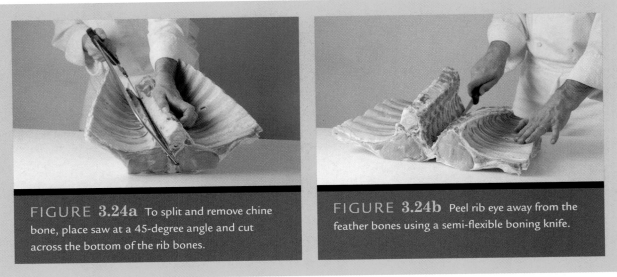

FIGURE **3.24a** To split and remove chine bone, place saw at a 45-degree angle and cut across the bottom of the rib bones.

FIGURE **3.24b** Peel rib eye away from the feather bones using a semi-flexible boning knife.

(Continues)

(Continued)

FIGURE **3.24c** Peel away cap meat through natural seam from rib bone side down.

FIGURE **3.24d** Pull away the yellow elastin band that is located along bottom edge. This is now considered a veal rack, chop ready, seven rib (NAMP 306B). Removing the last rib chop from the chuck end creates the veal rack, chop ready, six rib (NAMP 306C).

VEAL RACK / FRENCHED

The rack of veal can be Frenched or, by exposing the rib bones, create a refined presentation. Once Frenched, the rack can be cut into portions. Two pieces of Frenched rack can be tied to make a *crown roast*.

1. Measure away from the eye.

2. Make score line across bones

3. Score membrane on each individual bone.

4. Peel membrane away from bone.

5. Cut into portions.

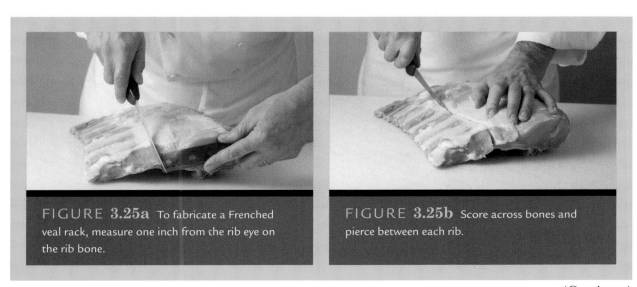

FIGURE **3.25a** To fabricate a Frenched veal rack, measure one inch from the rib eye on the rib bone.

FIGURE **3.25b** Score across bones and pierce between each rib.

(Continues)

FIGURE **3.25c** From the rib side, score across all rib bones.

FIGURE **3.25d** Score down the middle of each rib bone, loosening the membrane that surrounds each rib.

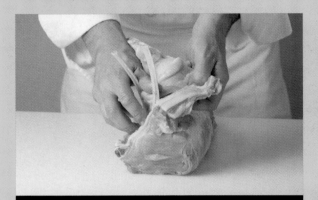

FIGURE **3.25e** Pop the bones out from where the score marks were made.

FIGURE **3.25f** Peel meat and membranes away from bones. Scraping bones may be required.

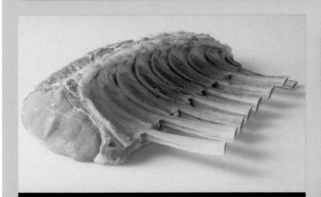

FIGURE **3.25g** Veal rack Frenched (NAMP 306D).

FIGURE **3.25h** To cut Frenched chops, lay the rack meat side down. Cut between each bone, paying attention to the rib eye meat portion as opposed to the bone structure. It is important that the meat is cut evenly.

(Continues)

(Continued)

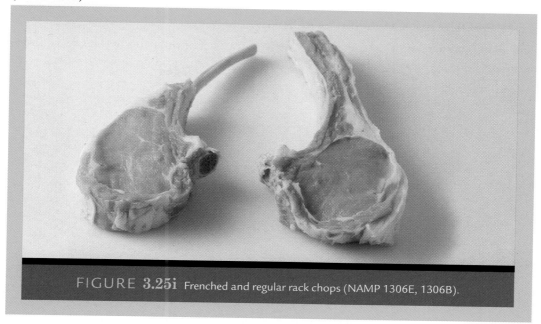

FIGURE **3.25i** Frenched and regular rack chops (NAMP 1306E, 1306B).

VEAL SHOULDER OR CHUCK FABRICATION

The veal shoulder can be cut into roasts, stew, or used for grind. Some retail stores sell it as bone-in chops, but this is not a typical foodservice application. The veal shoulder has many seams and connective tissues. If braising, many of the connectives can be left intact to provide more flavor.

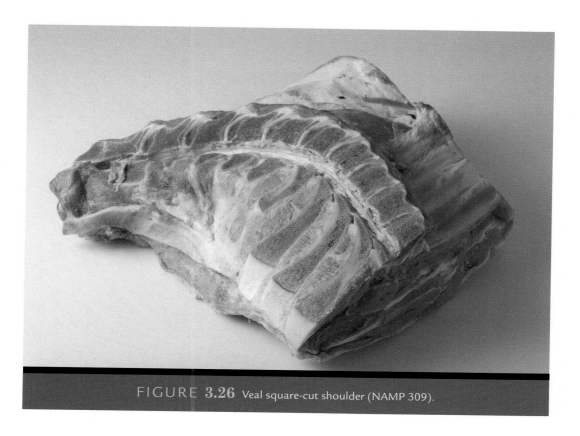

FIGURE **3.26** Veal square-cut shoulder (NAMP 309).

VEAL SHOULDER CLOD INTO ROASTS

The shoulder clod contains some of the largest muscles in the primal and can be fabricated into quality roasts. These roasts can be braised in liquid or slow roasted.

FIGURE **3.27a** The square cut shoulder contains the shoulder clod and the chuck roll sections. To separate the two, cut through the natural seam above the rib bones.

FIGURE **3.27b** The top section containing the blade bone and large humerus is the clod.

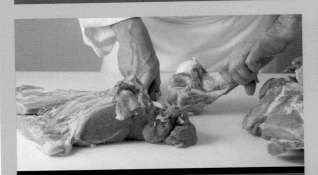

FIGURE **3.27c** To bone the clod, first remove the large humerus bone.

FIGURE **3.27d** Remove the blade bone by peeling along the edges and outline the bone. Remove the small chuck tender and top blade for smaller individual roasts.

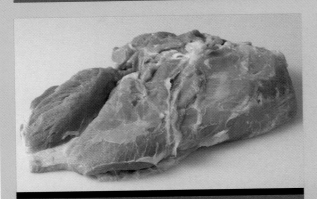

FIGURE **3.27e** Veal shoulder clod (NAMP 310A).

FIGURE **3.27f** The clod can be trimmed and tied into a solid roast.

VEAL CHUCK INTO STEW

Dividing the veal chuck, neck, or any of the smaller parts into stew is easily done in the kitchen. Larger connective tissues and fat are removed. Keep cuts even sized for even cooking.

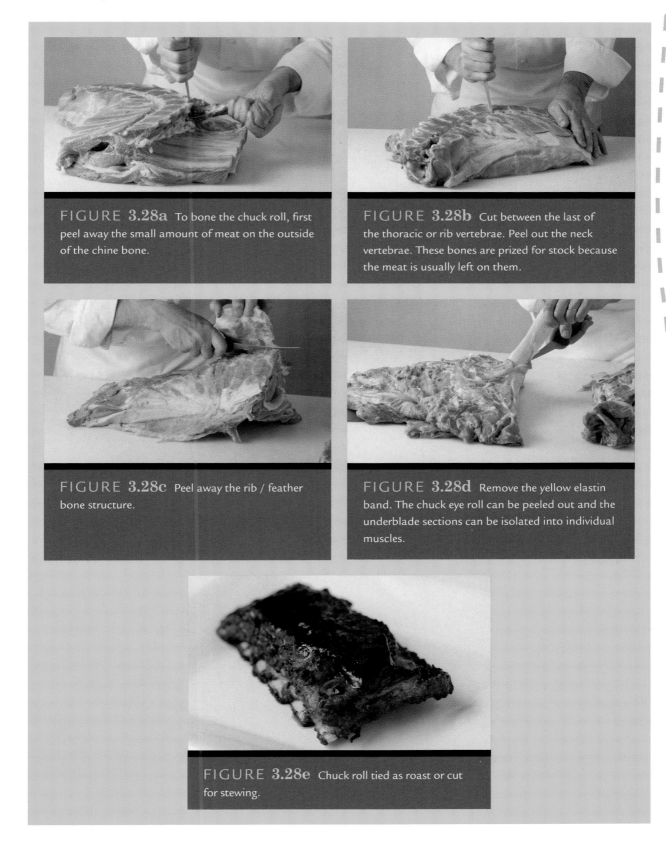

FIGURE **3.28a** To bone the chuck roll, first peel away the small amount of meat on the outside of the chine bone.

FIGURE **3.28b** Cut between the last of the thoracic or rib vertebrae. Peel out the neck vertebrae. These bones are prized for stock because the meat is usually left on them.

FIGURE **3.28c** Peel away the rib / feather bone structure.

FIGURE **3.28d** Remove the yellow elastin band. The chuck eye roll can be peeled out and the underblade sections can be isolated into individual muscles.

FIGURE **3.28e** Chuck roll tied as roast or cut for stewing.

VEAL BREAST

The veal breast is very inexpensive and can be fabricated into a number of quality dishes. Veal breast can be boned and butterflied or pocketed open for stuffing. Part of it can be fabricated into short ribs for braising. Quality stew can be cut from the brisket end and the bones from the breast make a quality stock. An advanced fabrication would be to bone and cure the breast meat and then smoke it as bacon.

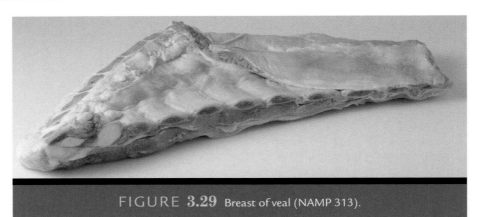

FIGURE **3.29** Breast of veal (NAMP 313).

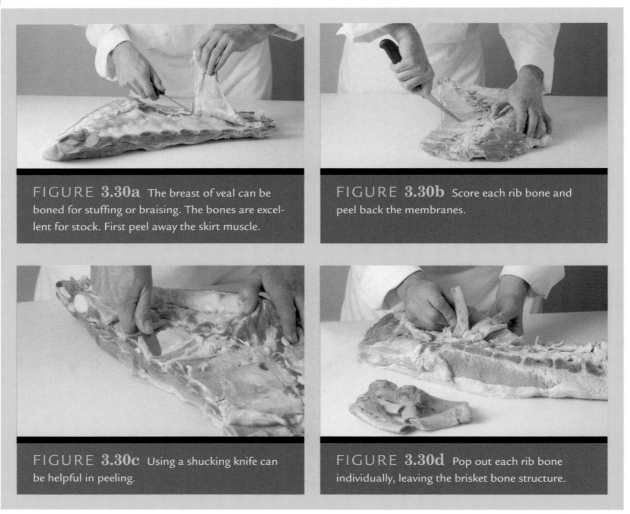

FIGURE **3.30a** The breast of veal can be boned for stuffing or braising. The bones are excellent for stock. First peel away the skirt muscle.

FIGURE **3.30b** Score each rib bone and peel back the membranes.

FIGURE **3.30c** Using a shucking knife can be helpful in peeling.

FIGURE **3.30d** Pop out each rib bone individually, leaving the brisket bone structure.

(*Continues*)

(*Continued*)

FIGURE **3.30e** Start to peel the brisket bones from the thick corner.

FIGURE **3.30f** Be careful to eliminate any small bone fragments.

FIGURE **3.30g** Yield includes boneless veal breast, usable trim, and bones for stock. Boneless breast can be butterflied or pocketed for stuffing.

FIGURE **3.30h** The breast of veal can be semi-boned and Frenched to create a rack–like look. Score the bones about two inches from the end and pop them out of the membrane. Remove all brisket bones.

FIGURE **3.30i** Stuff the center of the breast and roll into a spiral shape.

FIGURE **3.30j** Tie between each bone to hold shape.

VEAL OFFAL

The veal liver requires peeling to remove a tough exterior layer and may require some removal of large blood vessels. The kidney requires taking out the blood vessels in the center. Sweetbreads need peeling, as do calves brains.

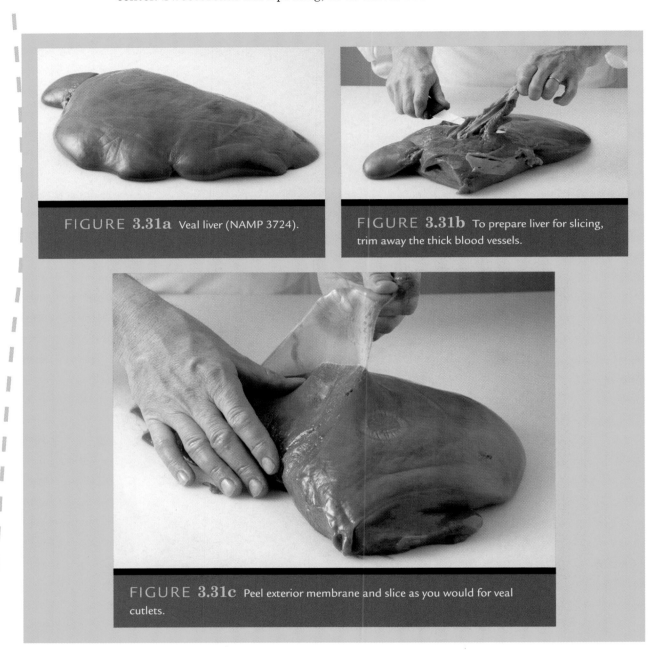

FIGURE **3.31a** Veal liver (NAMP 3724).

FIGURE **3.31b** To prepare liver for slicing, trim away the thick blood vessels.

FIGURE **3.31c** Peel exterior membrane and slice as you would for veal cutlets.

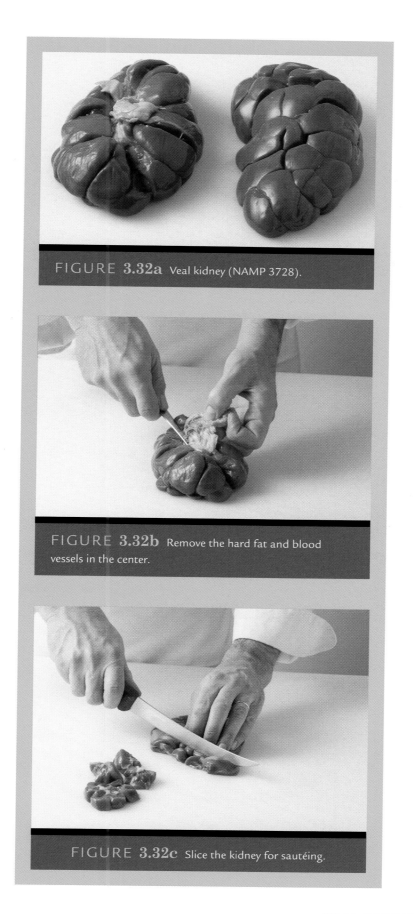

FIGURE **3.32a** Veal kidney (NAMP 3728).

FIGURE **3.32b** Remove the hard fat and blood vessels in the center.

FIGURE **3.32c** Slice the kidney for sautéing.

FIGURE **3.33a** Veal sweetbread (NAMP 3722).

FIGURE **3.33b** The sweetbread is often poached and chilled. After poaching, peel away the exterior membrane.

FIGURE **3.33c** Press the sweetbread to shape.

FIGURE **3.33d** The pressed and chilled sweetbread can now be sliced for sautéing.

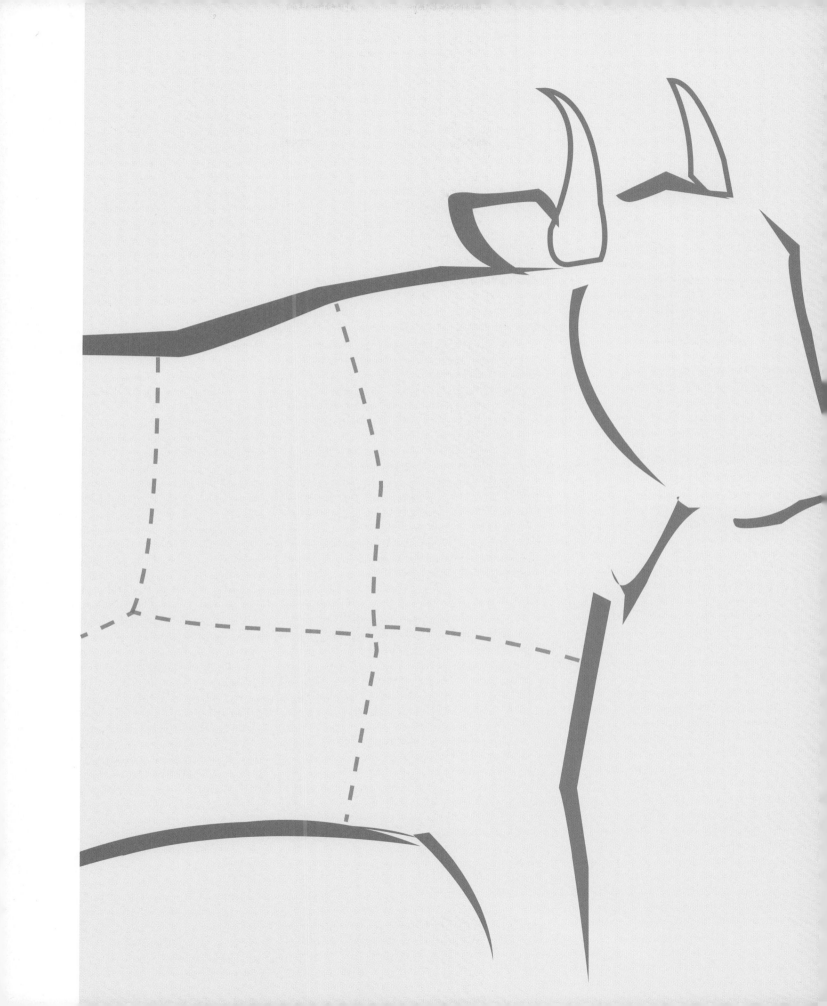

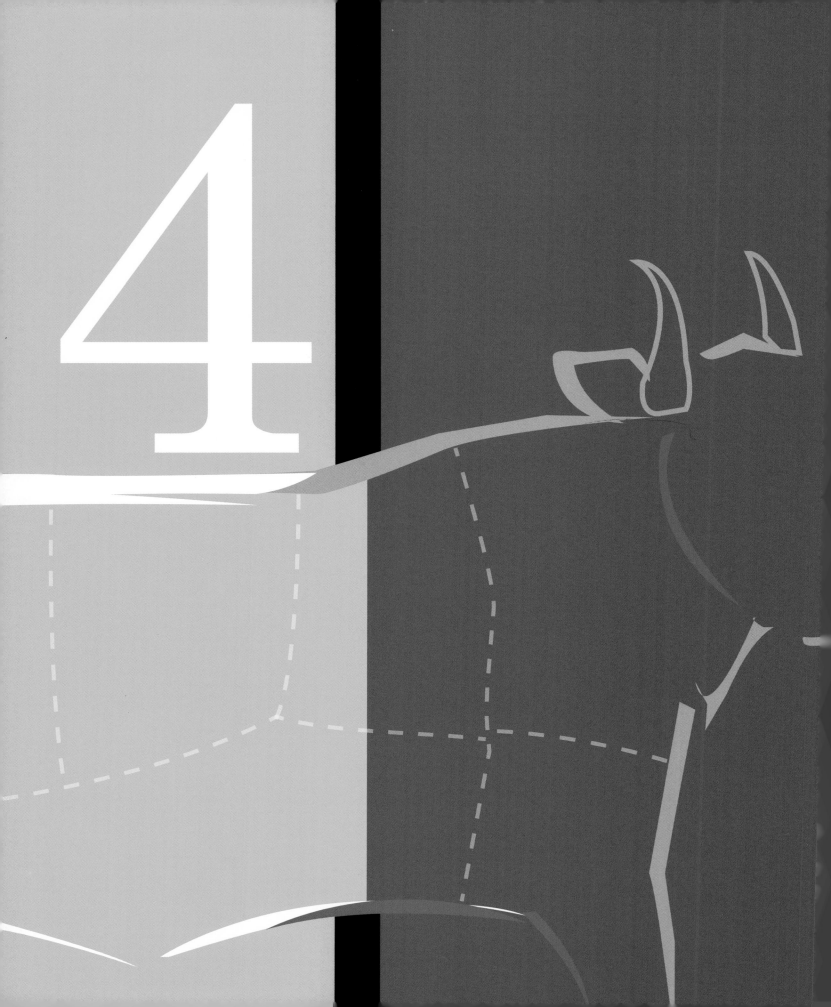

PORK

The term hog is used to describe a member of the domestic pig family, *Sus scrofa*. Pork is the meat produced from the domestic breeds of hog that descended from the Eurasian Wild Boar. The word pork comes from the Latin word porcine.

One of the earliest animals to be tamed, hogs were first domesticated around 6000 to 7000 BC, in what was the Fertile Crescent of the Middle East. While early nomadic herdsmen could follow grazing herds of animals, the domestication of the hog required a civilization that was stationary. Hog production required shade and forage from nut trees, so early hog raising existed in the northern regions of the Near East. There is, however, evidence that hog production existed in China before its appearance in the Middle East. Bone fragments and carved figures indicate that very early hog farming was part of China's culture.

Ancient people used the byproducts of the hog to produce a variety of tools, such as brushes from the stiff hair, called bristles, and shields and shoes from the hide. This continues in modern times, and those familiar with sports know that the American football was originally made from the hog hide giving it the name pigskin.

China is the world's largest pork producer, followed by the United States, Brazil, Canada, Russia, Poland, Japan, South Korea, Philippines, and Mexico. China annually produces about 75 pounds per person, with the bulk consumed by its own population.

During the Roman occupation of England, pork followed beef and mutton as the favored meat. In the Anglo-Saxon period, around 800 to 1000 AD, the pig became more of a substantial meat source. These early hogs were smaller than their modern counterparts are and took about three years to mature. They were forage fed, which included nuts, roots, certain barks, and tree buds. They had longer legs that enabled them to run and escape predators, such as wolves. Later, European domestic pigs were crossed with Chinese breeds, giving us many of the modern breeds we find today.

Pork is a staple meat in many nations. Pound for pound it is the highest consumed meat in the world. Farming of hogs spread throughout Asia, Europe, and Africa and eventually to the Americas. It is the dominant meat of China, Korea, Vietnam, much of Southeast Asia and the European Union, and is popular in North and South America, Russia, and Eastern Europe. Production is also found in some African nations. Due to dietary restrictions in the Jewish and Muslim religions, pork production is highly regulated in most Muslim-dominated nations, such as Saudi Arabia, Iran, and Oman, and is produced in relatively small amounts in Israel. The pig was considered a "dirty" animal because of its living and eating habits and the fact that it is not a ruminant or grass eater and cannot be considered Kosher.

The hog is an omnivore, meaning it is relatively easy to feed and can eat a large variety of foodstuffs. This allowed humans to feed hogs waste from villages and early cities. On farms, the pig would eat the leftover crops and excesses from the garden, as well as byproducts from other animals. In cities, the hog would be fed waste from bakeries, restaurants, and inns and tailings from breweries and distilleries; any leftover and usually spoiled food was fed to pigs. As previously stated, pigs were also allowed to graze and forage. In the fall, many of the deciduous trees in northern climates drop a large variety of nuts, which pigs would fatten on. The meat from these pigs was, and still is, considered the most flavorful.

Early European explorers, such as Hernando de Soto, brought hogs with them to the New World and released these animals into the wild to allow food for settlers coming later. Hogs were an important food source for pioneering settlers and provided food that could be preserved well beyond its traditional harvest time in the fall. The salting and curing of pork provided a source of protein and fat for travelers, explorers, and military troops. Soldiers were often given a ration of salted pork to be boiled with other foods for added flavor.

Today, most hogs are raised on large farms where they are housed in integrated feeding barns. They are born, raised, and fed on the farm and reach slaughter weight very rapidly. Most modern hogs reach market live weight, approximately 250 to 270 pounds, within six to eight months. They are raised on a variety of diets with corn based being the most common. The goal for feeders is to achieve a rapid gain, which can be upwards of two pounds per day on average; feeds are formulated to give energy and protein to achieve this.

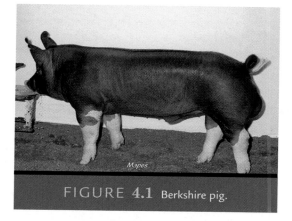

FIGURE **4.1** Berkshire pig.

FIGURE **4.2** Cheshire White pig.

FIGURE **4.3** Duroc pig.

FIGURE **4.4** Hampshire pig.

Large hog farms and concentration in feeding have presented new challenges. These farms require large amounts of water and produce enormous waste. There are efforts to convert waste into electric energy or fuel.

HOG BREEDS

Wild boars were once greatly feared, due to their large tusks, bristle coat, thick hide, and because they are a "thinking" animal, able to outsmart an opponent. Domesticating such an animal must have taken extreme skill by early farmers. Modern breeds developed by breeding European wild pigs with domestic breeds from China. Modern hog breeding and selection is dependent on a number of factors: average litter size; gain, or the ability of the animal to grow rapidly from birth; disease resistance; fat to lean ratio; overall length and width of the animal; and marbling, color, and texture scores of the lean muscle. All of these features can be bred into pigs by selective breeding. Many of the market-style hogs we find today are a combination of breeds.

TYPICAL HOG BREEDS

BERKSHIRE

Berkshire pigs have a high-quality flavor and the ability to marble well. The meat can be slightly darker than other breeds. In Japan, it is known as kurobuta pork (black hog), where it is as much prized as kobe beef.

CHESHIRE WHITE

Large litters and good meat quality make this breed a typical choice for modern farmers. This is a low-stress breed and has a good demeanor with others.

DUROC

This breed is red in color, fast growing, has large muscles, and produces a good litter size.

HAMPSHIRE

Hampshires have an excellent fat-to-lean ratio, with a large loin eye and without huge fatback. Markings are black with a wide white stripe around the middle. This breed is known historically as a good forager and is able to fatten on its own if allowed to roam.

LANDRACE

Known for being very good mothers, Landrace pigs have large litters, are fast growing, have white hides, and have a very good fat-to-lean ratio. They originate from Denmark.

POLAND CHINA

This breed is actually a mix of many different breeds, including Berkshire. It is a large pig with very stout bone structure and a mild demeanor, which makes it an excellent mixing breed. They are known for large litters.

SPOTTED

Closely related to the Poland China, the Spotted is a fast reproducer and has a good yield.

YORKSHIRE

The Yorkshire, also known as the "English Large White," is the most recorded breed in the United States and Canada. Fast growth rate, good muscle scores, and large litters make it the most popular. Most of the pork raised in the Midwest region of the U.S. is the Yorkshire breed.

Each of these commercial breeds developed in various parts of the United States, with most of their heritage coming from Europe or England. Because early farmers and homesteaders did not travel much, certain breeds became more popular in specific areas. Today, however, hogs are bred to be high performing, but a more homogenous herd is the result.

Although the pork industry is dominated by a few breeds, there are many other breeds worldwide. There are niche-market producers that are developing herds of unique "heritage" breeds that may not fit in the large hog farm system. A couple of breeds, such as the Tamworth and Ossabaw Island, are unique in their fat production and provide different flavors. The Tamworth, with long legs and a very thick belly, would have been known as a "bacon" pig years ago. The Ossabaw is a direct descendant of Spanish breeds that were abandoned on an island east of Georgia. These pigs are almost extinct due to their general physiology, which is not "normal" for modern pigs.

Other pigs, such as the Meishan and Minzhu from China, represent a style that requires the hog to create a large amount of lard and have rich flavor. These breeds are also known to resist diseases and reproduce rapidly.

FIGURE 4.5 Landrace pig.

FIGURE 4.6 Poland China pig.

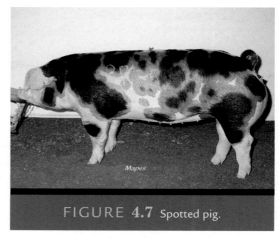
FIGURE 4.7 Spotted pig.

FIGURE 4.8 Yorkshire pig.

PORK EVALUATION AND GRADING

The evaluation of live hogs for today's commercial market depends on a few basic features, which include: thickness of the fatback, size and shape of the loin eye, length of the loin in general, width and muscling of the ham and shoulder, and width and thickness of the belly section. The USDA has a grading system for hogs that is based on these criteria. However, the USDA grade is not reflected in finished product, as it is in beef, veal, or lamb. There is only "acceptable" and "unacceptable" pork. Unacceptable pork is used for processed products and not sold as whole muscle cuts. Acceptable pork is divided according to yield on a one to four scale, one being the leanest.

Most pork producers have their own grading system as far as what they will sell as commercial or whole muscle cuts. Many will use the guidelines developed by the National Pork Producers Council, which would identify texture, color of lean muscle, and marbling scores.

Breed-specific and niche-market pork have gained in popularity among some chefs in recent years. An example of breed-specific pork would be Berkshire pork. Berkshire is known for its high marbling scores and rich flavor characteristics. Placing the term Berkshire on the menu increases potential value by implicating a higher-quality product. Other terms may be natural, which may have different connotations, ranging from the basic fact that there are no injected ingredients to the way the animal was raised or fed. The buyer must be diligent in understanding what sort of pork they are selling and not misrepresent terms on the menu. Be sure to research a product and not invent information that may not be true.

PORK CARCASS BREAKDOWN

The whole market hog is split down the middle, creating sides or halves. A typical half hog weighs around 100 pounds and is about five to six feet long, making it difficult, but not entirely unmanageable, to break down in a kitchen setting. The hog has an extremely high utilization rate and all of it can be used in some way. Pork has a sort of dual personality in that it can be used as a fresh meat, like veal or beef, or it can be cured to make a multitude of hams, bacons, sausages, and literally hundreds of other products. A chef who wants to experiment in creating his or her own specialty cured meats can certainly utilize every portion of the hog.

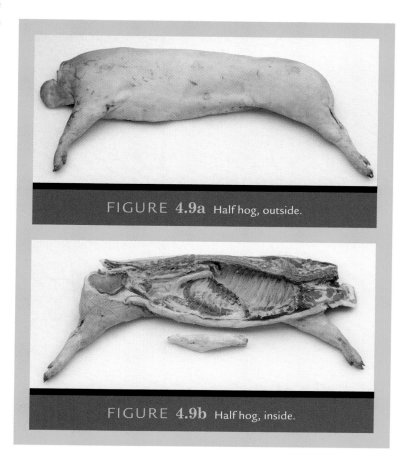

FIGURE **4.9a** Half hog, outside.

FIGURE **4.9b** Half hog, inside.

FIGURE **4.10** Half Hogs.				
ITEM AND NAMP NUMBER	**DESCRIPTION/ FABRICATION**	**SUGGESTED COOKING METHOD/ APPLICATION**	**AVERAGE SUGGESTED WEIGHT IN POUNDS**	**TYPICAL PACKAGE SPECS**
400 Pork Carcass	Market-style hogs are typically sold split and can be purchased as a half hog.	Can be roasted whole; typically fabricated into market cuts	90–110	Sold as hanging meat
400a Roasting pig/Suckling pig	Sold whole, unsplit; can be semi boned and stuffed	Roast whole, spit/ rotisserie, roast flat	Suckling 18—35; Roasting 40–60, 60–80, 80–100	Sold whole, hanging

As with other meats, pork can be purchased as pre-trimmed fabricated cuts. A large variety of specs can be found for each specific pork cut. Pork producers develop trim levels and specific measurements for cuts depending on customers' needs and also profitability.

PRIMAL CUTS

In this book, we will examine the pork cuts according to North American standards and cutting styles. In other regions of the world, pork is fabricated in a different manner. Divisions of the carcass can vary depending on intended uses and cultural differences.

Most meat carcasses have four primals, but due to the value of the belly section of pork, it, too, must be included as a primal.

- Ham
- Loin
- Boston Butt
- Picnic
- Belly with Spare ribs

MARKET FORMS

There are cuts that are not traditionally found attached to the primals. Certain sections are trimmed off and sold separately as market items.

- Neck bones
- Hock
- Fatback
- Jowl

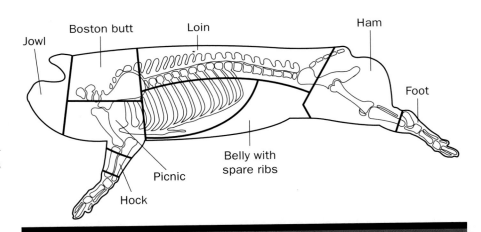

FIGURE **4.11** Swine skeletal structure with primal cuts.

PORK HRI CUTS

When purchasing pork items it is important to establish proper specifications with the vendor. Understanding average weights and requesting logical sizes ensures a consistent portion. Pork is sold with a large variety of trim levels and many bone-in, semi-boneless and completely boneless items. Attached are typical package sizes and counts per bag and box. These are general specs and can change from processor to processor. Every processor has some items they choose to package differently than others.

Pork is often processed into a large variety of cured, smoked, ground and seasoned products. This section will identify the "fresh" pork items first and then categorize the cured products.

Much of today's pork is lean without much marbling. This can lead to pork being too dry when overcooked. Many pork items, especially loin cuts, are sold as "enhanced" or pumped with water holding agents such as salt and sodium phosphate. These agents will allow pork to stay moist even if overcooked. Enhanced pork will be labeled with the added ingredients. Be specific with the processor about ordering enhanced or non-enhanced products. Some chefs choose to enhance pork themselves by adding their own brine or solution. Another option is to seek high marbling scores that will ensure more moisture.

The North American Meat Processor's Meat Buyer's Guide has established a standard number code system for meat purchasing. These numbers would be recognized by most salespeople.

HAM

The pork ham or back leg is the largest muscle section of the hog. It contains the same basic muscle groups, or subprimals, as the round of beef, including the top round, bottom, eye, heel, knuckle, shank or hock, and a small section of the sirloin. It has four basic bones: the femur, aitch, kneecap, and a portion of the shank. The ham is sold skin on unless requested otherwise. It can be sold fresh or cured. Cured hams are sold in two basic forms, dry or brine cured.

Examples of dry-cured ham include country style or Smithfield ham from Virginia, but other forms can be found throughout the southeastern United States. Many are smoked or peppered and require soaking to release some of the heavy salt flavor before using. Other forms of dry-cured product include the Italian Prosciutto style ham. These hams require an exacting procedure of salting and storing for many months to create the delicate flavor of this specialty. The Spanish Serrano Ham is selected from specifically fed hogs, carefully salted, and stored to create a fine and unique flavor. Other dry-cured hams include the French Jambon Bayonne, the heavily smoked German Bauernschinken (Farmer's Ham), and the Chinese Yunnan Ham. Many dry-cured hams are sliced very thin and served as an appetizer or included as an ingredient in other dishes.

Wet or brine-cured hams are manufactured by taking a raw ham and injecting it with a brine solution or soaking it in a salt brine. This type of ham is mild in flavor and is often smoked and precooked. Typically sold as deli-style ham, popular brine-cured

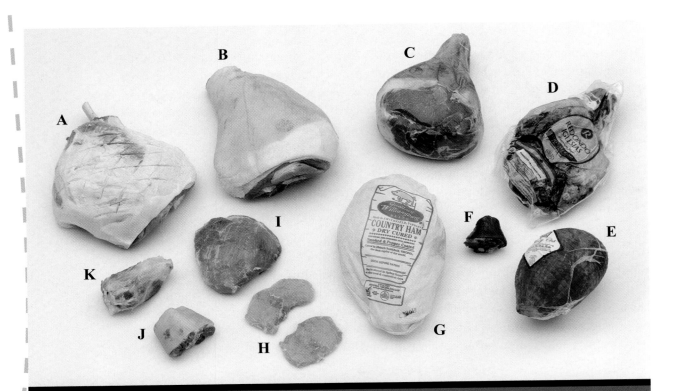

FIGURE **4.12** A: Fresh ham steamship, B: Pork Fresh ham, C: Prosciutto ham, D: Serrano ham, E: Smoked ham (ready to eat), F: Smoked ham hock, G: Smoked country ham/Smithfield ham, H: Pork top round cutlets, I: Pork inside ham/top round, J: Fresh pork ham hock, K: Pork shank skinless.

FIGURE **4.13** Fresh Hams.				
ITEM AND NAMP NUMBER	DESCRIPTION/ FABRICATION	SUGGESTED COOKING METHOD/ APPLICATION	AVERAGE SUGGESTED WEIGHT IN POUNDS	TYPICAL PACKAGE SPECS
401 Fresh ham (primal)	May be trimmed and semi-boned, boned rolled and tied or sectioned into subprimals. The ham can be cured and smoked	Roast whole, roast as smaller sections, cutlets Hock section braised	20–25	3 per case
401a Fresh ham/short shank	Same as above. Tougher hock section removed	Roast whole, roast as smaller sections, cutlets	18–20	3 per case

(Continues)

(Continued)

ITEM AND NAMP NUMBER	DESCRIPTION/ FABRICATION	SUGGESTED COOKING METHOD/ APPLICATION	AVERAGE SUGGESTED WEIGHT IN POUNDS	TYPICAL PACKAGE SPECS
402 Fresh ham skinned	Skin removed for easier carving. Sold with specific fat trim	Roast whole, cutlets	14–16	3 per case
Fresh ham, steamship	Skinned, shank bone exposed, pelvic bone removed, for easy carving	Roast whole, carving item	12–14	3 per case
402c Fresh ham, boneless	Sold rolled and tied, can be further fabricated and trimmed	Roast whole, roast as smaller sections, cutlets	10–12	3 per case
402e Out-side ham	Bottom and eye round sub-primals sold trimmed and defatted	Small inexpensive roast	4–5	2 per bag, 4 bags per box
402f Inside ham	Inside/top round sold trimmed and deffated, may need to peel cap muscle off top	Very good for cutlets, thin julienne slices, small roasts	4–5	2 per bag, 4 bags per box
417a Fresh ham Stock	Short shank section of ham	Flavor agent for soups, vegetables, braise as osso buco	1–2	varies
Fresh pork shank	Full shank of pork, sold skinless	Braised whole, cut in half for osso buco style braise	1.5 –2.5	varies

hams include boiled ham, "pit" hams, bone-in spiral cut hams, ham steaks, and a huge variety of smoked hams.

The ham can be separated into sub primals and sold as smaller cuts. The hock is sold alone as a flavoring agent for soups and stews. The top round, otherwise known as an inside ham, is sold as a separate subprimal and is excellent for cutlets.

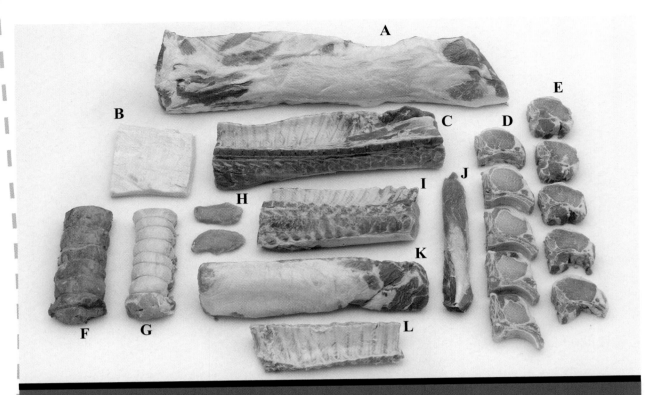

FIGURE 4.14 A: Primal pork loin. B: Pork fat back, C: Center cut pork loin, D: Rib end chops, E: Pork lion chops, F: Canadian Bacon, G: Boneless loin roast. H: Pork loin cutlets, I: Pork rack, J: Pork tenderloin, K: Boneless center cut loin, L: Baby back ribs.

LOIN

The pork loin consists of the entire back of the hog containing both a rib end and a loin end. In other species, such as veal, the two would be separated into two parts, a rack and a loin. The pork loin is typically dry cooked and is generally the highest value of the primals. When fabricated or boned, the loin yields a loin eye muscle, a tenderloin, and baby back ribs, all of which are high-value items. The loin is sold as a primal or as a center cut. The primal has a section of sirloin on one end and a section of blade or shoulder on the other end. The center cut has those removed and is more uniform in shape. Those end pieces can be purchased separately and are generally inexpensive. The loin can be purchased pre-cut as chops. Chops can vary in size and quality; be sure to specify exactly what chops are desired. Center cut chops are any chop that is cut from the center cut loin. Loin or porterhouse chops are cut from the loin end and would contain a piece of the tenderloin and a t-bone structure. Rib or rack chops would have the curved rib bone structure and can be Frenched. Sirloin and blade chops are cut from the end pieces and tend to be considered lesser quality.

The baby back ribs have become extremely popular in foodservice and there are a variety of specs to choose from when ordering. They are often sold by the number of ribs in the rack as well as the length of the rib. They can be purchased pre-cooked and flavored and with a large variety of marinades. Baby back ribs hold a lot of value and consistently out price even the boneless loin!

The loin is also sold as a cured item. Smoked pork loin or Kassler Ribchen would have the flavor of ham. Boneless smoked pork loin is often known as Canadian Bacon.

FIGURE **4.15** Pork Loin HRI Cuts.

ITEM AND NAMP NUMBER	DESCRIPTION/FABRICATION	SUGGESTED COOKING METHOD/ APPLICATION	AVERAGE SUGGESTED WEIGHT IN POUNDS	TYPICAL PACKAGE SPECS
410 Pork loin primal	Full primal cut, includes sirloin section and blade rib end section, some fat cover. Requires some fabrication, trimming. If boned, creates baby back ribs as a byproduct.	Roasting, chops, cutlets	18–22	2 per bag, 2 bags per box
412 Pork loin, center cut, sold as 8–11 rib cut with varying trim levels	Center piece of loin without sirloin or blade ends, can be boned for roast or cutlets	Roasting, center cut chops (loin end and rib end chops)	9–14	2 per bag, 2 per box
413/412 b/c Boneless pork loin, center cut boneless loin	Sold with varying trim levels, boneless, may be trimmed for cutlets	Roast, cutlets, medallions, boneless chops	6–12 (Size varies with specs)	1 per bag, 6 per box
415 Pork tenderloin	Sold with side muscle on or off. May require membrane removal. Can be cut into medallions.	Medallions, pan-seared, roast, broiled whole	1–1.5	2 per bag, 6 per box
Pork rack/rib end loin	Contains 8–10 ribs (rib end only), chine bone removed, fat capped, trimmed	Roast w/Frenched bones, chops, Cowboy chop	3–4	4 per box
1410 Pork loin chops/ sold with varying specs	Full loin cut into chops; contains quality chops from center and some odd shaped chops from end pieces	Grill, broil, pan sear, sauté, breaded, stuffed	Requested by purchaser	Varies
1412 Pork loin center cut chops	Uniform center cut chops, can be sold bone in or boneless with varying trim levels	Grill, broil, pan sear, sauté, breaded, stuffed	Requested by purchaser	Varies
Pork porterhouse	Contains a large piece of tenderloin with each t-bone-shaped chop, high quality	Grill, broil, pan sear, sauté, breaded, stuffed	Requested by purchaser	Varies
Rib chops	Contains only rib cuts with curved rib bones. Can be Frenched	Frenched, chops, grill, broil, sauté, stuffed, breaded	Requested by purchaser	Varies

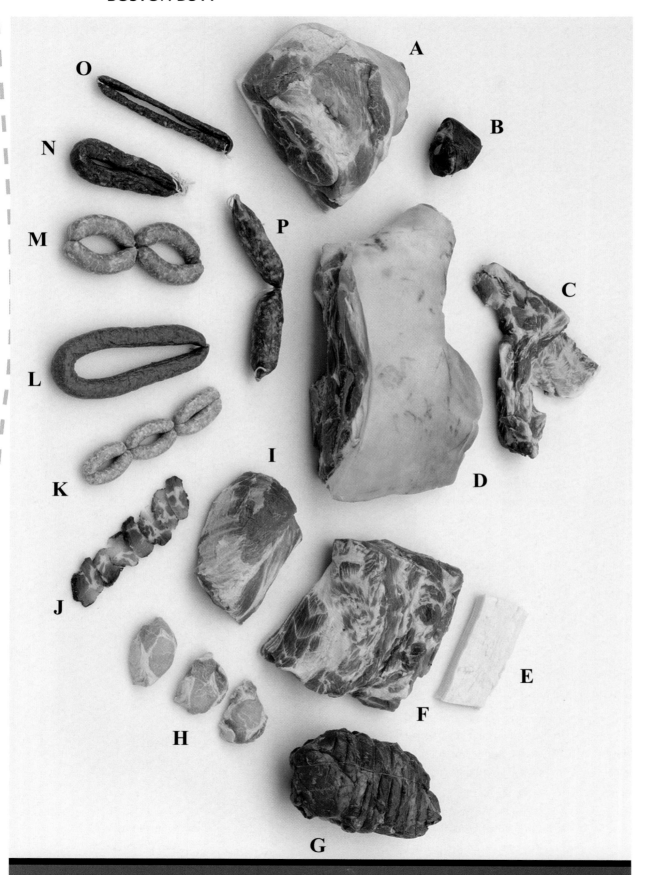

FIGURE 4.16 A: Pork picnic, B: Smoked pork hock, C: Pork neck bones, D: Full pork shoulder. E: Pork fatback, F: Pork Boston butt, G: Smoked pork butt, H: Pork butt cutlet/steak. I: Boneless cottage butt, J: Coppa ham. K: Breakfast links, L: Kilbasa, M: Italian Sausage, N: Dried chorizo, O: Caceiatore salami, P: Sopressatta.

ITEM AND NAMP NUMBER	DESCRIPTION/ FABRICATION	SUGGESTED COOKING METHOD/ APPLICATION	AVERAGE SUGGESTED WEIGHT IN POUNDS	TYPICAL PACKAGE SPECS
406 Boston butt	Sold bone in, skinless; trim levels vary with processor's specs. Typically 75% lean, 25% fat. Super-trimmed versions available.	Slow roasting, barbecue, pulled pork, slow braising, stewing, grinding, forcemeats, sausage, kebab cubes	6–8	2 per bag, 4 bags per box
406a Boston butt, boneless	Boneless, with varying amounts of trim; sold rolled and tied also	Slow roasting, barbecue, pulled pork, slow braising, stewing, grinding for sausage	5–7	2 per bag, 4 bags per box
407 Butt cellar, cottage butt	Center cut section of pork butt, well trimmed	Roasting, sliced and stuffed (braciola),	3–5	Varies

FIGURE **4.17** Boston Butt HRI Cuts.

The front of the hog is known as the pork shoulder. It can be purchased whole and some restaurants will buy it that way to cook as barbecue. It is traditionally broken into the Boston butt and the picnic. The Boston butt is the top section of the shoulder and, therefore, is the tenderer of the two. It is sold without skin and fatback and can be purchased either bone-in or boneless. It contains a blade bone and requires a relatively simple boning technique. There is a center section that is also known as the cellar or cottage butt, and this item is where the pork loin eye extends into the shoulder.

The Boston butt contains a fat ratio of about seventy-percent lean to thirty-percent fat, depending on its trim spec. Much of the fat is internal, making the butt a moist and very flavorful roast, and it is typically used for slow-cooked barbecue and pulled pork. The fat-to-lean ratio also makes it a superior choice for sausage fabrication.

The smoked pork butt is cured and smoked for a ham-like flavor or dry cured as Coppa ham or spiced to form the cappacola-style ham.

PICNIC

The picnic is the lower part of the shoulder. It is leaner than the Boston butt and is typically sold with the skin on. It is a lean cut and can be purchased boneless and skinless if required and can be sold as a BRT (boned, rolled, tied) roast. The price of the picnic tends to be very low, and therefore many pork processors will use the picnic for lean to mix with fat when making sausage products. It can also be cured and smoked as a picnic ham.

FIGURE **4.18** Pork Picnic HRI Cuts.

ITEM AND NAMP NUMBER	DESCRIPTION/FABRICATION	SUGGESTED COOKING METHOD/APPLICATION	AVERAGE SUGGESTED WEIGHT IN POUNDS	TYPICAL PACKAGE SPECS
403 Whole shoulder	Entire front section of hog; contains picnic and Boston butt; includes skin and heavy fat back and bones	Used for slow-cooking barbecue, grinding for sausage, braising	16–20	2 per box
405 Picnic	Leaner bottom section of the shoulder, sold skin on; can be boned for lean usable trim	Slow roasting, barbeque, slow braising, stewing, grinding	8–10	2 per bag, 4 bags per box
405a Picnic, boneless	Sold as whole, boneless section or as trimmed individual lean cushion meat	Slow roasting, barbecue, pulled pork, slow braising, stewing, grinding	6–8; Cushion is smaller, 2–3 pounds each	Varies

BELLY AND SPARE RIBS

The belly is considered a commodity meat item and prices of pork bellies are quoted daily in the *Wall Street Journal*. Traders will buy and sell futures of bellies on the Chicago Mercantile Exchange. Pork belly is used for a large variety of culinary applications. Number

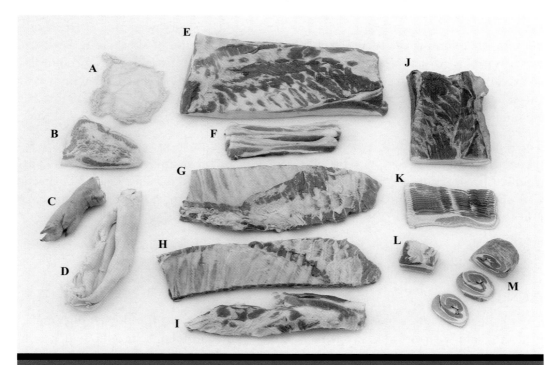

FIGURE **4.19** A. Caul fat, B. Fresh jowl, C. Pig's foot, D. Leaf lard, E. Fresh pork belly, F. Fresh belly slices, G. Spare ribs, H. St. Louis style ribs, I. Pork brisket bones, J. Slab bacon, K. Sliced bacon, L. Salt pork, M. Pancetta.

FIGURE 4.20 Pork Belly and Spare Ribs HRI Cuts.				
ITEM AND NAMP NUMBER	DESCRIPTION/ FABRICATION	SUGGESTED COOKING METHOD/ APPLICATION	AVERAGE SUGGESTED WEIGHT IN POUNDS	TYPICAL PACKAGE SPECS
422 Baby back ribs	Contains at least 8 ribs; result of boning the pork loin; may need to be peeled; sold with varying bone lengths	Slow cooked as barbecue racks; sectioned and coated and cooked individually; can be steamed first to tenderize	1.5–2	2 per bag, 6 per box; packaging varies with company
416 Pork Spareribs	11–13 ribs from belly region; may need breast bone removed or notched	Slow-cooked barbecue; can be steamed or simmered to tenderize.	3–5	2–3 per bag, 3 per box; packaging can vary with processor
416a Pork spare ribs, St. Louis style/Chinese style	Trimmed belly ribs; blocked and trimmed for consistent shape and size	Slow-cooked barbecue; can be steamed or simmered to tenderize	2–4	3 per bag, 4 per box; packaging can vary
423 Country-style ribs	Butterflied; 3–4 rib end piece of loin; very meaty; chine bone must be cut, can be pounded flat	Grill, slow-cooked barbecue	2–4	2 per bag
408 Pork belly	Large, rectangular, flat side of the hog; traditionally sold with skin on but can be purchased trimmed and skin off. Thickness can be specified.	Typically cured for bacon; can be slow roasted or braised as a fresh belly; very flavorful.	12–18	1 per bag; 60 pound box
416b Brisket bones, 412 Neck bones	Inexpensive sections removed when creating St. Louis style ribs or pork shoulder; lots of bone; Sold cured and smoked	Slow cooked; flavor agent for soups; greens; inexpensive riblets	Varies	Varies
420 Pigs feet	Sold in varying lengths; front and back available	Flavor agent; can be hollow boned and stuffed as Zampone	Bulk packaged	

one on the list must be bacon. Smoked belly bacon, sliced and fried, has been a breakfast mainstay for many years. Bacon is used as an ingredient in many culinary favorites.

The belly can be purchased fresh, smoked, or cured in various ways, such as salt pork or pancetta. Fresh belly is often slow roasted or braised and can be served as a stand-alone main course or as a side dish. The cured versions can be used as a flavor agent, giving dishes a salty, crispy boost.

The pork spare ribs are the rib cage that coincides with the pork belly cut. Often known as belly or rack ribs, they are wider and generally meatier than their baby back rib cousin. There are a variety of specifics to consider when purchasing. Overall rack weight and length of the bones can be requested and processors may offer a variety of rib products. The full spare rib can be purchased without the brisket bones and trimmed to make a more uniform rib. These are often known as St. Louis Ribs and are, normally, slightly higher priced. Ribs can be purchased enhanced (marinated or basted) or even pre-cooked.

OFFAL AND MARKET ITEMS

Beyond the primals, there are other items that hold a fair amount of value. Pork fat-back is the subcutaneous fat found over the loin and Boston butt area. This fat is very solid and clean and can be used for barding and larding. The leaf lard is the lumbar fat found on the inside of the carcass and is used for shortening in baking recipes.

The pork neck bones are sold fresh and smoked and used as a flavor agent.

Offal include the liver, intestines, caul fat, and kidneys. A classic use for pork liver is the French pate provencale or a country-style pate. Caul fat is used to wrap and bard other meat items. The intestines are used for sausage casings or can be sold as chitterlings.

PORK FABRICATION

When fabricating pork, be sure to cut separately from other meats. Pork, although relatively safe, is considered a danger and cross-contamination should be avoided.

DIVIDING HALF HOG

Although a half hog is large and not a typical purchase for most restaurants, it is not entirely out of the question. Fabricating the hog requires a handsaw and a large six-foot tabletop. The whole hog yields a lot of fatback and usable trim that can be used if the chef desires to explore the art of char-cuterie. The belly and ham can be cured and smoked; the hocks and feet can be used for flavor. Nothing really goes to waste.

HAM OR LEG

The ham can be used bone-in, semi-boned, or boneless. It is sold skin on, unless otherwise specified.

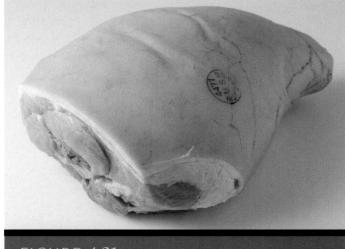

FIGURE 4.21 Pork fresh ham (NAMP 401) can be purchased skin on or off and with the shank or hock cut shorter. The fresh ham can also be purchased pre-divided into subprimals.

Boning the Ham

Remove hock or shank by making a straight cut with a saw. Remove aitch bone, cut between the inside round and the knuckle to remove femur, then cut around and remove kneecap. Once boned, the ham can be divided onto subprimals for cutlets or smaller roasts.

FIGURE **4.22a** The fresh ham can be boned and tied for roasting, also semi-boned and Frenched for a quality presentation. Using a stiff boning knife, remove the hipbone by cutting along the pelvic bone through the ball and socket joint.

FIGURE **4.22b** To French the shank bone, peel away meat and skin and cut away. There is a small extra bone that must be removed.

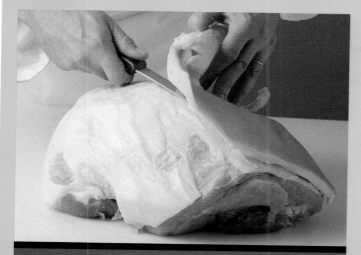

FIGURE **4.22c** Peel the skin away from the exterior. The skin can be used as a protective cover and pulled away before serving.

FIGURE **4.22d** The Frenched pork fresh ham may be trimmed of some fat and scored for presentation.

LOIN

Making a Primal Loin into a Center Cut

To make a primal loin into a center cut, remove three to five ribs off the shoulder end of the loin and remove the sirloin at the end of the pelvic bone.

The primal loin has the sirloin and rib end that may be removed. Cutting the loin for chops can be done by hand or with a band saw. Boning the loin requires some knowledge of the backbone vertebrae and some skill, but is manageable. Cutting the baby back ribs away from the rest of the bone structure may require a saw. The rib end can be Frenched for an upscale presentation.

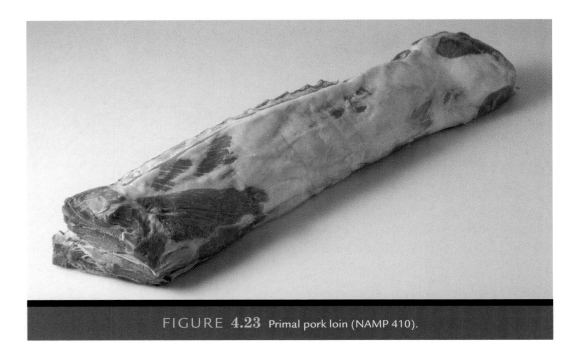

FIGURE **4.23** Primal pork loin (NAMP 410).

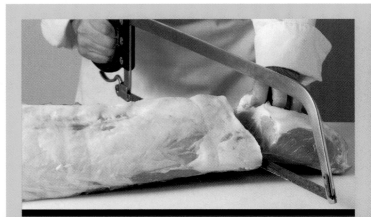

FIGURE **4.24a** The primal loin contains a sirloin end and a blade bone end that can be removed to create the center cut loin. The sirloin is removed at the end of the pelvic bone.

FIGURE **4.24b** The blade is removed three to five ribs into the eye, about four inches from the end. The ends can be cut off with a knife and basic hand saw.

Boning a Center Cut Pork Loin

From a center cut, remove the tenderloin by scooping it away from the chine and finger bones. Cut down rib cage, freeing the main eye muscle from the ribs and feather bones and creating a V-shape as you cut. Cut down finger bones to complete. Trim edges and tie into roast.

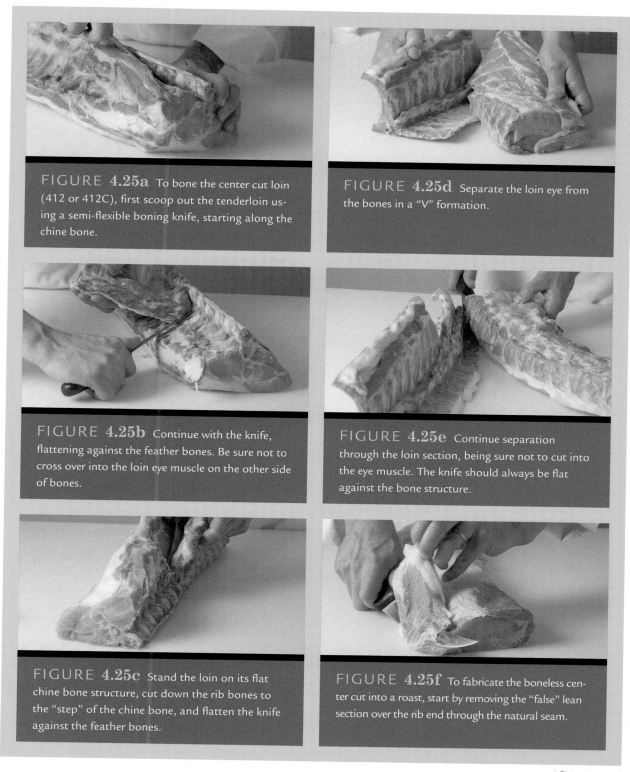

FIGURE **4.25a** To bone the center cut loin (412 or 412C), first scoop out the tenderloin using a semi-flexible boning knife, starting along the chine bone.

FIGURE **4.25b** Continue with the knife, flattening against the feather bones. Be sure not to cross over into the loin eye muscle on the other side of bones.

FIGURE **4.25c** Stand the loin on its flat chine bone structure, cut down the rib bones to the "step" of the chine bone, and flatten the knife against the feather bones.

FIGURE **4.25d** Separate the loin eye from the bones in a "V" formation.

FIGURE **4.25e** Continue separation through the loin section, being sure not to cut into the eye muscle. The knife should always be flat against the bone structure.

FIGURE **4.25f** To fabricate the boneless center cut into a roast, start by removing the "false" lean section over the rib end through the natural seam.

(*Continues*)

(Continued)

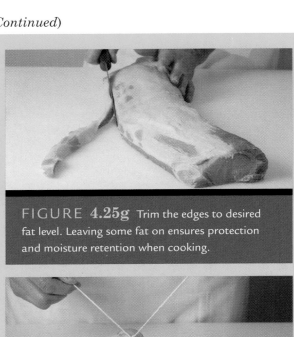

FIGURE **4.25g** Trim the edges to desired fat level. Leaving some fat on ensures protection and moisture retention when cooking.

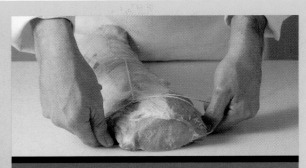

FIGURE **4.25k** Bring the loop over the far end of the loin.

FIGURE **4.25h** To tie the roast using a continual knot, start by tying a normal slip knot one inch from the end of the eye muscle. Do not cut the string.

FIGURE **4.25l** Set the knot an inch and a half from the previous knot.

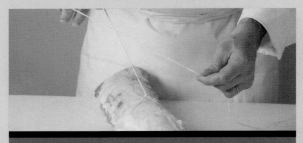

FIGURE **4.25i** Create a loop by making a "U" shape with the string and twist.

FIGURE **4.25m** Cinch the knot tightly and repeat.

FIGURE **4.25j** Twist the string again.

FIGURE **4.25n** Once the top side is secure, flip the roast and cut the string about double the length of the roast.

(Continues)

(Continued)

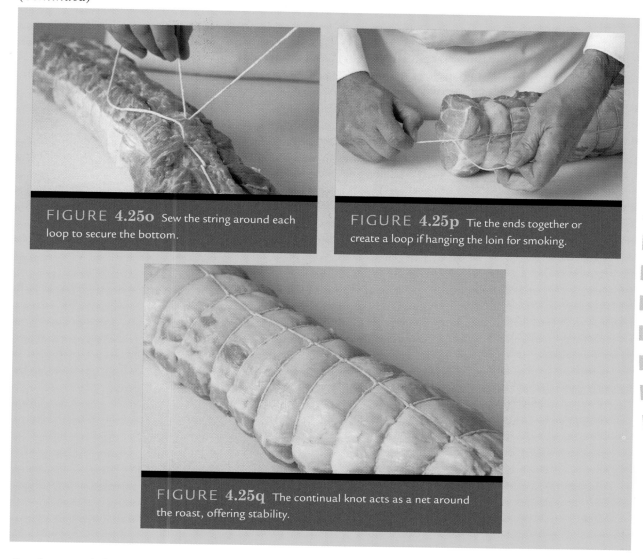

FIGURE **4.25o** Sew the string around each loop to secure the bottom.

FIGURE **4.25p** Tie the ends together or create a loop if hanging the loin for smoking.

FIGURE **4.25q** The continual knot acts as a net around the roast, offering stability.

Cutting Medallions or Cutlets from the Boneless Loin

Completely denude the loin of all silverskin and fat, cut towards the loin side on a bias across the grain with palm flat on the surface. Use a slicer knife or scimitar for best results.

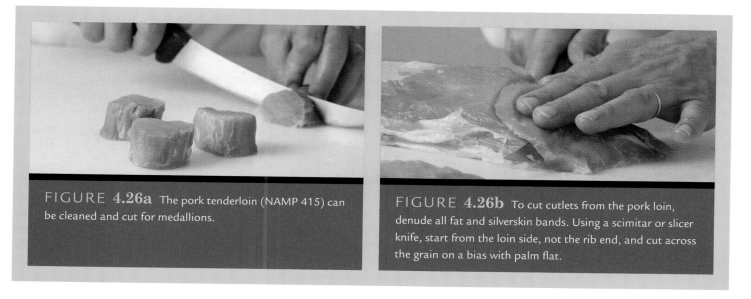

FIGURE **4.26a** The pork tenderloin (NAMP 415) can be cleaned and cut for medallions.

FIGURE **4.26b** To cut cutlets from the pork loin, denude all fat and silverskin bands. Using a scimitar or slicer knife, start from the loin side, not the rib end, and cut across the grain on a bias with palm flat.

Cutting Baby Back Ribs

The bone structure of the pork loin can be cut into valuable baby back ribs by removing the chine bone.

FIGURE **4.27a** The rib cage is fabricated into baby back ribs (NAMP 422) by cutting the chine and feather bones away from the base of the ribs. This is easier done with a band saw, but can be done with a small stiff boning knife or cleaver.

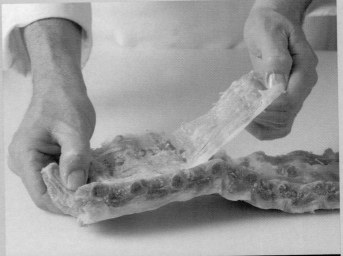

FIGURE **4.27b** The back ribs have a thin membrane that should be removed before cooking. Peel up one corner and pull it off by hand.

Cutting Chops

Be sure the bones are cut first if using a band saw. If cutting by hand, use a heavy meat cleaver, not a vegetable cleaver or chef's knife.

FIGURE **4.28a** To cut pork chops on a band saw, start from the loin end, using the same basic technique as a porterhouse steak. Cut with the fat side flat on the saw and start by cutting the bones section first. Use the measuring guide to ensure even cuts.

FIGURE **4.28b** To cut loin chops by hand, use a cleaver and scimitar. First, cut through the meat about an inch and a half with the knife, and then clip through the bone, using a heavy meat cleaver. The cleaver should do most of the work. Repeated chopping can lead to bone fragments and chips. To practice with the cleaver, chop usable trim chine bones or neck bones.

(Continues)

FIGURE **4.28c** On the left is a rib or rack chop; on the right is a loin or porterhouse chop.

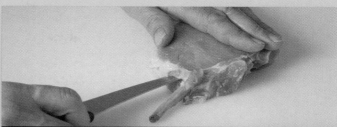

FIGURE **4.28d** To create a pocket for stuffing, use a thin boning knife and poke a hole above the rib bone. Open the pocket without expanding the original hole, therefore minimizing shape and moisture loss.

FIGURE **4.28e** Push the filling in with a spoon or, depending on the density, pipe it with a pastry bag.

FIGURE **4.28f** The typical yield of an eight-ounce pork chop from a center cut pork loin.

Frenching the Rib End

Cut along the lip of the eye muscle, piercing between each rib bone. Score each bone and scrape away excess meat.

FIGURE **4.29a** The pork rack or rib end of the loin can be Frenched for a quality presentation. First, remove the chine and feather bone structure by cutting across the base of the ribs using a handsaw.

FIGURE **4.29b** The rib end of the pork loin or pork rack may have the chine bone attached. To remove it using a band saw, hold the ends of the rib bones and cut the chine off at about a 45-degree angle, separating it from the rib and feather bones. Be sure the loin is dry and hands are clean to avoid slipping.

(Continues)

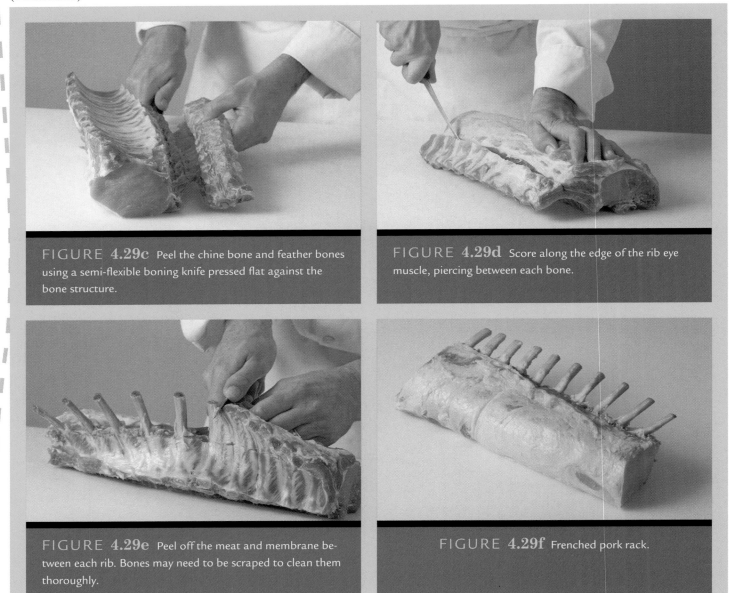

FIGURE **4.29c** Peel the chine bone and feather bones using a semi-flexible boning knife pressed flat against the bone structure.

FIGURE **4.29d** Score along the edge of the rib eye muscle, piercing between each bone.

FIGURE **4.29e** Peel off the meat and membrane between each rib. Bones may need to be scraped to clean them thoroughly.

FIGURE **4.29f** Frenched pork rack.

SHOULDER

The pork shoulder is the entire front section of hog made up of the Boston butt and picnic and includes skin and heavy fat back and bones. It is typically used for slow cooking barbecue, grinding for sausage, and braising.

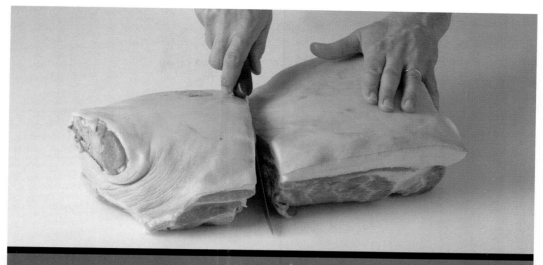

FIGURE **4.30** Pork shoulder (NAMP 403). The shoulder contains the picnic (NAMP 405, left) and the Boston butt (NAMP 406).

Boston Butt

Boston butt can be boned and rolled into a roast or cut for sausage, stew, or kebobs. The butt has only one bone and is relatively easy to fabricate.

Place the meat fat side down. Remove the "cottage" butt by following the natural seam above the bone. Following the curved bone structure, peel the meat away using the knife for leverage. Trim to desired fat level for roast or cubes.

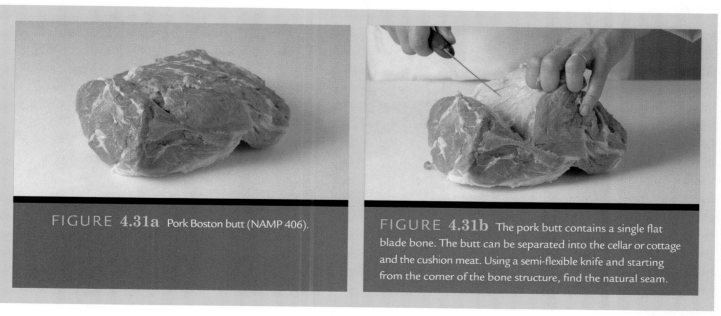

FIGURE **4.31a** Pork Boston butt (NAMP 406).

FIGURE **4.31b** The pork butt contains a single flat blade bone. The butt can be separated into the cellar or cottage and the cushion meat. Using a semi-flexible knife and starting from the corner of the bone structure, find the natural seam.

(Continues)

(Continued)

FIGURE **4.31c** The cottage can be trimmed for roasting or curing. Remove the small blood vessels found on the side.

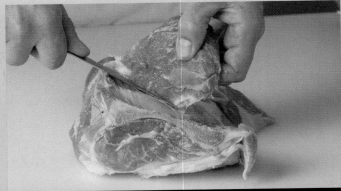

FIGURE **4.31d** Peel off the cap of the Boston butt, following the natural seam.

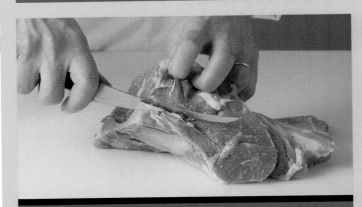

FIGURE **4.31e** Remove the flat blade bone by outlining the bone, following through the curve of the structure.

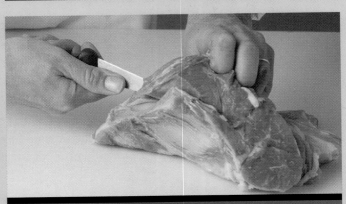

FIGURE **4.31f** The bone curves up, so be sure to curve your knife up, keeping the blade along the bone structure.

FIGURE **4.31g** Remove the blade bone. Notice the shape of the bone.

FIGURE **4.31h** Remove the gland that is found on the side.

(Continues)

(Continued)

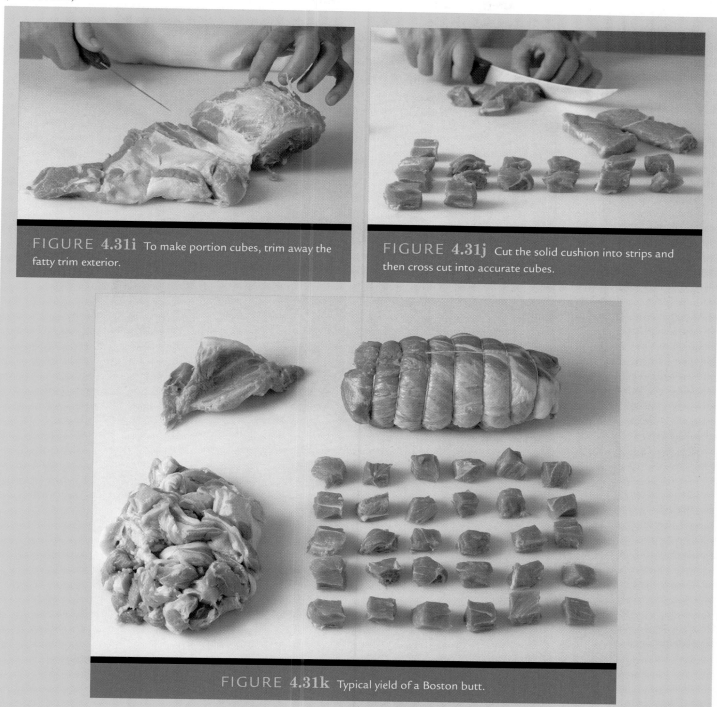

FIGURE **4.31i** To make portion cubes, trim away the fatty trim exterior.

FIGURE **4.31j** Cut the solid cushion into strips and then cross cut into accurate cubes.

FIGURE **4.31k** Typical yield of a Boston butt.

Picnic

The picnic comes with the skin on and a simple bone structure. It can be boned for a BRT roast or used for sausage.

FIGURE **4.32a** The picnic (NAMP 405) is sold skin on or off. It contains one bone structure containing the humerus. To bone the picnic, start by outlining the humerus bone, lifting it from one end.

FIGURE **4.32b** Remove the humerus bone and release it from the meat.

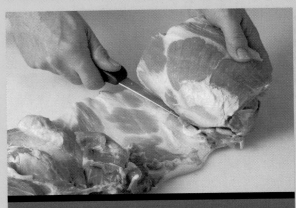

FIGURE **4.32c** The picnic contains the shoulder clod section, which is solid.

FIGURE **4.32d** The picnic can be skinned for sausage trim and a small roast.

FIGURE **4.32e** Typical yield of the picnic.

PORK BELLY

The belly can be purchased fresh, smoked, or cured in various ways, such as salt pork or pancetta.

FIGURE **4.33a** The pork belly (NAMP 408) is sold skin on or off (NAMP 409). The belly is often cured and seasoned for creating bacon or pancetta.

FIGURE **4.33b** A cured and seasoned belly is rolled tightly.

FIGURE **4.33c** The rolled belly is then tied tightly and allowed to air dry to make Italian pancetta.

Spare Ribs

The spare ribs are cut away from the belly and can be trimmed into the more refined St. Louis style ribs.

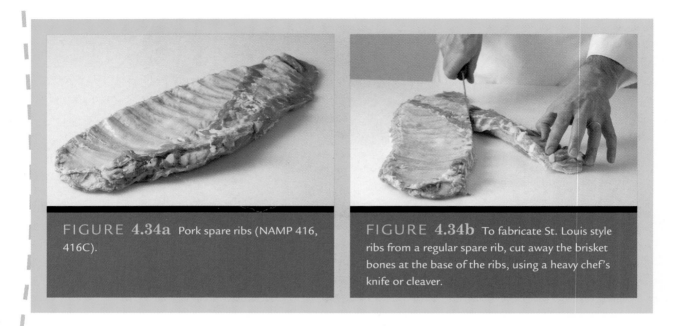

FIGURE **4.34a** Pork spare ribs (NAMP 416, 416C).

FIGURE **4.34b** To fabricate St. Louis style ribs from a regular spare rib, cut away the brisket bones at the base of the ribs, using a heavy chef's knife or cleaver.

SUCKLING PIG

The suckling pig is typically twelve to thirty pounds and only about three to six weeks old. It is primarily milk fed, therefore very mild in flavor, and extremely tender. The suckling is usually roasted whole, either bone in or semi-boned and stuffed. The Italian porchetta, or semi-boneless stuffed roasted pig, is a dish created by removing the bones, except for the feet, and stuffing the inside. It is considered an Italian heritage dish.

The suckling pig is sold with the head on and skin intact. This results in a relatively poor yield and requires about one pound of pig to each portion. Therefore, a twenty-five-pound suckling feeds around twenty-five people.

When roasted correctly, the suckling develops a fine crackling skin that is eaten almost like a chip. The crispy seasoning-laden skin is prized at pig roasts.

Because the farmer who raises the suckling never gets to realize the full potential yield of the market-sized hog, the suckling remains a fairly expensive meat.

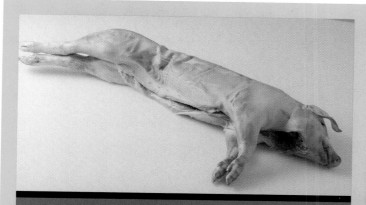

FIGURE **4.35a** Suckling pig (NAMP 400A).

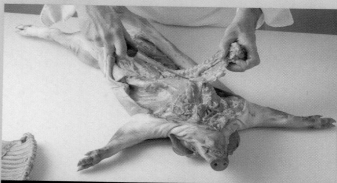

FIGURE **4.35d** Peel out the spare ribs from the base of the ribs out to the sternum.

FIGURE **4.35b** The suckling pig can be boned without damaging the skin, so it can be stuffed and roasted. With a stiff boning knife, score along the base of the rib bones along both sides of the spine.

FIGURE **4.35e** Remove the pelvic bone structure, carefully cutting through the ball and socket joints and around the tailbone. Remove the femur and arm bones by scraping down each to the joint, leaving the feet attached.

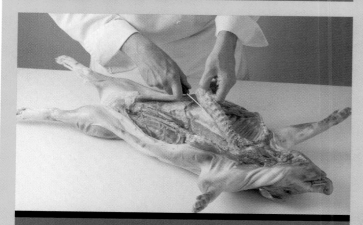

FIGURE **4.35c** Work knife along the spine, removing it in sections. Be very careful not to cut through the exterior skin.

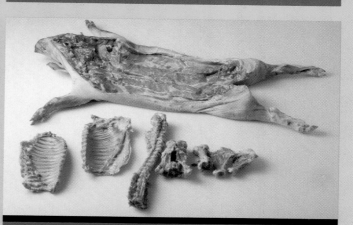

FIGURE **4.35f** Typical yield from a semi-boneless suckling pig; the suckling pig is now ready to be stuffed and tied as roast.

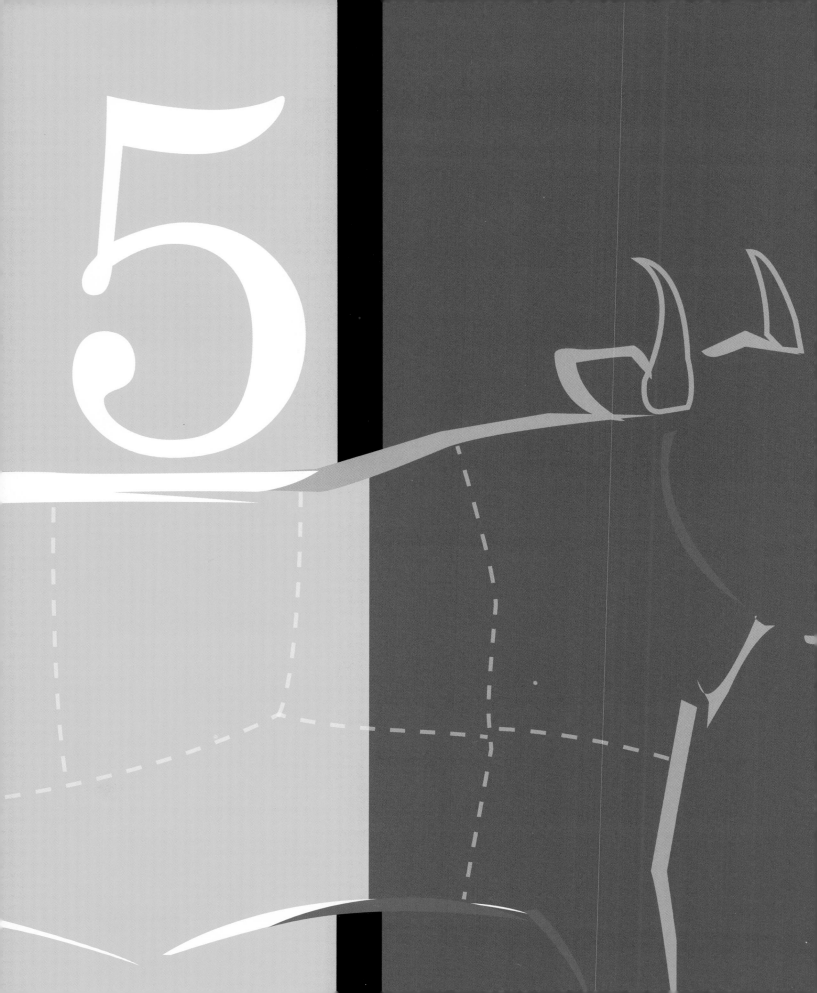

LAMB

Sheep and goats are herd animals, making them a logical choice for early humans to domesticate. Most modern sheep breeds stem from the domestication of the Asian Mouflon *(Ovis orientalis orientalis)*, which is found in the mountains of Iran and Asia Minor to this day. The European Mouflon *(Ovis orientalis musimon)*, found on Corsica, is another early relative of modern breeds. Sheep were domesticated between 6000 and 8000 years ago, making them the second-earliest animal to be domesticated, after dogs.

Early civilizations first spun wool into yarn around 3500 BC. This yarn established a renewable resource for clothing and textiles; thus, the domestication of sheep allowed people to migrate to northern regions without having to hunt for food or manufacture clothing by weaving. Wool fleece was a valuable commodity and was often traded like money.

There are many mentions of sheep and wool during biblical times. Shepherds kept flocks of sheep on the hillsides surrounding many ancient cities and woolen garments were traded in marketplaces.

Sheep are found on every continent with the exception of Antarctica. The genetic diversity found in sheep has allowed the species to adapt to all sorts of weather conditions and graze on a variety of vegetation, making them a viable farm animal. Sheep are prolific grazers and have been blamed for the desertification of lands when they are allowed to over-graze. They will eat grasses to the roots and, in times of drought, these plants will not grow back.

In the times of early global exploration, wool provided income to fund voyages, and live sheep were taken along as a food source. Viking voyages to Iceland brought sheep to the island in the tenth century. The sheep helped maintain human populations during the harsh winters. Christopher Columbus left sheep on the island of Santa Domingo during his second voyage to the new world in 1493. Many of the early explorations by the Spanish Conquistadors were funded by the thriving Spanish wool industry. The Spaniard Hernando Cortez brought sheep to Mexico, and these were later captured by Navajo tribes and became the Navajo Churro, which is the oldest breed existing in North America and is still raised today. Churro wool is used to make the famous and artistic Navajo rugs.

One of the reasons the American Colonies wished to break from England was the increasing taxation on goods including wool imported into the colonies. The new colonies had an established population of over one million sheep by the mid eighteenth century. Massachusetts had a large wool industry and spinning wool into yarn was a skill taught in most farm houses. England wanted domination of this industry due to the independence that it afforded the colonist. The colonies resisted. George Washington kept sheep on his farm as a form of defiance.

Captain James Cook, the famed British explorer circumnavigated the New Zealand islands in 1770 and charted its bays. Upon returning in 1773 he brought sheep to aid in colonizing the islands. Sheep farming rapidly developed in New Zealand due to the lack of natural predators, and the country is now the world's largest exporter of lamb and wool with over 45 million sheep in pasture. New Zealand exports over ninety-five percent of its lamb production and it is found commercially worldwide.

In the American West, from the 1870s to around 1900, there were many conflicts between sheep farmers and cattlemen. These "Sheep Wars" were a result of the introduction of sheep into the western cattle lands. Sheepherders were restricted to specific areas, but often ranged sheep beyond those vague lines. Nomadic sheep farmers were accused of denuding grazing lands by over grazing their livestock. Bloody feuds between established sheep farmers and cattle ranchers over water rights and droving routes often occurred. Laws established in the 1880s to regulate sheep herding were difficult to enforce.

Beyond wool, sheep provide milk and meat. Milk is preserved as yogurt or cheese. Some of the world's finest cheeses derive from sheep milk. The Manchego cheese of Spain, the Pecorino Romano from Italy, and the Roquefort blue cheese from France are just a few of the numerous high-quality sheep milk cheeses found worldwide. Sheep's milk is more pungent than cow's milk is, but less so than goat milk. Its high butterfat content translates to a creamy and rich cheese.

Sheep are used as a source of quality meat as well as cheese. The market for lamb, which is similar to veal, arose as a direct result of the dairy sheep industry. Male offspring are not needed in great quantities and, therefore, are sold and consumed when young. Today, we find lamb raised specifically for meat and breeds will reflect high meat quality.

BYPRODUCTS

The wool, or hair, found on sheep is prized for its ability to insulate and repel water. Various wool grades are determined by length and fineness and some are extremely expensive. Hair sheep, as opposed to wool sheep, can produce fine, soft strands and their hide is made into fine leather goods.

Sheep also produce lanolin, sometimes known as "woolgrease," which is an oil found in the wool. Lanolin is used in a large variety of hand lotions, creams, and balms. In earlier times, lanolin was used to grease machines and axles.

BREEDS OF SHEEP AND LAMB

There are literally hundreds of sheep breeds and they vary in size, shape, and use. Reading the names of all the worldwide breeds is like a lesson in linguistics. Names such as the Hu from China, the Kooka raised in Pakistan, the Oxford from England, the Steinschaf from the Bavarian region of Germany, indicate the diversity of sheep worldwide. There are over forty registered breeds found in the United States alone.

Sheep are raised in many extreme environments. Dessert shorthaired breeds, high-mountain Alpine sheep, and Norwegian wool sheep all have an ability to thrive in less-than-perfect conditions. The look of sheep can vary greatly; some have large horns that present a formidable protection against predators; others grow long, shaggy locks that extend to the ground, creating a wooly blanket.

Sheep are raised for three main uses: wool or hair, milk, and meat. Breeds that are known for wool or hair, such as the Icelandic or Merino, are valuable for making fine cloth. The Icelandic is probably the oldest true continuous pure-bred domestic breed still in existence today. This sheep was brought to Iceland by the Vikings, and, for the most part, has not been crossbred with other breeds as are most other modern breeds. It is also considered a high-quality meat animal.

Other breeds are known for the qualities of their milk. The Spanish Manchega is a unique breed used for making the Manchego cheese.

Many breeds are combinations of other breeds and have established and reproducible traits. Certain breeds are considered better for meat production because of their ability to "gain" rapidly; in other words, they achieve a marketable size and weight faster than other breeds. Although there are hundreds of recognized breeds around the world, this book will restrict the breeds discussed to those that are most typical for meat production.

TYPICAL MEAT BREEDS

CHEVIOT

Origin: England

Cheviot sheep are smallish, have a good yield, and are excellent mothers. They are hardy lambs and do well in adverse climates.

COLUMBIA

Origin: England

Columbia sheep are large, fast growing, have good conformation, and produce quality meat.

DORSET

Origin: England

The Dorset breed is fast gaining, relatively lean, and durable.

DORPER

Origin: South Africa

The Dorper is a high-quality meat breed. Dorpers are prolific breeders, have thick muscling, and do well in adverse dry conditions.

HAMPSHIRE

Origin: Southern England

Hampshires are fast gaining and have good yield and meat-to-bone ratio.

FIGURE **5.2** Columbia.

FIGURE **5.3** Dorset.

FIGURE **5.1** Cheviot.

FIGURE **5.4** Hampshire.

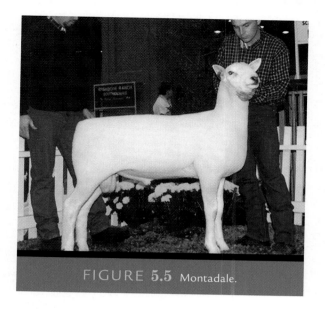

FIGURE **5.5** Montadale.

FIGURE **5.6** Oxford.

MONTADALE

Origin: United States

Montadale sheep are prolific breeders, have a high yield, and are low in fat.

OXFORD

Origin: England

The Oxford is a large, prolific breeder. Oxfords are often crossed with other breeds.

SUFFOLK

Origin: England

Another fast gainer is the Suffolk breed. It is very popular in the United States and is large with a good yield.

TEXEL

Origin: Netherlands

Like the Hampshire, the Texel has a very good meat-to-bone ratio with high muscle score.

FIGURE **5.7** Suffolk.

TUNIS

Origin: Tunisia

The Tunis arrived in the United States in 1799 and is a large, prolific, and very popular in breed, particularly in the Southern States.

NEW ZEALAND ROMNEY

Origin: England and New Zealand

The Romney is the largest breed in New Zealand, with good meat and wool production.

FIGURE **5.8** New Zealand Romney.

MERINO

Origin: England

The Merino was the first sheep brought to New Zealand. It has fine hair and good muscling but is small. Many sub-breeds of Merino exist throughout the world.

FIGURE **5.9** Merino.

LAMB GRADING AND EVALUATION

Lamb is evaluated on two basic factors: color and marbling scores of the lean muscle tissues and conformation of the carcass. Lamb is graded as a whole carcass and evaluation is determined first by age. Age is determined by looking at the *breakjoint* at the end of the front trotter bones. A *crowned* breakjoint will indicate less bone ossification and, therefore, a younger animal. Marbling and color of the lean muscle is judged at the flank area, just inside the carcass. Fatty streaks in the flank and a bright reddish color indicate high quality. Lamb meat is very tender.

Lamb is divided into four basic classifications for grading: young lamb (under six months), older lamb (under one year), yearling mutton (under sixteen months), and mutton (older than sixteen months). Young yearling mutton can still achieve a choice grade if it is highly marbleized and has good conformation. A younger lamb does not require an extremely high marbling score because of the tenderness and fineness of fibers.

Lamb grading is similar to both beef and veal grading. Older animals are graded more like beef and the younger more like veal. This implies some variation in size and can be somewhat problematic when trying to achieve consistent portions. Be sure to specify average weights of HRI cuts when ordering lamb.

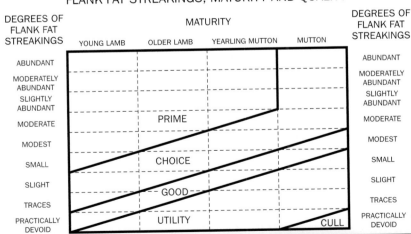

FIGURE **5.10** Chart demonstrating relationship between flank fat streakings, maturity, and quality of lamb.

Most lamb produced in the United States is graded choice and prime with very little allowed to fall below to the "good" grade. Lamb raising practices have ensured a very high level of quality and the customer base, which is primarily higher-end foodservice and specialty meat markets, demands only higher-quality lamb. Recalibrations in the quality criteria in the 1950s and 1960s adjusted the choice category to encompass more variety. Approximately 98 percent of all lamb falls into the prime or choice categories.

LAMB GRADES

- Prime
- Choice
- Good
- Utility
- Cull

THERE ARE TERMS USED IN THE LAMB INDUSTRY THAT IMPLY CERTAIN SIZES

HOT-HOUSE LAMB

A small, very young lamb that would be used for roasting whole. Generally milk-fed and considered a niche market item.

SPRING LAMB

A term that implies the animal is younger. In the past, lamb was a seasonal product and spring lamb was available from March through October. Generally, it was considered smaller and tenderer. Today we have farming techniques that enable "lambing" year round, so the seasonality is minimized somewhat.

LAMB

Any graded lamb product.

KOSHER LAMB

The Jewish religion has strict dietary laws; lamb that is raised and slaughtered within these guidelines is deemed Kosher. Kosher lamb follows a process that checks for disease and proper preparation procedures beyond the USDA inspection. (See also Kosher Beef, page 21.)

HALAL LAMB

Lamb that is processed in accordance to Islamic law can be deemed Halal. The Koran has guidelines for what can be considered Halal. It is usually sold fresh and minimally processed. (See also Halal Beef, page 22.)

YIELD GRADING

Lamb fat is considered waste and is not palatable. It contains branched chain fatty acids that tend to leave a stronger taste on the palate. Meat flavor can be altered by varying feeding methods and breeding for traits. Certain breeds, those with high-quality wool, tend to have a stronger, "lamby" flavor, while hair breeds tend to be milder.

Lamb can acquire a lot of excess fat, therefore yield grading on lamb is very important. Due to its size, lamb is often purchased as whole, untrimmed primals and the entire exterior fat can be included. Lamb is also relatively expensive, so the combination of wasteful fat and high cost means lamb yield grades are a very important factor when creating purchasing guidelines.

YIELD GRADES

1. Leanest, usually very young lamb

2. Considered best buy

3. Also considered normal and a good buy

4. Fatty and considered expensive, often found on larger, high-quality lamb

5. Very fatty, wasteful

NEW ZEALAND AND AUSTRALIAN LAMB GRADING

Both New Zealand and Australia sell a large amount of lamb products worldwide. New Zealand is the world's largest exporter of lamb and it is a major industry in that nation. Lamb from New Zealand tends to be smaller and somewhat leaner than U.S. lamb. This is because New Zealand sheep farmers are raising breeds that are somewhat smaller and feeding them on pasture. Their market is primarily the European Union and the United Kingdom, as smaller lamb is preferred in those markets.

Lamb in New Zealand is graded according to carcass weight and fat scores. Scores are given as a letter grade. Standard export grades are determined to ensure consistency for lamb sent abroad. Modern computer grading, using a pixel breakdown of the rib eye area, is being applied on a small scale but may be growing in the future.

Australian and New Zealand lamb is primarily sent pre-fabricated as trimmed or boneless cuts. This is to minimize weight for transport.

Australian lamb is graded according to guidelines set up by Meat and Livestock Australia Ltd., a private concern that grades meat for export. Australian and New Zealand lamb is considered naturally raised, which implies primarily pasture raising.

Brand Name Lamb

As with the Certified Angus Beef program, high-quality lamb is often sold for a higher price as a "branded" product. For instance, the American Lamb Board promotes Fresh American Lamb. The promotion is supported by a small fee paid for each animal. This lamb must be assessed according to the Lamb Board's criteria and is generally sold fresh, as opposed to frozen.

Brands such as Cedar Springs Lamb are guaranteed to be a certain size and age. Shepherd's Pride is a brand that ensures a "natural" raising technique; in other words, no antibiotics or growth hormones were used during the feeding time. Both of these are brand names of the Mountain States/B. Rosen Co., which presents these as higher-quality products that have undergone a higher scrutiny than the USDA grade.

Niche-Market Lamb

Lamb produced by small co-ops or small farming operations that differentiate from the normal raising practices can be considered niche market. These may include grass-fed or pasture-raised lamb. It may mean the animal was not fed any growth hormones or antibiotics. Much of the niche-market product is consumed locally and is minimally processed. Some chefs are seeking this sort of lamb because of its unique flavors and marketable attributes. The flavor can be deeper or richer depending on the feeding method.

Caution should be used when purchasing niche-market products. An understanding of quality and fabrication techniques is necessary because most small-market lamb is not USDA graded nor is it fabricated to the level that most large companies produce.

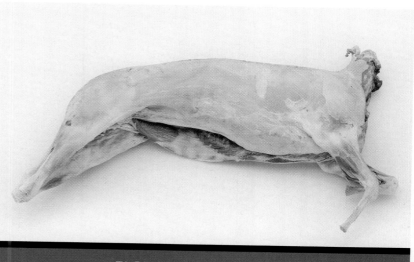

FIGURE **5.11** Lamb carcass.

LAMB CARCASS BREAKDOWN

The lamb carcass is divided in a manner similar to veal. It is not split or sectioned at the time of slaughter; therefore, it is sold in saddles. This implies that most cuts are sold as pairs.

PRIMAL CUTS

LEG

The leg of lamb is often roasted whole, but it can be fabricated into manageable semi-boneless or boneless roasts. Smaller subprimals can be used for mini roasts, steaks, cutlets, or broiling items. Often the leg is denuded and cut into kebab for grilling. The shank section is typically braised and can be cut osso buco style.

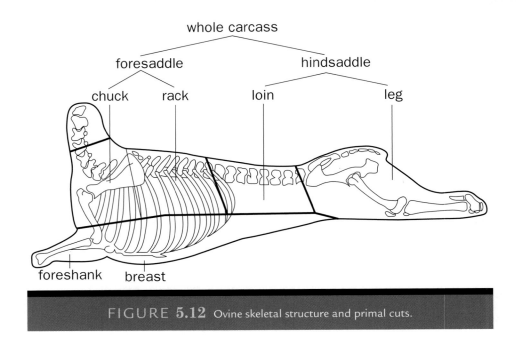

whole carcass

foresaddle

hindsaddle

chuck rack loin leg

foreshank breast

FIGURE **5.12** Ovine skeletal structure and primal cuts.

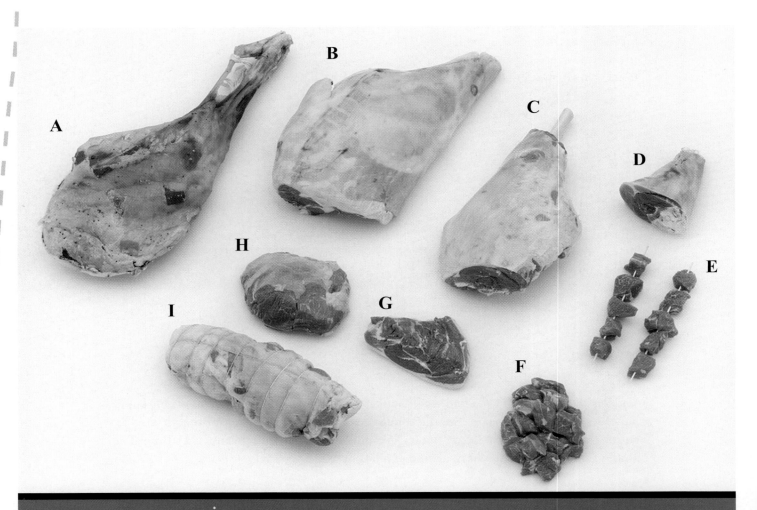

A

B

C

D

H

E

I

G

F

FIGURE **5.13** A: dry cured lamb prosciutto, B: leg of lamb, C: leg of lamb steamship, Frenched, D: lamb shank, E: lamb leg kebabs, F: lamb shank cubes, G: lamb sirloin, H: lamb top round, I: leg of lamb BRT.

FIGURE **5.14** Lamb leg HRI cuts.

ITEM AND NAMP NUMBER	DESCRIPTION/FABRICATION	SUGGESTED COOKING METHOD/ APPLICATION	AVERAGE SUGGESTED WEIGHT IN POUNDS	TYPICAL PACKAGE SPECS
233 Lamb legs 233a Lamb leg, trotter off	Full primal leg, typically sold with trotter bone cut off, can be sold in pairs, requires trimming and possible boning	Roasting, divided into smaller roasts	9–13	1 per bag, 6 per box
233c Lamb leg, semi-boneless 233e Lamb leg, Frenched, sirloin off (steamship)	Semi boneless leg is easier to carve; may require trimming and Frenching of shank bone	Roast whole for carving; quality presentation at carving station	6–10	1 per bag, 6 per box
234 Lamb leg, boneless 234a Lamb leg, boneless, shank off	Typically sold netted, shank off is higher quality, can be reformed and further trimmed, butterflied, sectioned	Roast whole, butterfly and grill like steak, divide into small subprimal roasts, cut as cubes for kabab	6–8	1 per bag, 8 per box
233f Lamb hind shank	Sold whole; small, single portion	Braise slow, can be Frenched for presentation	1–2	2 per bag, 12 bags per box
234d Lamb leg, outside 234f Sirloin tip (knuckle) 234g Sirloin	Trimmed bottom round, knuckle, sirloin sections of leg, may require minor trimming	Small roast, cut for small butterflied leg or kabab	1–3	1 per bag, 12 per box
234e Lamb leg, inside	Trimmed top round section, solid, high quality	Small roast, cut for small butterflied leg, kabab, steaks, cutlets	1–2	1 per bag, 12 per box
295a Lamb kabab	Ready to cook	For skewers	Specify size	Varies

LOIN

The loin can be purchased whole, split, boneless, or portion cut. Most chefs sell the loin cut as chops. Chops from the loin resemble small t-bones or porterhouse steaks. Cutting an even chop may require the use of a band saw.

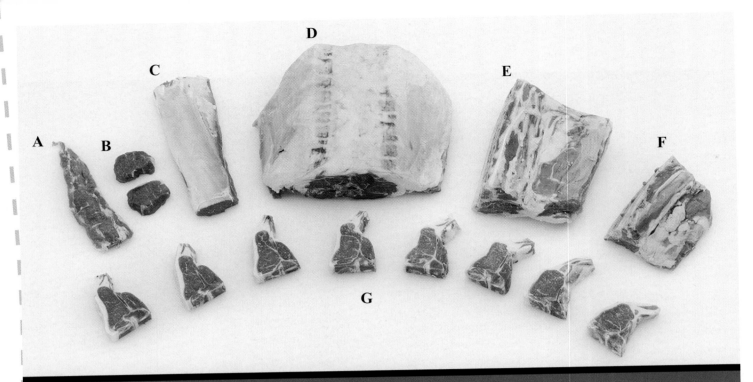

FIGURE **5.15** A:lamb tenderloin, B: lamb loin medallions (noisette), C: lamb loin boneless, D: lamb loin trimmed (saddle), E: lamb loin split, F: New Zealand lamb loin, G: lamb loin chops.

FIGURE **5.16** Lamb loin HRI cuts.

ITEM AND NAMP NUMBER	DESCRIPTION/ FABRICATION	SUGGESTED COOKING METHOD/ APPLICATION	AVERAGE SUGGESTED WEIGHT IN POUNDS	TYPICAL PACKAGE SPECS
231 Lamb loins 232 Lamb loins, trimmed	Full primal loins; require trimming, splitting, and band saw to cut into chops; can be boned	Cut for chops, bone or notch for roast	8–12; be sure to specify yield grade!	1 per bag, 6 per box
232a Lamb loins, trimmed and split	Cut into chops with band saw or hand cut with cleaver	Cut for chops, notch for roast, bone out for roast	2–3	1 per bag, 12 per box
232b Lamb loin boneless, single or double	Can be purchased with or without exterior fat, may require trimming	Roast whole, cut into medallions or noisette, cut thin for carpaccio	1–1.5	2 per bag, 6 per box
246 Lamb tenderloin	Very small, may need some trimming	Grill, broil, sauté, mini medallions, appetizers	3–8 ounces	Varies
1232a Lamb loin chops	Small, t-bone style chop, may need some exterior fat or tail trimmed	Grill, broil, pan sear, sauté	Specify size	Varies

HOTEL RACK

The rack of lamb is traditionally sold unsplit but is not common today. The rack is fabricated to a variety of trim levels, the least of which would be "split and chined." It can also be purchased Frenched with the rib bones exposed or boneless. When purchasing pre-Frenched, it may be necessary to specify the length of the lip of fat left on the eye. Many chefs choose to French the racks in-house to guarantee quality. The boneless rack is very expensive.

If purchasing portion cut chops, be sure to specify trim levels.

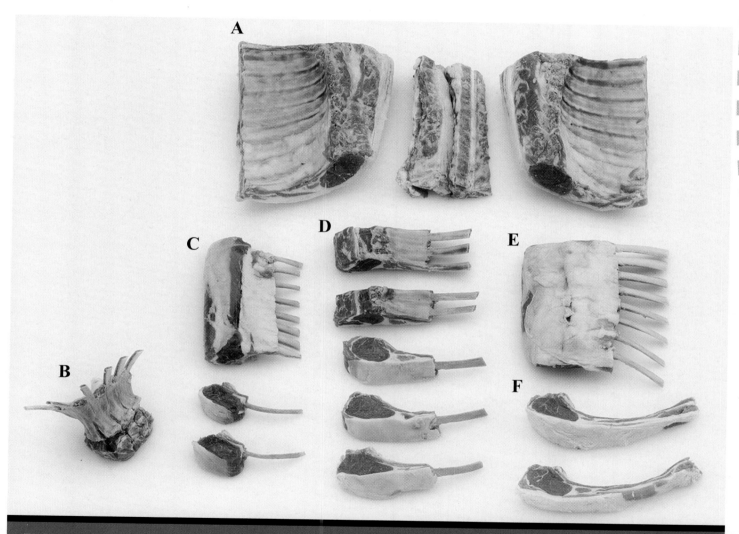

FIGURE 5.17 A: lamb rack split and chined, B: Mini crown roast, C: New Zealand lamb rack and chops, D: Various lamb rack chops, Frenched, E: US lamb rack, Frenched, F: lamb rack chops, untrimmed.

FIGURE **5.18** Lamb rack HRI cuts.

ITEM AND NAMP NUMBER	DESCRIPTION/ FABRICATION	SUGGESTED COOKING METHOD/ APPLICATION	AVERAGE SUGGESTED WEIGHT IN POUNDS	TYPICAL PACKAGE SPECS
204 Lamb rack	Full primal, requires splitting with saw and trimming	Roast, grill, broil, sauté, pan-sear	7–9; be sure to specify yield grade	1 per bag, 6 per box
204a Lamb rack, split and chined	Requires trimming, can be Frenched	Roast, grill, broil, sauté, pan sear	7–9; be sure to specify yield grade	1 per bag, 6 per box
204c Lamb rack, Frenched 204d	May require extra cleaning of bones	Roast, grill, broil, sauté, pan sear	2–3	1 per bag, 12 per box
204e Lamb rack, boneless	Ready to cook, very expensive item	Roast, grill, broil, sauté, pan sear	1–1.5	2 per bag, 12 per box
1204b Lamb rack, chops	May require extra trimming; sold as single, double, or triple bone chops	Grill, broil, sauté, pan sear	Specify size	Varies
1204c/d Lamb rack chops/Frenched	Trim levels can vary; sold as single, double, or triple bone chops; lollipop chops are trimmed to the eye muscle	Grill, broil, sauté, pan sear, lollipop chop served as appetizer	Specify size	Varies

SQUARE CUT CHUCK/SHOULDER

The lamb shoulder can be purchased whole as a bone-in item or boneless as a BRT (boned, rolled, and tied). The shoulder can be cut into portion chops or cut into stew. Boning the shoulder in-house could be considered difficult.

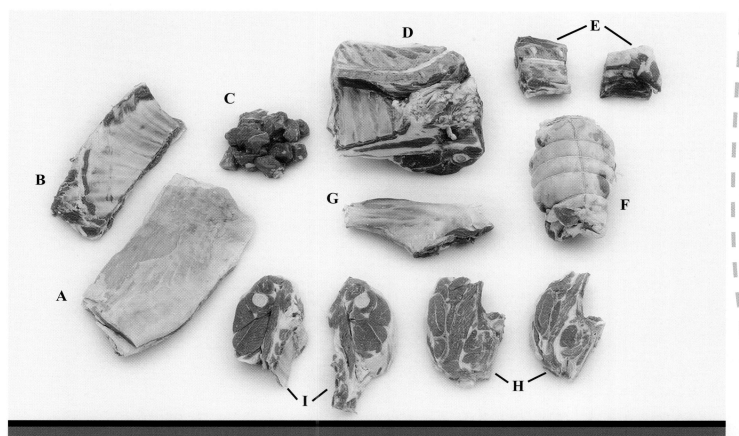

FIGURE **5.19** A: lamb breast, B: lamb Denver ribs, C: lamb shoulder cubes, D: lamb square cut shoulder, E: lamb neck, F: lamb shoulder BRT, G: lamb foreshank, H: Blade shoulder chops, I: Arm shoulder chops.

BREAST AND FORESHANK

The lamb breast is similar to pork spare ribs, with plenty of meat between each rib. Lamb ribs can be purchased as Denver-style ribs that are trimmed and prepped for grilling. Lamb ribs have a fair amount of excess fat and may need to be par–cooked to reduce flair up on a char-grill.

An alternative method for preparing lamb ribs is to cut a pocket lengthwise and stuff the breast in a manner similar to the veal breast.

The foreshank is typically purchased whole for braising but can be cut into an osso buco.

ITEM AND NAMP NUMBER	DESCRIPTION/FABRICATION	SUGGESTED COOKING METHOD/ APPLICATION	AVERAGE SUGGESTED WEIGHT IN POUNDS	TYPICAL PACKAGE SPECS
207 Lamb shoulder/ chuck, square cut	Full primal bone in lamb shoulder, may require boning, trimming	Roast whole, slow braise, stew	6–8	1 per bag, 6 per box
208 Lamb shoulder, boneless	Sold BRT (boned, rolled, and tied) may require some extra trimming	Roast whole, slow braise, stew	3–4	1 per bag, 6 per box
209b Lamb short ribs	Cut from the shoulder	Braise, slow roast, very flavorful	2–3	1 per bag, 12 per box
1207 Lamb shoulder chops, Arm chops, Blade chops	May require fat trimming and partial bone removal	Broil, grill, sauté, pan sear, braise	6–8 oz each	Varies
210 Lamb foreshank	Sold whole or blocked	Braise whole or cut as osso buco	1–2	2 per bag, 12 per box
Lamb neck	May be split	Slow braise, pulling meat, stew	1–2	Varies
209 Lamb breast	Requires trimming, can be cut with pocket for stuffing, inexpensive	Braising, grilling, slow roasting	2–3	2 per bag, 6 per box
209a Lamb Denver ribs	Trimmed, ready to grill	Braising, grilling, slow roasting	1–2	2 per bag
295 Lamb stew	Cut from leg or shoulder	Stewing	Varies	Varies
296 Ground lamb	Ready to cook	Burgers, ingredient in other dishes, flavor agent	Varies	Varies

FIGURE **5.20** Lamb square cut chuck/shoulder HRI cuts.

FABRICATION OF LAMB CUTS
LEG OF LAMB

The leg of lamb can be roasted whole with the bones but sections are difficult to carve. Boning the leg and tying it into a roast allows servers to carve the leg easily. The leg can be sectioned into its subprimals to fabricate small roasts. The shank can be taken off and braised separately.

FIGURE 5.21 Leg of Lamb (NAMP 233, 233A).

STEAMSHIP ROAST

The lamb steamship is simply the leg of lamb with the shank bone Frenched and the pelvic bone removed. Peeling the meat away from the shank bone creates a handle that can be held while carving. The steamship roast is often used as a carving station item. The presentation of the leg of lamb, nicely roasted and carved in front of the customer, can make for a quality catering item. Typically, the price is relatively low in comparison to the loin or rack cuts, making this an attractive purchase.

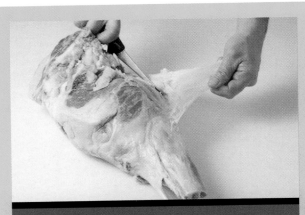

FIGURE **5.22a** The leg of lamb has an exterior membrane that must be peeled.

FIGURE **5.22b** The end of the shank can be Frenched for presentation.

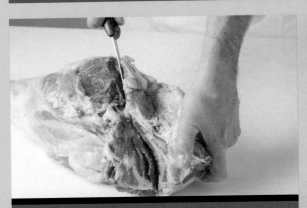

FIGURE **5.22c** Remove the pelvic bone by cutting along the aitch bone.

FIGURE **5.22d** Cut through the ball and socket and roll out the pelvic.

FIGURE **5.22e** Tie the sirloin end up using a trussing needle (NAMP 233C).

FIGURE **5.22f** Lamb steamship roast.

BONE ROLL AND TIE THE LEG OF LAMB

- Process begins with steps for steamp ship toast Fig 5.22a – 5.22d
- Cut away the flank flap.
- Loosen the tenderloin.
- Cut along aitch bone through the ball and socket joint. Be aware of the small hook-shaped bone near the top round.
- Remove the shank (either bone it or remove it whole for braising).
- Remove the kneecap.
- Take out the small fat clods which contain glands.
- The leg can be divided into subprimals for small roasts.
- Roll and tie using single knots.

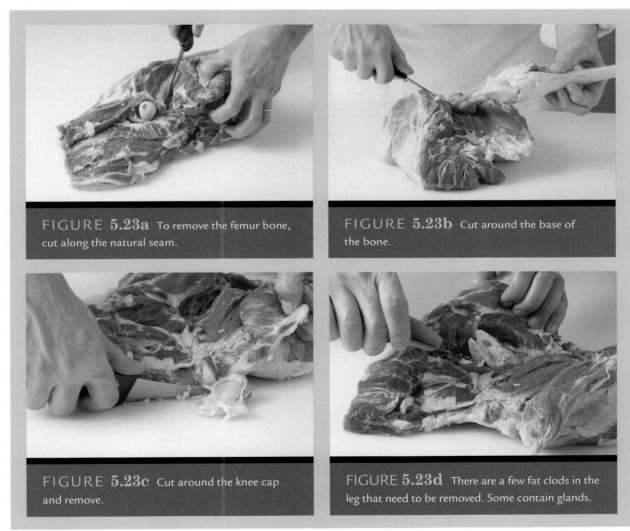

FIGURE **5.23a** To remove the femur bone, cut along the natural seam.

FIGURE **5.23b** Cut around the base of the bone.

FIGURE **5.23c** Cut around the knee cap and remove.

FIGURE **5.23d** There are a few fat clods in the leg that need to be removed. Some contain glands.

(*Continues*)

(Continued)

FIGURE **5.23e** The boneless leg tied into roast shown with usable bones and trim.

BUTTERFLIED LEG OF LAMB FOR GRILLING

- Follow instructions for boning leg, excluding the last step.
- Make a cut through the center of the top round and knuckle sections.
- Pound leg to even thickness.
- Leg can be divided into subprimals and each can be butterflied for quicker grilling.

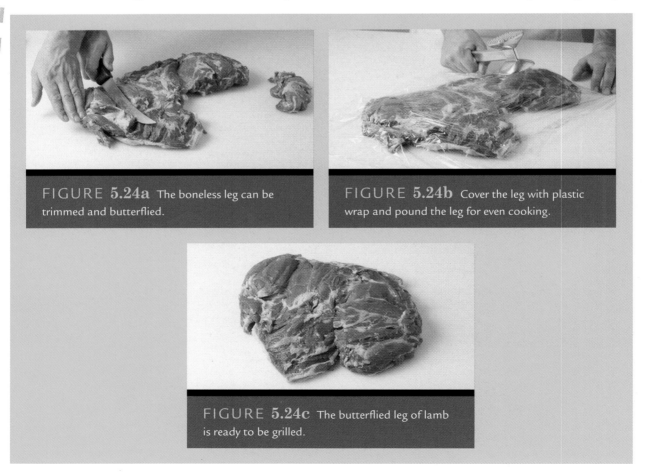

FIGURE **5.24a** The boneless leg can be trimmed and butterflied.

FIGURE **5.24b** Cover the leg with plastic wrap and pound the leg for even cooking.

FIGURE **5.24c** The butterflied leg of lamb is ready to be grilled.

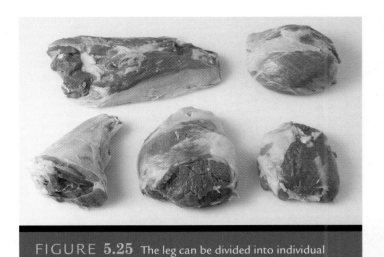

FIGURE **5.25** The leg can be divided into individual subprimals. The rop round or inside (NAMP 234E) is the largest section.

FIGURE **5.26** The inside sliced as steak or medallions. Be sure to cut across the grain.

LAMB LOIN

The lamb loin is often cut for chops. Loin chops resemble small t-bones and are usually purchased as portion cuts, but can be cut inhouse. The loin can be purchased whole or split.

The loin can also be fabricated boneless for a roast or medallions.

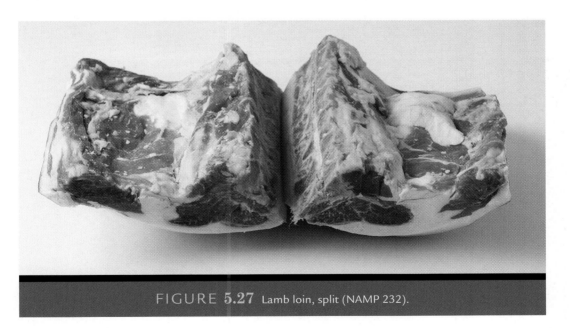

FIGURE **5.27** Lamb loin, split (NAMP 232).

CUTTING LOIN CHOPS

Split loin down the center of the chine bone or purchase pre-split.

Trim exterior fat and tail to desired thickness.

Cut chops on band saw or with meat cleaver. Be sure to make even cuts to ensure even cooking.

FIGURE **5.28a** To cut chops, first trim the flank fat one inch from the eye.

FIGURE **5.28b** Trim the fat exterior to one-quarter inch.

FIGURE **5.28c** Cut through the loin eye with slicer or scimitar.

FIGURE **5.28d** Using a meat cleaver, chop through chine bone.

FIGURE **5.28e** Yield of chops and medallions or noisette from loin (NAMP 1232A, 1232C).

BONING LAMB LOIN FOR DOUBLE EYE ROAST (SARATOGA)

- Trim excess fat and tail to desired thickness.
- Remove tenderloin.
- Remove thirteenth rib bones.
- Insert knife under finger bones and cut eye muscle away from backbone.
- Be sure to leave thin layer of membrane between two eye muscles.
- Roll and tie into roast.

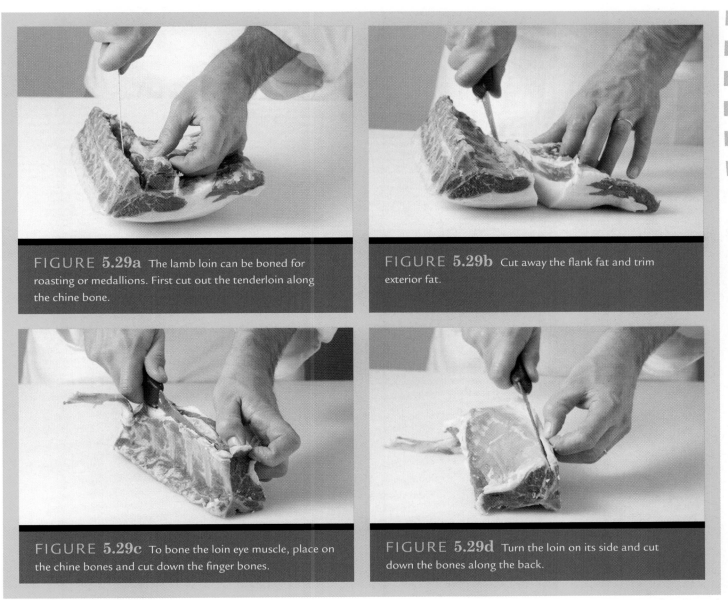

FIGURE **5.29a** The lamb loin can be boned for roasting or medallions. First cut out the tenderloin along the chine bone.

FIGURE **5.29b** Cut away the flank fat and trim exterior fat.

FIGURE **5.29c** To bone the loin eye muscle, place on the chine bones and cut down the finger bones.

FIGURE **5.29d** Turn the loin on its side and cut down the bones along the back.

(Continues)

(*Continued*)

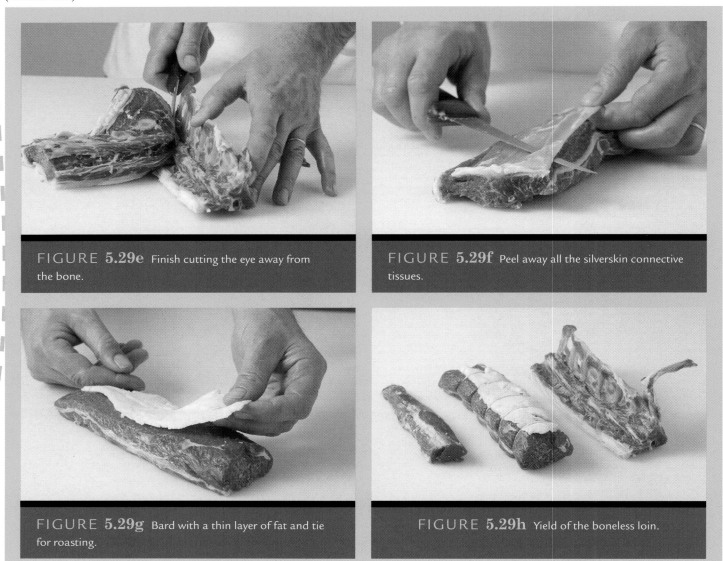

FIGURE **5.29e** Finish cutting the eye away from the bone.

FIGURE **5.29f** Peel away all the silverskin connective tissues.

FIGURE **5.29g** Bard with a thin layer of fat and tie for roasting.

FIGURE **5.29h** Yield of the boneless loin.

MEDALLIONS

- Follow instructions for boning loin.
- Denude loin, removing all silverskin.
- Cut portion into even sections.

LAMB RACK

The lamb rack can be purchased whole or split; splitting a whole hotel rack can be done either by hand or with a band saw. Pre-Frenched lamb racks are available but often require extra cleaning before cooking. Frenching racks can be time consuming and enough time needs to be allowed to complete multiple racks.

Hand Cut Method

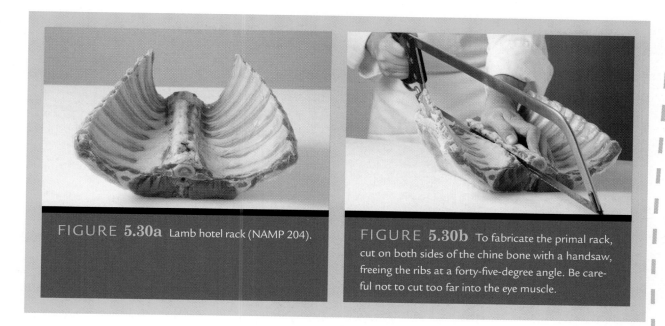

FIGURE **5.30a** Lamb hotel rack (NAMP 204).

FIGURE **5.30b** To fabricate the primal rack, cut on both sides of the chine bone with a handsaw, freeing the ribs at a forty-five-degree angle. Be careful not to cut too far into the eye muscle.

Band Saw Method

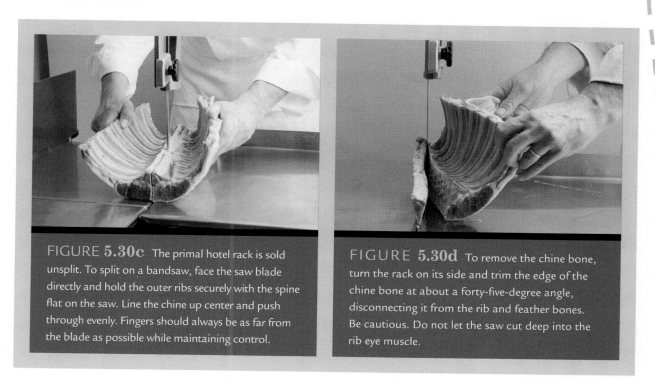

FIGURE **5.30c** The primal hotel rack is sold unsplit. To split on a bandsaw, face the saw blade directly and hold the outer ribs securely with the spine flat on the saw. Line the chine up center and push through evenly. Fingers should always be as far from the blade as possible while maintaining control.

FIGURE **5.30d** To remove the chine bone, turn the rack on its side and trim the edge of the chine bone at about a forty-five-degree angle, disconnecting it from the rib and feather bones. Be cautious. Do not let the saw cut deep into the rib eye muscle.

FRENCHING A SPLIT RACK OF LAMB

- Place half rack bone side down.
- Remove feather bones, if attached.
- Peel out blade bone.
- Measure one to two inches from eye muscle (measurement can vary depending on desired presentation).

FIGURE **5.31a** Using a semi-flexible boning knife, cut down the feather bones to free the eye muscle. Use caution not to cut into the meat. The result is a rack of lamb, chined (NAMP 204A).

- Score across fat cap.
- Pierce between each rib bone.
- Score each individual bone, scraping away membrane.
- Push bones through and scrape clean.
- Peel cap away from eye muscle.
- Remove elastin (yellow band along bottom of eye).
- For an alternative method, starting from step six:
- Cut between each bone.
- Tie string at base of bone.
- Pull rapidly to remove all debris.

FIGURE **5.31b** To French the rack, remove the flat blade bone by peeling back the cap and cut under and then over each side.

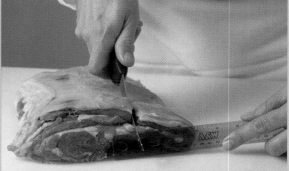

FIGURE **5.31c** Measure desired length from the end of eye (one-inch measurement pictured) on each side of rack. Score across the cap, connecting the measurements.

FIGURE **5.31d** After scoring, pierce between each rib in a straight line.

FIGURE **5.31e** Turn over rack and cut across the rib bones on the pierce line.

(Continues)

FIGURE **5.31f** Score down each rib bone, being sure to stay in the center of each. The scoring is to free the membrane that covers each bone.

FIGURE **5.31g** Loosen membrane over each bone using a shucking knife or butter knife. Apply pressure while scraping.

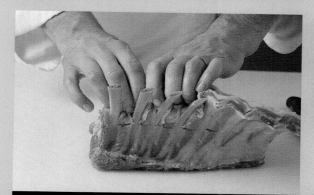

FIGURE **5.31h** Stand the rack on the eye and pop the bones out of the membranes. Each rack may need extra scraping.

FIGURE **5.31i** Another method for Frenching is to score bones as previously explained, then cut between each bone, leaving a finger of meat around each bone.

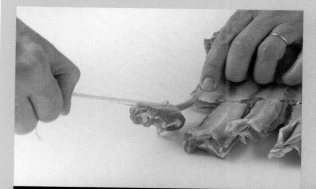

FIGURE **5.31j** Tie a long piece of twine around the base of each bone and pull rapidly to "floss" the bones.

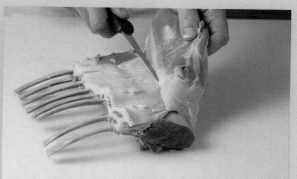

FIGURE **5.31k** Peel the exterior cap fat and muscle from the rib, bone side down.

(Continues)

FIGURE **5.31l** Remove the yellow elastin band along the bottom of the eye muscle.

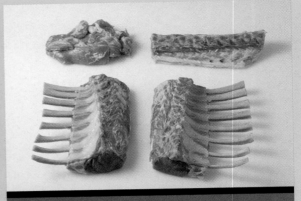

FIGURE **5.31m** Rack of lamb, Frenched (NAMP 204C); yield shown with trim and chine bone.

FIGURE **5.32a** To cut chops, place the rack meat side down and cut between each bone. Be sure to cut the eye muscle evenly.

FIGURE **5.32b** Portion cut rack chops (NAMP 1204D).

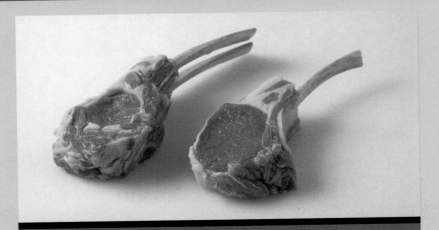

FIGURE **5.32c** The chop on the right is from the loin end of the rack and is a solid muscle. The chop on the left is from the chuck side and has more sections and intermusclar fat.

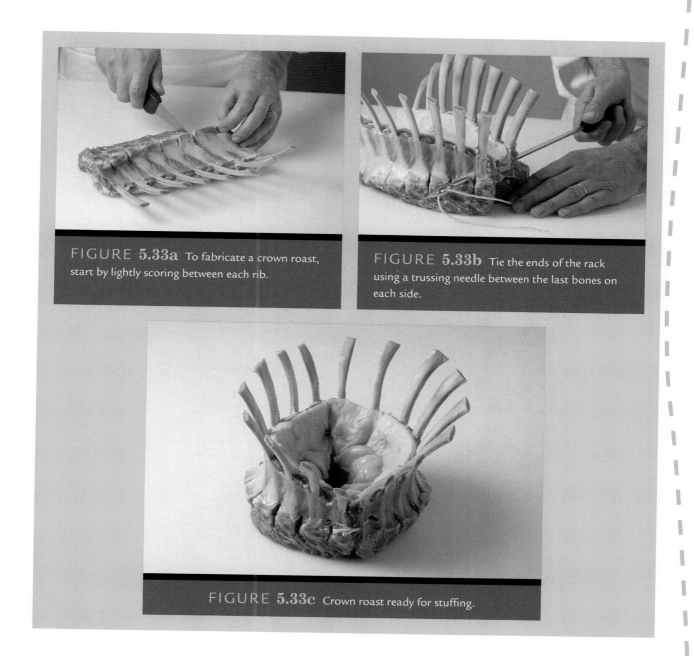

FIGURE **5.33a** To fabricate a crown roast, start by lightly scoring between each rib.

FIGURE **5.33b** Tie the ends of the rack using a trussing needle between the last bones on each side.

FIGURE **5.33c** Crown roast ready for stuffing.

SQUARE CUT LAMB SHOULDER/CHUCK

The shoulder is always a good value and can be a high-profit item but it has a complicated bone structure and is a challenge to fabricate. One fabrication is to simply cut it into shoulder chops. These tend to be difficult for the customers to navigate because of the many bones. Creating semi-boneless chops is another option.

The shoulder is often boned and rolled into a roast. Because of the many sections of muscle, it may make sense to stuff the shoulder with something that binds, giving a better look and higher value. The boneless shoulder can easily be cut into stew pieces.

FIGURE **5.34** Lamb shoulder, square cut (NAMP 207).

BONE, ROLL, AND TIE THE SHOULDER

- Remove the neck and rib bones.
- Open from side to remove arm bone.
- Peel cap off blade bone and work knife around small ridge in center of blade bone.
- Remove any large pieces of fat or connective tissues.
- Roll and tie into roast.
- Shoulder can be split in two to make smaller roasts.

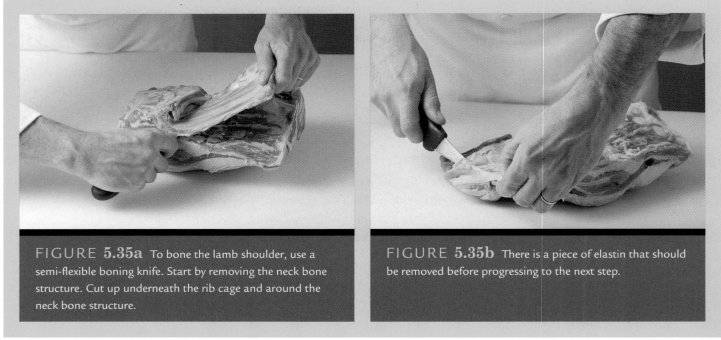

FIGURE **5.35a** To bone the lamb shoulder, use a semi-flexible boning knife. Start by removing the neck bone structure. Cut up underneath the rib cage and around the neck bone structure.

FIGURE **5.35b** There is a piece of elastin that should be removed before progressing to the next step.

(Continues)

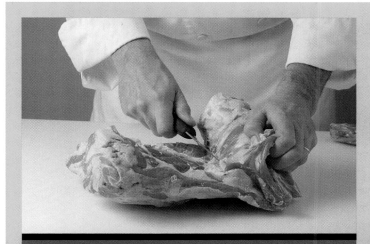

FIGURE **5.35c** The shoulder can be divided into two roasts. Split the shoulder through the natural seam.

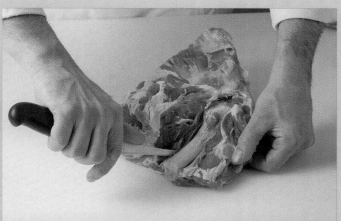

FIGURE **5.35d** Remove the arm bone through the socket joint.

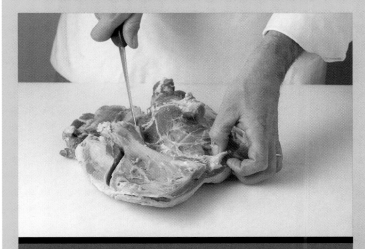

FIGURE **5.35e** Outline the blade bone and peel it out.

FIGURE **5.35f** Trim and tie each section.

FIGURE **5.35g** Yield from shoulder.

LAMB SHANK

The fore or hind shanks can be purchased whole or blocked or squared off. Frenching the end of the shank can give it a quality presentation. The shanks can also be cut shorter into osso buco.

For photos, please refer to page 90 of Chapter 3: Veal.

BREAST OF LAMB

An untrimmed lamb breast is typically a very good value. It requires trimming of the excess fat and removal of the sternum or brisket bones. Once trimmed, the breast can be cooked as a riblet or short ribs. An alternative is cutting a pocket for stuffing.

For photos, please refer to page 86 of Chapter 3: Veal.

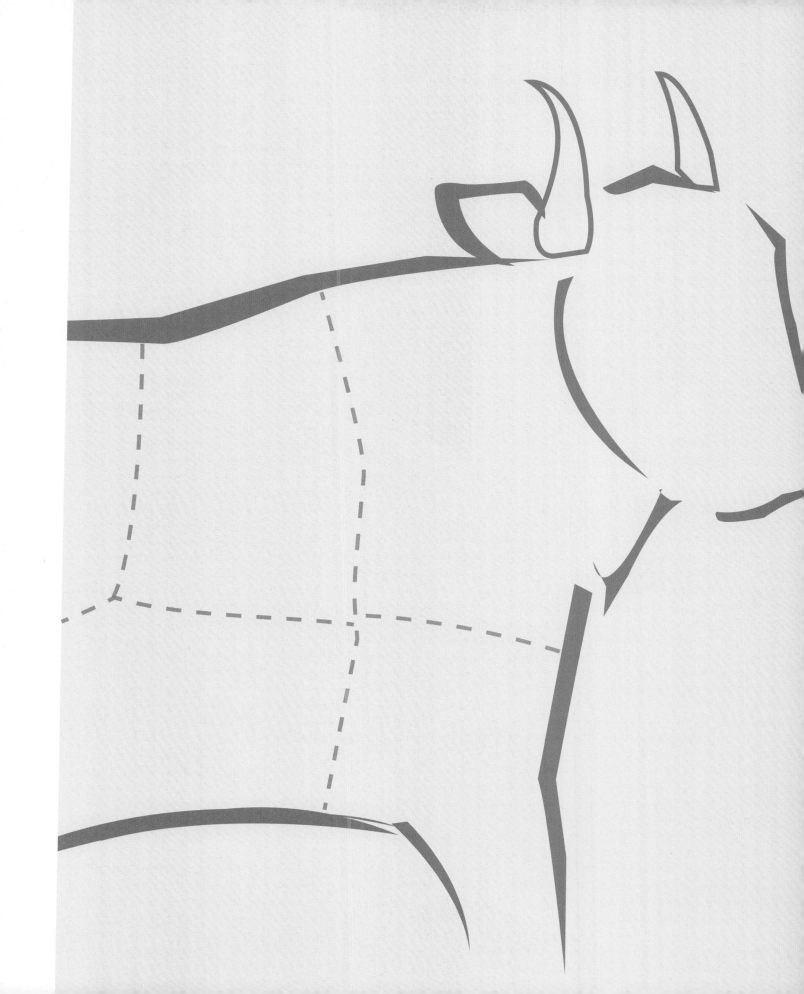

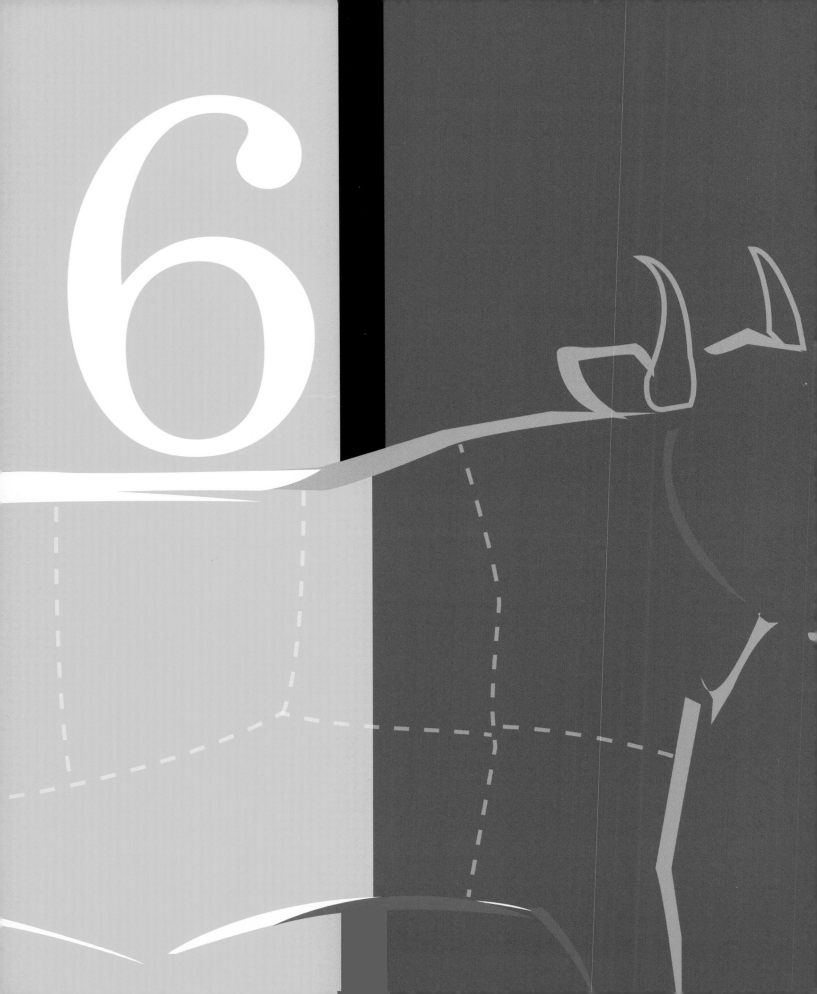

GAME

Game meats are those that are traditionally hunted. Humans have been hunting and gathering for thousands of years and the type of game found varies from region to region. Chefs have often turned to creating game dishes to showcase different flavors and to highlight their skills. Game presents challenges that other meats may not. Stronger flavors, extra lean cuts, tougher flesh, and customers' hesitancy to accept game meats are just a few of the challenges.

Game offers seasonality to menus. Fall is the traditional hunting season and certain game dishes are more appealing during these months. That is not to say that game isn't appealing year round. Many chefs choose to place game prominently on the menu through the entire calendar year.

Today, we find game animals that are farm raised and fed in a manner similar to their domestic cousins. So what makes them game? Commercially raised game has not been altered out of its natural breed; therefore, it can require different fabrications and cooking techniques. Often, feeding practices are not that much different from what we may find in the wild. Animals are typically allowed to forage or graze depending on the farm. Only a small amount of grain feeding and mineral supplements added to ensure health and quality may be part of the process, not to the extent that we find in domestic animal feeding. This ensures the game will possess the stronger game flavors that are desired in the product. The more foraged diet will create more robust flavors. Do not assume all game animals are running wild though; some are feed lot finished, similar to their domestic counterparts.

Processing is done by smaller operations and each has its own style of cutting and packaging. Game is not regulated the same way other meats are and may not require USDA inspection. Be sure to purchase from reputable distributors. There are some distributors that specialize in game and fancy, unique meats. Heirloom breeds of various meats may not be considered game but may be part of this type of purveyor's product list. Heirloom breeds are those not popularly used in modern meat production. They tend to have unique and sometimes game-like flavors. Be prepared to pay much higher prices for game and heirloom items. Consider using underutilized cuts, such as those from the chuck area, to minimize costs.

GAME MEATS

Although there are thousands of game animals worldwide, we choose to focus on those that are typically available from vendors:

- Bison / American Buffalo
- Venison
- Antelope
- Elk
- Rabbit
- Wild Boar

BISON/BUFFALO

Although the terms *bison* and *buffalo* are used interchangeably, bison are not true buffalo, a family whose members include the African cape buffalo and the Asian water buffalo. Early European settlers used the term *buffalo* to describe the wooly bison because of the similarity between the body types. The bison is actually more closely related to beef cattle.

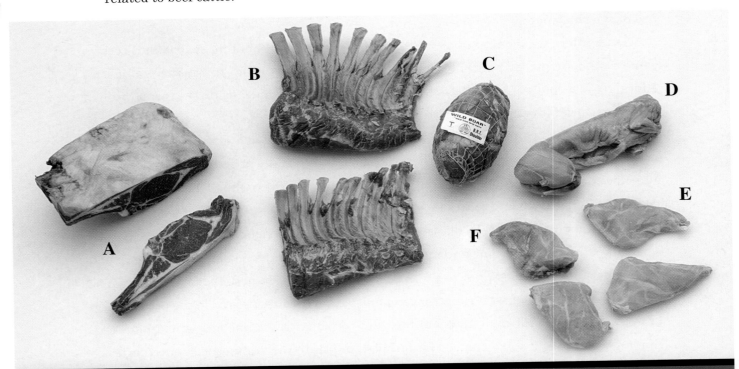

FIGURE **6.1** Assorted game: A. Bison ribeye; B. Wild boar racks; C. Wild boar shoulder; D. Fryer rabbit; E. Rabbit leg, hind; F. Rabbit shoulder and leg.

Bison are large, ranging from 1000 to 2000 pounds, and are very agile. Although they are typically seen grazing lazily in open pasture, they can actually charge at thirty-five miles per hour and even jump gullies and streams. They stand up to six feet high at the shoulder when mature and have a large, muscular front end. They are highly respected in the animal world and are considered more dangerous than any animal in North America, except the huge Alaskan brown bear or grizzly bear, or a large male moose in rut. They grow thick hair for the winter season and can survive in very cold weather.

American bison once dominated the landscape. They were found from coast to coast, with the largest populations located in the Great Plains of the Midwest. Their range extends from Canada to Mexico and they are prolific grazing animals. The great plains of North America were created in part by the roaming of the huge bison herds which naturally mowed, tilled, and fertilized the land. Their actions naturally rotated pastures by their continual roaming and migrating. It is estimated that up to 60 million bison lived in North America when Christopher Columbus first voyaged to the continent. Herds were seen by settlers crossing the great plains in the 1840s that extended for more than fifty miles long and twenty mile wide. The ground would shake with the movement of herds. In the 1870s trains running from Topeka, Kansas to Santa Fe, New Mexico were actually by derailed the thousands of buffalo ramming into the moving train during their migrations. The bison were thought to be an inexhaustible supply of meat. In the 1880s, bison were mercilessly slaughtered. The invention of the repeating rifle and the fact that bison were "in the way" of western progress allowed for their demise. This happened in part to eliminate the food source for aboriginal Indian tribes. The plains Indians such as the Sioux depended on the buffalo for survival. These were nomadic peoples following the herds and were starved without them. Thousands of buffalo were wasted and left to spoil on the open plains by sportsmen and government troops alike. Elimination was actually part of military campaigns to control Indian populations, forcing them to take government handouts of beef rather than starve. Some of the buffalo were skinned for their robes which were prized in the east and the tongues harvested as they were considered a delicacy at the time but many were simply wasted. In twenty short years there were few buffalo left on the open plains. This horrific extinction almost wiped out the species, but it was saved by a few concerned naturalists. By 1889 it was estimated by William Hornaday, the first director of the Wildlife Conservation Society, that only 1091 bison were left. In 1905 Hornaday convinced Theodore Roosevelt to form the American Bison Society and preservation of the species began.

Considered a national heritage species, bison are now protected. Wild herds are found in Yellowstone National Park and hunting is limited to specific seasons by the federal government. Today, they are no longer endangered and herds have grown substantially to the point where bison can now be considered for meat again. A herd of approximately 500,000 currently exists between the United States and Canada, most of which are raised on private ranches with very few actually in wild herds.

Bison meat has steadily gained ground in the culinary field and is seen regularly on menus around the United States. Ted Turner, the media magnate, founded Ted's Montana Grill, a restaurant chain based around bison; it now has over thirty locations.

ITEM AND NAMP NUMBER	DESCRIPTION/ FABRICATION	SUGGESTED COOKING METHOD/ APPLICATION	AVERAGE SUGGESTED WEIGHT IN POUNDS	TYPICAL PACKAGE SPECS
Bison has a small round and very large chuck, the rib eye is larger than the striploin.				
Top round, bottom round flat, eye round, knuckle	Sold whole, typically well trimmed or divided as tied roasts	Roasts, steaks, very lean, can be dry. Best marinated and tenderized.	Varies with cut 10—15 pounds each	1 item per bag
Shortloin 174	Sold with tail trimmed to 2x3, 1x1, minimal fat coverage	Fabricated as porterhouse, t-bone, and shell steaks; slightly smaller than beef	17–20	1 per bag
Striploin bone in/Boneless 175/180	2x3, 1x1, 0x1 trim, minimal fat cover	Cut for striploin or shell steaks, roasted whole, split for medallions	8–10 if well trimmed	1 per bag
Tenderloin PSMO 189a	Peeled, side muscle on. Requires trimming and removal of silverskin.	Steaks, medallions, filet mignon, roast whole	4–6	1 per bag
Flank steak, Skirt steak, Hanger steak	May need exterior membranes peeled.	Grill as steak, fajita, marinate or tenderize (can be tough but very flavorful)	1–2	2–4 per bag
Rib, export style 109 d	Rib bones in, fat lip trimmed to two inches (trim level can vary)	Bone in rib eye steak, cowboy steak, roast whole as bison "prime rib"	12–16	1 per bag (sometimes sold split in half)
Rib eye, boneless lip on 112a	Rib eye with two-inch lip of fat	Boneless rib eye steak, Delmonico steak	8–12	1 per bag

FIGURE **6.2** NAMP HRI cuts for bison.

(Continues)

(*Continued*)

ITEM AND NAMP NUMBER	DESCRIPTION/ FABRICATION	SUGGESTED COOKING METHOD/ APPLICATION	AVERAGE SUGGESTED WEIGHT IN POUNDS	TYPICAL PACKAGE SPECS
Short ribs	Cut short, "flanken," or "Korean" style	Braise, slow cook, barbecue	2–3 each; size can vary with processor	4 per bag
Chuck/Shoulder/Hump	Various chuck sections, roasts, bison has a larger chuck section, including a "hump"	Braise, slow cook, stew, grind	3–7	1 per bag
Brisket	Sold trimmed, fresh, or corned	Braise, slow cooked, as barbecue	4–8	1 per bag
Portion cuts				
Porter house steak, T-bone steak, Bone-in or boneless rib eye, Sirloin steak, Filet mignon medallions	Portion cut to specs	Dry cook, grill, broil, sauté, pan sear	Varies	Most items packaged individually or as pairs but can vary with processor.
Stew, from chuck or trim pieces.	1- 2–inch pieces	Stew, braise, chili	Customer specified	Typical five pounds per bag, can vary
Ground bison	Bulk or formed as burgers	Very lean, best not well done if used as burger	Varies	Varies
Bison products: jerky, sausages, hot dogs, marinated or cured products	None	Ready to eat	Varies	Varies, be sure products include proper ingredients

Meat from bison resembles beef and is sometimes described as "beefier than beef" due to its high iron count and rich, robust flavor. Bison is typically range fed and may be finished on some grain, but it tends to be leaner than beef. Most bison processors use the same cutting techniques as for beef and vendors typically use the beef NAMP numbers and descriptions. Typical purchases are the bison striploin, rib eye, and tenderloin PSMO. Short ribs for barbecue are another popular item. Many casual dining establishments use bison burger. Use the same specs for beef when purchasing bison.

VENISON

The term "venison" encompasses a number of genera and species of the *Cervidae* family. This includes the many wild breeds of deer, elk, antelope, and moose. Most commercially produced venison is from European and Asian breeds of deer that have been domesticated over many years. Many wealthy kings and noblemen kept stags to be released for hunting. Hunting stag in England during the sixteenth century was considered necessary to keep the wealthy lords in shape for battle and military fitness. Hunting was an integral part of manor life for the wealthy. These hunting breeds became the basis for most of the commercially available venison meat today. In the United States there are certain wild breeds of deer that are protected by game laws and cannot be raised for meat.

Historically, menus would only feature venison during hunting season, typically in the fall. Venison is now found year round due to modern farming techniques, which allow for a steady supply, and the desire of chefs to experiment with this versatile meat.

Deer are raised for byproducts beyond meat. The horns are prized for ornamental purposes and as a vitamin supplement. Chinese scrolls dated to 168 AD describe the use of deer antlers in medicinal recipes. The later Ming dynasty raised deer for antlers in the sixteenth century and the powder of them was mixed with tortoise shell and ginseng to make elixirs. Today we find China and Korea still using large amounts of antler for medications. New Zealand, which is a major producer of venison, exports large amounts of antler to Korea. Deer antlers are high in glucosamine and chondroitin, as well as other valuable minerals believed to affect arthritis and blood functions. The antlers that are not fully ossified are desired for medicines. This is known as the antler "velvet" or the softer exterior of the horn. The older horns are used to make gelatin that also has medicinal value.

Early German bakers would burn the antlers to create a powder called *Hirschhorn salz* or potassium carbonate. This carbonate was used in place of modern baking powder to help aerate bread with CO^2.

Deer horns grow back year after year, making them a renewable resource.

Deer hides make a fine, supple leather. High-quality gloves and clothing command a high price. The leather is thin enough to be sewn into many shapes and clothing styles. Early European settlers arriving in North America noted the quality of the Indian garb made from deer. The deer leather industries as well as the aforementioned antler industry continue to complement the meat harvest and provide much of the revenue realized from deer farming.

Venison is a lean, dark red meat that is very high in iron and zinc, giving it a distinct flavor and texture. Wild venison, such as the White Tail deer, tends to have a stronger, slightly "gamey" flavor, while most domesticated breeds are much milder. Venison is considered a healthful meat with much less saturated fat than beef. Because it lacks fat, venison should be cooked as you would veal; quick grilling, sautéing, and broiling are typical methods.

Deer are grazing animals and will eat a variety of plants; they do not do well as a feedlot animal. Typically, venison is not given steroids or other growth hormones. Deer need space to graze and are typically fed a natural diet. A venison farm will consist of large, grassy pasture with ten-foot electric fences to keep the animals from escaping.

There are thousands of venison farms in the United States and Canada, located coast to coast. Large farms are found in Texas, Kansas, Pennsylvania, and New York, but many more exist in numerous states.

New Zealand is the world's largest exporter of venison and there are large Red Deer populations. The climate is ideal for deer and there are no predators. The Red Deer was brought to New Zealand from Europe as a hunting animal, but the population exploded, giving birth to the deer meat industry. The Cervena brand is a state-certified co-op of farmers and processors that produce an extremely consistent product.

Australia also produces a large amount of venison for export. The Australian outback is well suited for venison raising.

BREEDS
- Fallow deer
- Red Tail deer
- Axis deer
- Sika deer
- Elk
- White Tail

FIGURE 6.3 NAMP HRI cuts for venison and antelope.

ITEM AND NAMP NUMBER	DESCRIPTION/ FABRICATION	SUGGESTED COOKING METHOD/APPLICATION	AVERAGE SUGGESTED WEIGHT IN POUNDS	TYPICAL PACKAGE SPECS
Venison/Antelope				
Leg, whole (similar to veal leg)	Entire bone-in leg, lean; Requires fabrication, boning, removal of silverskin, dividing into subprimals	Roasts, portion cut steaks, cutlets, medallions, (stew, grind from trim)	18–22	1 per bag
Leg, Denver style	Leg divided into subprimals, denuded, shank and trim excluded, very good yield	Roasts, portion cuts, medallions	10–12	Subprimals packaged separately
Shank, osso buco	Sold as whole shank or portion cut as osso buco	Braise, stew	2–3	1 shank per bag, portion cuts, package varies
Saddle, contains loin and rack section	Sold whole, unsplit; requires band saw to cut bone in portions; can be boned to create medallions or steaks	Roast, grill, broil, pan sear, sauté; very lean, may require added lipids, such as butter, fat, or oil	18–20	1 per bag
Short loin, trimmed, split	Cut for porterhouse, t-bone, chops	Grill, broil, sauté, pan sear	3–4	1 per bag
Rack, 8–10 bones; Sold as split rack, often Frenched	Cut for chops, may require removal of silverskin	Grill, broil, sauté, pan sear	3–4	1 per bag
Chuck/Shoulder boneless	Cut as roasts or stew, grind, remove heavy silverskin	Braise, stew, slow cook	10–15	1 per bag
Breast, ribs/short ribs	Peel silverskin, membranes	Braise, slow cook, barbecue	2–3	Varies
Portion cuts chops, cutlets, medallions	May require minor trimming	Grill, broil, sauté, pan sear	Varies, customer specified	Varies

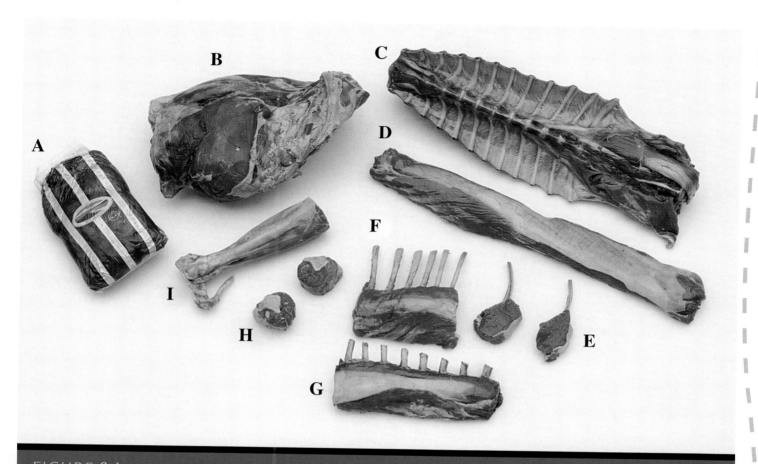

FIGURE **6.4** Venison cuts: A. Venison Denver leg; B. Venison leg, shank off; C. Full venison saddle; D. Boneless venison loin; E. Venison rack chops; F. Venison rack, long bone and Frenched; G. Venison rack, short bone and Frenched; H. Venison osso buco; I. Venison shank.

VENISON FABRICATION

Venison is fabricated in the same manner as lamb or veal. The carcass is not split down the spine, so there are saddles and pairs available. The carcass is divided into legs, loin, rack, and chuck. The loin and rack can be sold as one large piece, known as a saddle.

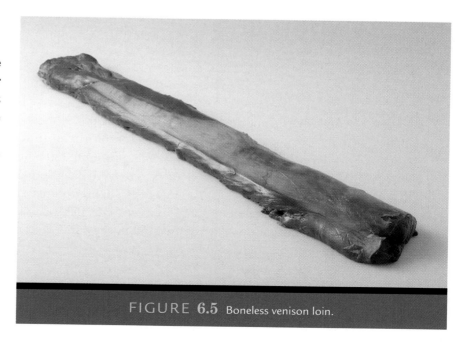

FIGURE **6.5** Boneless venison loin.

FIGURE **6.6a** To prepare the loin for medallions, use a semi-flexible boning knife and peel the exterior silverskin. The silver extends into the eye muscle on the rib side. It may require opening the rib muscle to remove.

FIGURE **6.6b** Cut the loin into medallions.

FIGURE **6.6c** Tie the medallions with butcher's twine to hold shape.

ANTELOPE

Antelope is sometimes sold as venison and the meat is similar to deer. The antelope raised for food are the Nilgai breed, typically of Indian and Nepalese descent. They are larger than most deer, averaging around 280 pounds. Antelope meat is mild and very lean and, like deer, is dark red. Like deer venison, it is high in iron, making it a very nutritious meat. Because it is slightly milder than deer meat, Antelope can be appealing as a grill or sauté item without heavy masking spices. Antelope is sold in the same format as deer, fabricated in the same method as lamb or veal. Racks, loins, saddles, legs, and shoulders are typical cuts.

RABBIT

The rabbit has a prominent place in many cultures. It is one of the twelve zodiac signs associated with the ancient Chinese lunar calendar. The rabbit was introduced into Europe through Spain about 4000 years ago. It was prized by the Romans for its meat and quality fur. The rabbit made its way through the farm lands of Europe and reached England in the eleventh century. The development of farms and pasture lands gave the rabbit a quality habitat. Its rise in population coincides with the rise in agriculture worldwide.

The term *rabbit* once referred to only young animals; an adult was called a *coney*. The term coney stems from the Greek word for rabbit, *kuniklos*.

Medieval monks were the first to raise rabbits for food. Young rabbits very soon after birth, were not considered meat but an aquatic lifeform and therefore could be eaten during Lent. French Monks between 500 AD and 1000 AD are responsible for mixing breeds and changing hair colors by cross-breeding.

Coney Island in New York is so named because the island was once overrun by rabbits; they were protected from predators by the water barrier separating them from the mainland. Coney Island was a favorite hunting ground for New York residents for many years.

Rabbits and hares have been hunted for many thousands of years and have been introduced to all continents except Antarctica. Rabbit populations grow very rapidly and rabbits were and are still considered pests by vegetable farmers. The Romans introduced the rabbit from Spain to the Mediterranean including Italy by 230 AD. The Romans would capture wild rabbits and establish a large warren or protected land for them to semi-free range and then harvest from time to time. By 1066 rabbit was introduced to England, they were considered the ideal food because they multiplied rapidly and were just the right size to be eaten at one sitting. Their population exploded in the 1700s when property divisions and hedgerows were introduced to the landscape, giving the rabbit an ideal habitat. Rabbits were also introduced in Australia in 1788 and rapidly became unmanageable. Managing overpopulation of rabbits was and still is a concern for Australia. By the 1860s rabbits were hunted for bounty. Huge rabbit fencing was constructed to contain the populations. One such fence extended over eleven hundred miles. Viruses were purposely introduced into populations in the 1950s, but the rabbits became immune and populations grew again. The Australian Commonwealth Scientific and Industrial Research Organization introduced the Calicivirus in 1996 and it has helped control populations since.

Another rabit-like animal, the *European hare,* should also be considered when mentioning game meats. The hare is slightly gamey and has a much darker meat than rabbit. It can be purchased commercially but is harder to find. Hare is almost always braised or stewed and can be liberally spiced.

Meat from a young rabbit is similar to chicken. It is light in color, mild in flavor, and quite tender, without much fat. Rabbit is available from many purveyors and can even be found in some supermarkets today. China is the largest rabbit producer and rabbits are also farmed in the United States, Canada, the European Union, Japan, Korea, New Zealand, and Australia, as well as many other nations.

Meat is sold as a whole carcass divided by weight ranges and also as parts, such as the loin, front, or back legs. Whole rabbits are categorized as *fryers* or *roasting rabbits* in the United States. Fryers weigh up to three and a half pounds and are about twelve weeks old and roasters weigh up to four pounds and can be up to six months old, making the roaster much tougher.

BREEDS

New Zealand

New Zealand rabbits weigh from ten to thirteen pounds when mature. They are known for their ability to grow to market-ready fryers (four to five pounds) by eight weeks of age. Their average litter size is eight to ten bunnies. The breed was developed in the United States and has a full, well-muscled carcass.

Californian

The Californian is a good meat breed, also developed in the United States. At maturity, this breed weighs nine to ten pounds. It is plump and grows rapidly. The average litter size is six to eight bunnies. Breeders often cross New Zealand and Californians for quality meat.

Champagne D'Argent

This is one of the oldest breeds of rabbit. It has well-developed hindquarters. Champagnes are larger and weigh about ten to fifteen pounds at maturity.

Florida White

The Florida is a smaller rabbit, weighing only four to six pounds at maturity; it is better suited to the fryer market. This breed is becoming more popular for home meat production and crossbreeding. They have a compact, meaty body carcass. This breed was developed in the United States.

FIGURE **6.7** NAMP HRI cuts for rabbit.

ITEM AND NAMP NUMBER	DESCRIPTION/ FABRICATION	SUGGESTED COOKING METHOD/ APPLICATION	AVERAGE SUGGESTED WEIGHT IN POUNDS	TYPICAL PACKAGE SPECS
Rabbit				
Whole broiler/ fryer	Sold whole with giblets, Can be cut into parts	Roast, grill, braise, stew	2–4	1 per bag
Legs, hind/fore	May require partial boning, remove back bones	Roast, grill, braise, stew, pulled meats	2 per pack	4 legs per pack
Loin section w/ ribs	Can be boney, may need partial boning	Grill, broil, sauté	2 per pack	2 pieces per pack

RABBIT FABRICATION

Rabbits are fabricated in a method similar to poultry, although they have a bone structure similar to other mammals. Basic fabrication is to divide the carcass into front and back legs and the loin section. Rabbits are also sold with *giblets*, meaning a small bag of offal is included.

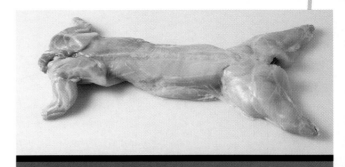

FIGURE **6.8** Fryer rabbit.

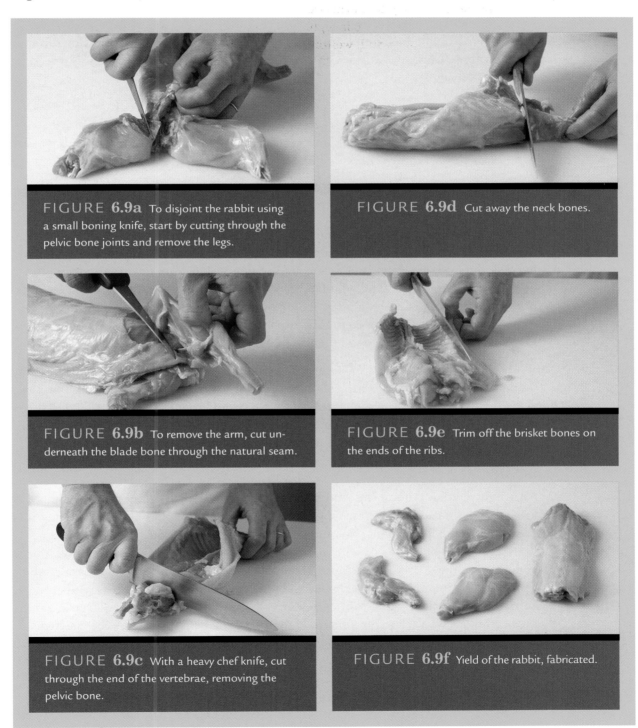

FIGURE **6.9a** To disjoint the rabbit using a small boning knife, start by cutting through the pelvic bone joints and remove the legs.

FIGURE **6.9d** Cut away the neck bones.

FIGURE **6.9b** To remove the arm, cut underneath the blade bone through the natural seam.

FIGURE **6.9e** Trim off the brisket bones on the ends of the ribs.

FIGURE **6.9c** With a heavy chef knife, cut through the end of the vertebrae, removing the pelvic bone.

FIGURE **6.9f** Yield of the rabbit, fabricated.

WILD BOAR

In history, the boar was considered one of humans' most feared adversaries. Ancient Greeks included the boar in many famous myths and tales. The boar, due to its ability to surprise its opponent and its fearlessness, was a prized hunting trophy. The boar was not only ferocious, it was highly destructive to farmers. It has a thick hide with coarse bristle-like hair and large tusks. A boar or herd of wild swine can destroy stored foods and wreak havoc on other small farm animals, putting farmers in jeopardy for months to come.

The Romans tamed boars and used them in formal parades and as fighting animals for spectators. The boar was a part of Roman life and it was often eaten as a festival food, roasted whole.

Throughout the Americas boars originated from swine brought from Spain in the 1500s that were traded with local Indians. Escaped swine developed into wild pigs. The term *razorback* refers to wild hogs in the Southern United States. The University of Arkansas uses the razorback as its mascot.

Wild boars are found in backwoods areas where temperatures stay mild year round and forage is available.

Modern wild boar is meat from feral swine or hogs that are allowed free range of territory to find food. Their diet is highly varied and diverse, consisting of root vegetables, berries, nuts, plants, bugs, and even small rodents. This diet ensures a strong flavor and dark color of meat. The wild boar is typically about half the size of commercial pork and the meat is much leaner. The fat on a feral swine is darker in color, yellowish, and softer than that of commercial pork. Depending on diet, the fat can have a higher level of Omega-3 fatty acid and can spoil faster than typical pork.

Wild boar can refer to any number of different breeds. Some of the feral domestic boars found in the United States are related to Spanish Iberico swine. Game and hunting clubs have introduced Eurasian and Russian boar to large game preserves. These are commercially sold as wild boar. There are also large feral domestic swine populations descended from animals that have escaped captivity.

BOAR CUTS

Although related to hogs, the wild boar is much smaller. Often, processors do not follow hog schematics when breaking down the carcass. The loin is often divided into rack and short loin sections. The ham includes all of the sirloin. Belly and bacon sections are about half the size of domestic pigs. The shoulders are sold as BRT roasts and not as typical Boston butts and picnics. Be sure to examine a vendor's spec sheet carefully before ordering. Boar meat can be very expensive and the purchaser must be ready to conduct further fabrication on certain items. For example, Frenched boar racks often arrive with a fair amount of debris on the bones that must be cleaned.

ITEM AND NAMP NUMBER	DESCRIPTION / FABRICATION	SUGGESTED COOKING METHOD / APPLICATION	AVERAGE SUGGESTED WEIGHT IN POUNDS	TYPICAL PACKAGE SPECS
FIGURE 6.10 NAMP HRI cuts for wild boar.				
Wild Boar				
Leg or ham bone in or boned, rolled, tied	Sold skin off, may require trimming; also sold cured and smoked	Roast, cut for portions	8–10	1 per bag
Short loin	Cut for chops, t-bone style	Grill, broil, sauté, pan sear	3–4	2 per bag; varies with processor
Boneless loin	Cut for medallions, cutlets	Roast, grill, broil, sauté, pan sear	4–5	2 per bag, varies
Boar rack, 8 bones	Usually sold Frenched; typically requires further fabrication and cleaning of bones.	Roast, grill, broil, sauté, pan sear	2–3	2 per bag
Shoulder whole/ boneless rolled and tied	Entire shoulder sold skin off and tied or netted	Slow roast, braise, pulled meat, barbecue	3–5	1 per bag
Spare ribs	Small compared to regular pork, may need to remove sternum bone	Slow roast, barbecue	1–2	2 per bag
Belly/bacon	Sold fresh or cured as smoked bacon	Roast or braise fresh belly, cook as strips for bacon	2–3; varies with processor	Varies

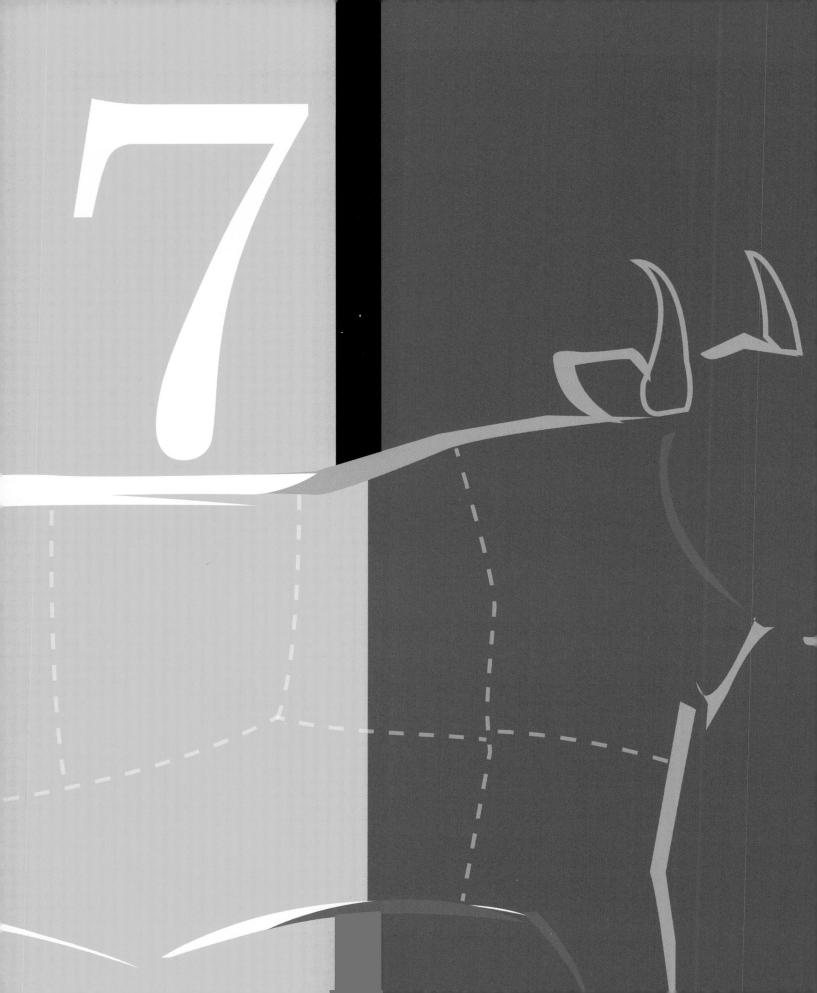

SAFETY AND SANITATION

BASIC MEAT FOOD SAFETY

Meat is highly susceptible to pathogens because it has a high water content. Great care must be taken when handling meat products. The risk of contracting or spreading a food-borne illness must be taken very seriously. Salmonella, *E-coli*, staphylococcus areoles, campylobacter, and listeria are examples of serious food-borne illnesses that can affect any consumer, especially young children, the elderly, and those with compromised immune systems. Basic guidelines implemented by the United States Department of Agriculture and the Food Safety and Inspection Service will help to ensure safety.

USDA INSPECTION

Inspection of meat dates back to medieval times in Europe. The ancient butcher guilds had elected officers who were responsible for meat safety. In England, the Market Act of 1674 established rules in which inspectors could seize meat and punish the offending butcher. If a town butcher was found selling pork with measles or other serious disease they were often fined and expelled from the guild. If the meat they sold was rancid or spoiled many were forced to ride through the town on horseback facing backwards and wearing the rancid meat around their neck. Written regulations were formed to control the excessive waste created by slaughter. The Market Act basically acted as the foundation for modern inspection.

In more modern times, the U.S. Meat Inspection Act was passed in 1906. The USDA, founded in 1862 by President Lincoln, was entrusted with enforcing the act. Changes in regulation occurred throughout the decades, with the beef grading system introduced in 1927 and the Poultry Products Inspection Act in 1957. The Food Safety and Quality Service was established in 1977, which later became the current Food Safety and Inspection Service. As the meat industry grew and changed, the type of inspection moved from simply looking for animal disease to inspecting meat and meat products for wholesomeness.

To ensure food safety, the USDA inspects meats on various levels. *Antemortem* inspection is conducted on the live animal. Cattle are checked for any diseases, broken bones, and, in some cases, irregular behaviors. *Postmortem* inspection occurs after slaughter when the carcass is visually inspected for pathogenic debris. Internal organs are examined for diseases. The USDA inspector can reject a carcass, which is then taken off line. In a large processing plant, a team of inspectors will observe a number of critical points. Key inspection points are during the evisceration, chilling, cutting, packaging, and storing, but all aspects of the fabrication come under the scrutiny of the USDA inspection team. Once meats pass inspections, they are stamped with a blue USDA stamp. This stamp will contain the processing plant's USDA establishment number. If a pathogen outbreak occurs, recalls can be coordinated by using these establishment numbers. Vacuum-packaged meats will be stamped with a circular stamp on the exterior. Boxes will have an inspection stamp, but it only valid if the box is sealed.

FIGURE 7.1 USDA inspection stamp.

HACCP

In the early 1990s, the USDA implemented the use of Hazard Analysis Critical Control Points, or HACCP, systems. This program was designed to reduce pathogens by having meat processors identify the most critical areas where pathogens can present problems, and set up systems to monitor all those critical areas. The program, which is now recognized worldwide, allows for a sharing of responsibility of inspection, rather than having a government agency in total control of all inspections. It is a system where the plant design, equipment, day-to-day production, packaging, storage, and everything to do with food safety is examined by the USDA and then monitored by the processors. The USDA inspects the systems in place as well as the actual production. This encourages the processors to be innovative in maintaining higher levels of food safety, because they are involved in the process. If deciding to sell meat on a wholesale level, you should become accustomed to HACCP plans and designs. The USDA Web site has examples of HACCP plans and tips to create your own plan for a variety of plant operations: http://www.usda.gov.

When deciding on a purveyor, it makes sense to tour the warehouse and cutting facilities. Be sure the facility is inspected and proper HACCP plans are in place and followed. A high-volume meat purveyor is normally USDA inspected and the inspector is typically on site during production times.

PACKAGE AND STORAGE

Traditionally, meats were transported as whole or split carcasses. Train or tractor trailer loads were delivered to meat processors close to their final destination. In the 1960s, the invention of vacuum packaging allowed for meat to be stored for much longer with minimal loss. Fabrication could be done much farther from the customer and in plants that were much closer to the farms. Plastic packaging made from polymers originally had some problems with leaking. Today this process has been improved to securely package meats—even those with bone-in—with minimal leakage. Meats should be inspected upon arrival for loose bags where air has entered. "Blown" bags or "leakers" should be returned, especially if there is discoloration and odor present.

Poultry items, such as broiler chickens, are often packaged in modified atmospheric packaging (MAP). This package is loose around the item and is filled with a CO_2 mixture to slow bacterial growth. Upon opening, there should be no strong sulfur odors and poultry should not be slimy.

Vacuum-pack machines vary in size and capacity. If considering the purchase of one, be sure to test machines beforehand to be sure the capacity fits the need. Some states require food-safety plans in place before operating. An investment in a vacuum machine can result in significant savings and improves the amount of options when considering in-house meat fabrication.

FIGURE 7.2 Meat Storage Times and Temperatures.

MEAT	VACUUM PACKAGED	EXPOSED (OUT OF VACUUM BUT COVERED)	FREEZER
Beef (fresh) Large HRI cuts	4–6 weeks from pack date	3–4 days	6–12 months
Veal (fresh)	3–5 weeks from pack date	2–4 days	6–9 months
Pork (fresh)	3–4 weeks from pack date	3–4 days	3–6 months
Lamb (fresh)	4–5 weeks from pack date	3–4 days	6–9 months
Ground beef, veal, and lamb	2–3 weeks from pack date	1–2 days	3–4 months
Ground pork	2 weeks from pack date	1–2 days	1–3 months
Variety meats	3 weeks from pack date	1–2 days	3–4 months
Sausage, fresh pork	2 weeks from pack date	3–4 days	2 months
Bacon	8–10 weeks from pack date	5–7 days	1 month
Smoked ham, whole	8 weeks from pack date	1 week	2 months
Beef, corned	8 weeks from pack date	1 week	2 weeks
Pre-cooked meat	4–5 weeks from pack date	1 week	2–3 months
Sausage, smoked	8 weeks from pack date	3–7 days	2 months
Sausage, dry & semi-dry (unsliced)	Can last many months	2–3 weeks	Preferred not frozen

Ideal temperature for raw meat storage is 28° to 32°F / −2° to 0°C. If storing in a typical restaurant cooler where temperatures are higher, use shorter storage times.

BASIC VACUUM PACKAGING INSTRUCTION

1. **PLACE** item in bag, allowing two inches of extra space.

2. **POSITION** bag in chamber so open end is draped over sealer bar but still within the machine.

3. **SET** vacuum pressure to appropriate level for task (most machines can be turned down for fragile items).

4. **CLOSE** lid and machine will automatically equalize pressure, vacuum out air, and seal the bag.

5. **PLACE** label with product name and pack date.

For fresh red meat, the ideal storage temperature is 28° to 32°F / −2° to 0°C. Most large meat processors will hold products in this range for up to a week before shipping. Items will hold for six weeks in a vacuum bag (slightly less for bone-in items). In a typical restaurant walk-in cooler, storing at 32° to 41°F / 0° to 5°C, vacuum-packed items will last around two weeks. Storage times will depend on the original pack date on the label. Most meats will be around one to two weeks old upon receipt. If no pack date is visible, the customer should look for excessive purge or meat juices left in the bag. Large cuts of meat exposed or opened will last about three to four days before exterior spoilage begins. Portion cuts last about two to three days. Fresh meats should be laid out or wrapped in meat paper that wicks away moisture and prevents oxidation. Other methods may be to wrap meat in cheese cloth or rub with vegetable oil. Poultry items last three to five days when topped with ice or stored in modified atmospheric packaging. Be sure ice is drained properly and does not contaminate floors or other shelves.

Correct procedures should be followed when purchasing and receiving meat items. Any delivery trucks should be checked for cleanliness and proper temperature (below 45°F / 7°C).

Creating a basic checklist ensures product is received and recorded correctly. Avoid leaving meat items out on loading docks or wherever temperatures are above safe holding temperatures. When meats are brought into the walk-in cooler, be sure to rotate stock and check pack dates. Throw out boxes and packaging that may be harboring pests.

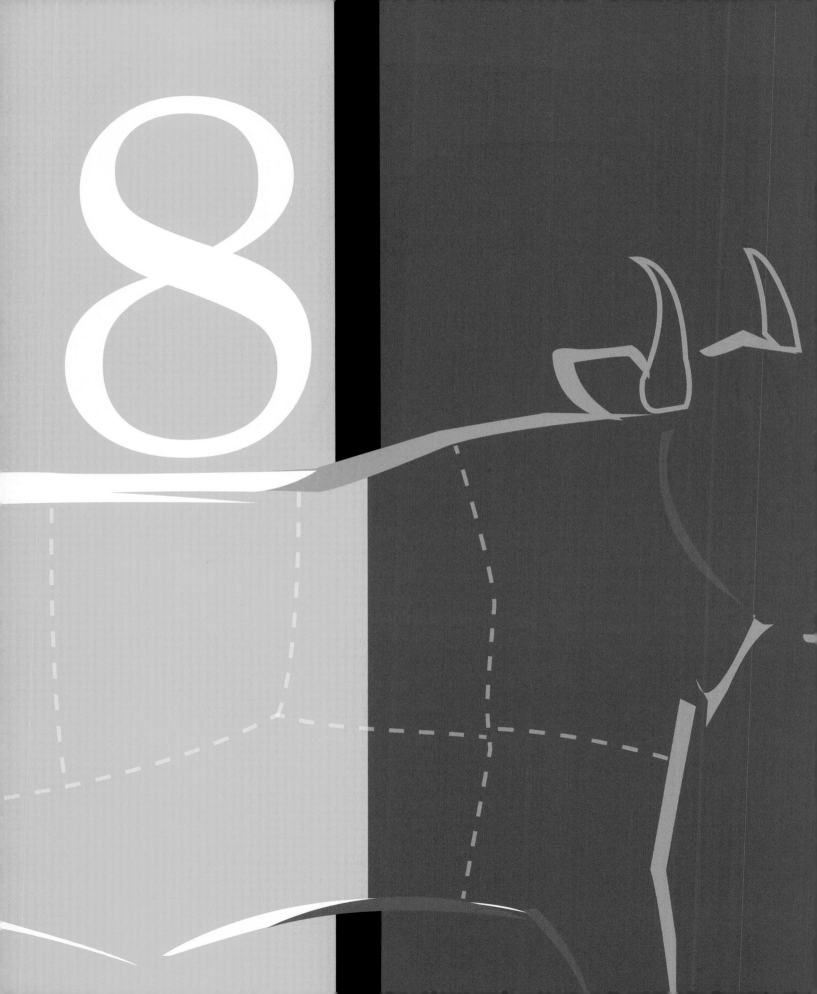

NUTRITION

Identifying the nutritional value of meats is important when creating dishes that will be scrutinized by the consumer. Foods created for institutions, schools, spas, and some corporate cafeterias may need to be broken down nutritionally. Even customers in a casual dining bistro may have nutritional concerns.

Meats are often the center of the plate item and contain a large amount of nutrients. Controversy and debate surround many meat items. Meats can contain large amounts of saturated fats and cholesterol, which can lead to many health problems, such as cardiovascular disease. Many studies have concluded that over-consuming large amounts of fatty meats can lead to a variety of serious health issues.

But "meat" is a general term. There is a huge variety of meats and meat products, all with different nutrient values. When consumed in moderate amounts, meats are a quality source of healthy vitamins and minerals. Red meats are high in digestible iron, calcium, zinc, selenium, phosphorous, vitamin E, and complex B vitamins. Digestible protein is abundant in meats. Even the fats and lipids in meat are essential to the diet. Fats and lipids can aid in absorption of other vitamins.

Meats from different animals have different levels of certain nutrients. Red meats from beef and lamb contain large amounts of iron and zinc, while pork is very high in thiamine. All meats have a certain amount of saturated and monounsaturated fats. The USDA quality grades will help differentiate between fat levels. The USDA has compiled a huge database of nutrients for thousands of meat items. When considering data created by the USDA, be sure to determine quality grades, fat trim levels, and whether the data is on cooked or uncooked items.

What animals are fed can alter the nutrient value and change the type of fat produced. Meats contain a certain amount of essential fatty acids (EFAs), which are divided into two basic groups: Omega-6 fatty acid and Omega-3 fatty acid. These two EFAs are found in the bloodstream and contribute to the flow of blood. Omega-6 is important for the ability for blood to clot while Omega-3 has the opposite effect, allowing for blood to flow freely, preventing clots. With an overabundance of Omega-6 in the diet, there is risk for blood clots and stroke. Animals on a grain-fed diet tend to have an imbalance, with more Omega-6 than Omega-3. This could imply that certain meats are healthier than others are. Recent efforts by the meat industry have resulted in changes in this imbalance in certain products. Feeding animals a diet high in lysine changes the fat content. Feeding an all-grass diet to cattle increases the Omega-3 content.

Other factors that can affect nutrients occur during processing. Exposing meats to high heat reduces fragile B vitamins, especially thiamine. Cooking meats in water or exposing them to light for prolonged periods depletes a variety of vitamins. Freezing is an effective preservation of vitamins if done rapidly, but cold can affect some micronutrients. Irradiation of meats, or "cold pasteurization," done either by electronic beam or gamma ray exposure, can reduce fragile B vitamins and micronutrients, depending on exposure levels and time. Irradiation of meats has been considered safe by FDA standards, but there is still controversy and resistance to the technology by some consumer groups. Altering pH or alkaline levels can affect certain vitamins. Some basic nutrients, such as protein, iron, zinc, and other minerals, are affected very little by cooking, freezing, or irradiation. Cooking is important to denature proteins, making them more digestible. Heating to specific temperatures is necessary to reduce pathogens. Fresh meat items, cooked the least amount of time, have the greatest vitamin content, but all meat items provide protein and basic minerals. As with other foods, the chef or foodservice operator decides on what type of product he or she will choose and how it is to be prepared.

How much meat is necessary in the diet? A typical American diet ranges anywhere from 1800 to 3,000+ calories daily. This amount is usually above what is needed, and, therefore, the end result is weight gain unless the person is able to utilize all the calories. Depending on gender, activity level, and age, the USDA recommends anywhere from five to six ounces of lean meat daily. A three-ounce tenderloin steak without any sauce contains only about 180 calories. However, a three-ounce portion is considered far too small for most menus. Many menus contain meat items that are in excess of what is needed daily, but it is up to the customer to decide what a satisfying portion is. A steak weighing twelve ounces is roughly double the suggested total daily amount required. That stated, a twelve-ounce steak contains about 720 calories and diets can vary. Processed grains and sugars in the modern diet result in a high calorie count with meat acting as only part of the problem. Trans fats and an increase in hydrogenated vegetable-based oils also contribute to an unhealthy diet.

As we decide what a "portion" is on the menu, this publication will attempt to show realistic portion nutrition data. A chef or foodservice operator that is providing information to the general public should be as accurate as possible. Charts with nutritional data are provided with typical portion sizes. Calorie counts are for meats only. Sauces, marinades, and any added ingredients will increase calories. The data for this publication are derived from the USDA nutrition database, available online.

DESCRIPTION	CALORIES	CALORIES FROM FAT	TOTAL FAT GRAMS	SATURATED FAT/GRAMS	MONO-UNSATURATED FAT/GRAMS	CHOLESTEROL MILLIGRAMS	PROTEIN GRAMS	CALCIUM MILLIGRAMS	IRON MG.	SODIUM MGRAM	ZINC MG	RIBO-FLAVIN	THIAMIN
Beef cuts													
12 oz Beef rib eye steak lean end, choice grade	768	360	39.72	16.08	16.8	276	95.28	44.04	8.76	240	23.76	.72	.36
12 oz Beef striploin steak	708	288	31.92	12.24	12.84	264	97.32	27.96	8.4	228	17.76	.72	.36
8 oz Beef striploin steak	472	192	21.28	8.16	8.56	176	64.88	18.64	5.6	152	11.84	.48	.24
8 oz Denuded tenderloin medallion, broiled	464	192	21.52	8.08	8.16	192	64	16	8.08	144	12.64	.64	.32
16 oz T-bone steak, choice grade	976	416	47.04	18.88	18.88	368	127.52	32	13.6	304	24.48	1.12	.48
1/4 pound hamburger 80/20 lean to fat ratio	304	184	20.24	7.96	8.88	100	28.48	12	2.52	88	6.16	.24	.04
Veal cuts													
6 oz Veal leg cutlet, unbreaded	312	72	7.86	2.22	2.82	180	56.4	12	1.5	132	5.76	.6	.12
12 oz Veal loin chop	600	216	23.64	8.76	8.52	360	89.52	72	2.88	324	11.04	1.08	.24
10 oz Veal rack chop	500	180	21.10	5.9	7.5	320	73.0	33.3	2.7	270	12.7	.8	.20
6 oz Veal top round, cap off, roast/cutlet	258	54	5.76	2.1	2.04	174	47.7	40.02	1.98	114	5.22	.54	.12
Pork cuts													
8 oz Pork loin roast portion	472	200	21.85	7.92	9.76	184	64.88	40	2.48	120	5.76	.72	1.68

Item													
5 oz Pork baby back ribs (estimated edible portion only, from 8 bone rack)	525	375	41.9	15.55	19.05	165	34.35	63.5	1.95	140	4.75	.3	.6
8 oz Pork baby back ribs (estimated edible portion only, from full rack)	840	600	67.04	24.88	30.48	264	54.96	101.6	3.12	224	7.6	.48	.96
10 oz Center-cut pork loin chop/broiled	570	210	22.9	8.4	10.3	230	85.5	87	2.4	170	6.7	.9	3.3
6 oz Pork tenderloin cleaned/roasted	276	72	8.16	2.82	3.3	132	47.82	10.2	2.52	96	4.44	.66	1.62
Lamb cuts													
6 oz Leg of lamb roasted/choice grade	324	120	13.14	4.68	5.76	150	48.12	13.98	3.6	114	8.4	.48	.18
6 oz Lamb shoulder roast	348	162	18.3	6.96	7.44	150	42.42	31.98	3.6	96	10.26	.42	.21
6 oz Lamb rack chops, broiled	360	198	22.02	7.92	8.88	156	47.16	28.02	3.78	144	8.94	.42	.21
6 oz Lamb loin chop, broiled	366	150	16.56	5.88	7.26	162	51	31.98	3.42	144	7.02	.48	.21
Offals													
6 oz Beef liver, sautéed	298	8	8	2	1.12	648	46	12	10	130	8	6	.36
6 oz Veal liver, sautéed	414	174	19.38	7.2	4.2	558	50.58	19.98	8.88	222	13.38	5.7	.42

This data, although from and accurate source, is only a guideline. Many other factors may influence nutrition for each meat item. Quality grade and marbling scores can greatly increase or decrease fat content. Prime meats will have a higher fat content while choice will be lower. Feed stuffs fed to the animal can change the type of fat and cholesterol levels. Animals that are fed grain tend to have higher saturated fat content as opposed to those that are grass fed. This chart does not always account for degrees of doneness. Meats that are cooked to well done may have less fat than those cooked rare. Vitamin content can be altered by over cooking. Some products may be sold as "enhanced" which would increase sodium content. Many pork products are sold enhanced today. Purveyors may have accurate nutrition data available on packaging. Be sure to check the portion size tested. Often data reflects unrealistic size portions such as 3 oz or 100 grams. These are not typical meat portions and may need to be adjusted or doubled. The USDA has done extensive testing on meat items and the data is available on their website.

Source: NAMP Meat Buyers Guide (multiplied by oz size portion)

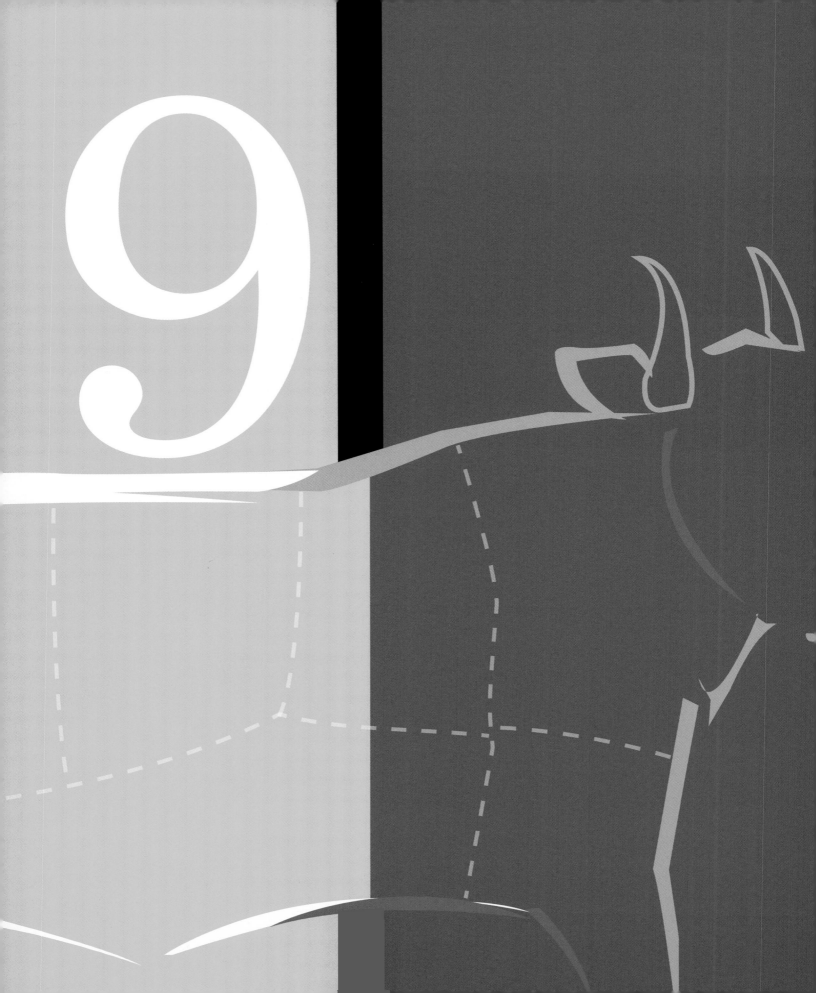

RECIPES

Beef Recipes

BEEF MATAMBRE

Matambre is a rolled steak stuffed with a variety of other meats and vegetables. This is a basic recipe, but the stuffing ingredients can be altered to create a variety of other dishes and the chef can allow for some creative freedom. Marinade is used in this recipe but may not be needed, depending on the flavor desired.

YIELD: 6 SERVINGS

Beef top round cap, trimmed, butterflied to 1/2 in/1 cm thickness and flattened	2–3 lbs/907–1361 g

MARINADE

Garlic cloves, chopped	4/4
Cilantro, chopped	1 Tbsp/15 mL
Canola *or* olive oil	1/2 cup/120 mL
Red wine vinegar	8 oz/240 mL
Salt	1/2 tsp/3 g
Freshly ground black pepper	1/4 tsp/1.5 g

STUFFING

Bread crumbs	6 oz/170 g
Hard-boiled eggs, coarsely chopped	3/3
Corn niblets	5 oz /142 g
Medium-sized carrots, cut into 1/2-inch strips	3/3
Medium onion, peeled and sliced with the grain	1/1
Chopped spinach, blanched	1 cup/240 mL
Cilantro, chopped	2 Tbsp/30 mL
Salt	as needed/as needed
Freshly ground black pepper	as needed/as needed

(Continues)

Canola *or* olive oil	1/4 cup/60 mL
Red wine	8 fl oz/240 mL
Brown beef stock	32 fl oz/960 mL
Demi-glace	2 cups/480 mL
Standard sachet d'epices, with a pinch of oregano	1/1

METHOD

1. In a large flat pan, combine all marinade ingredients; whisk together thoroughly to combine. Place meat into marinade and turn to coat, massaging the mixture into the meat. Cover with plastic wrap and place in refrigerator for 12–24 hours.
2. Remove meat from the marinade and lay flat. Spread bread crumbs evenly over one side of the steak. On top of the breadcrumbs, evenly layer the corn niblets, carrots, onions, spinach, and cilantro and season with salt and pepper.
3. Carefully roll the steak, making sure to keep all of the stuffing ingredients inside; then, using butcher's string, tie 5–6 knots to keep the roll in place. Start knots on ends of steak to prevent stuffing from seeping out.
4. In a rondeau or heavy-bottomed pot, heat oil over medium-high heat. Add the rolled steak and cook, turning occasionally, until well browned on all sides, about 8–10 minutes.
5. Remove the rolled steak from the pan, and reduce heat to medium. Add the wine and, using a wooden spoon, scrape all of the browned bits. Add the stock, demi-glace, sachet, and rolled steak into the pot. Cover and braise for about an hour over medium-low heat or until fork-tender.
6. Remove the steak and continue to cook the liquid until reduced, degreasing the liquid as necessary.
7. Slice the rolled steak about 1-inch thick and serve with the sauce.

FIGURE **9.1** Beef Matambre.

BEEF FAJITAS

Fajitas were traditionally made from skirt steaks, which are slightly tough but very flavorful, but many other cuts can be substituted instead. Sirloin end pieces, flank steak, tri-tips, sirloin flaps, flat iron (top blade) steaks, and other, less-expensive cuts can be used for fajitas.

Many chefs will trim tenderloins for large functions and catered events. The *chains* or long side muscles are often ground or discarded. If cleaned properly, they make a quality small grilling steak. Each chain can yield one or two portions.

YIELD: 10 SERVINGS

Beef tenderloin side muscle chain; clean and trim all silverskin and fat and pound slightly to an even thickness	6 8-oz pieces/6 227-g pieces

MARINADE

Chili powder	1 Tbsp/15 mL
Cumin, ground	1 tsp/5 mL
Coriander, ground	1/2 tsp/2.5 mL
Coarse sea salt	1 tsp/5 mL
Freshly ground black pepper	1 tsp/5 mL
Garlic cloves, finely chopped	2/2
Canola *or* olive oil	1 Tbsp/15 mL
Lime, juiced	1/2/1/2
Tortillas	

(Continues)

ACCOMPANIMENT OPTIONS

Salsa verde
Chopped avocado
Chopped jalapeño
Grilled poblano peppers
Sour cream

METHOD

1. In a large, wide dish, combine all marinade ingredients; whisk together thoroughly to combine. Add beef pieces and turn to coat. Cover with plastic wrap and let stand 4–6 hours.
2. Heat a grill pan or gas or charcoal grill over high heat. Grill the steaks, about 2–3 minutes on each side (depending on thickness) until cooked to medium rare.
3. Let the meat stand for a couple of minutes and then, on a bias, slice the meat about 1/4-inch thick.
4. Heat the tortillas briefly on the grill and top each with about 4–5 slices of steak. Top with desired accompaniments and roll.

SOUTHERN CALIFORNIA BEEF TRI-TIP SANDWICH

This sliced steak sandwich is a classic use for the tri-tip. The tri-tip is a quality cut, but there are numerous other cuts that could be used instead, such as the top round cap, sirloin flap, top sirloin cap, striploin "end" steak, flank steak, hanger steak, chuck "flat iron" steak, shoulder tender, or "teres major" steak. If using a lower-quality cut, a Jaccard knife could be helpful to slightly tenderize the meat.

The tri-tip sandwich is served with thick barbecue sauce and often it can be sliced and put on a section of crusty baguette.

YIELD: 8 SERVINGS

Beef Tri-Tip	1 1/2–2 1/2 lbs/680 g–1.13 kg

DRY RUB

Freshly cracked black pepper	1 Tbsp/15 mL
Garlic cloves, finely chopped	2/2
Dry mustard	1 tsp/5 mL
Paprika	1 tsp/5 mL
Cayenne pepper	1/4 tsp/1.25 mL
Salt	1 tsp/5 mL

SAUCE

Olive oil	1 Tbsp/15 mL
Red onion, finely chopped	1/2 cup/120 mL
Garlic, minced	1 tsp/5 mL
Chicken or beef stock	1/2 cup/120 mL
Ketchup	1/4 cup/60 mL

(Continues)

Red wine vinegar	2 Tbsp/30 mL
Parsley, finely chopped	1 Tbsp/15 mL
Worcestershire sauce	1 Tbsp/15 mL
Ground coffee	1 1/2 tsp/7.5 mL
Freshly ground black pepper	1/4 tsp/1.25 mL
Baguette	1/1

METHOD

1. In a small dish, combine all dry rub ingredients and stir to combine. Lay the meat down in a large, wide dish and liberally rub and massage the dry mixture on both sides of the meat. Cover with plastic wrap and allow the meat to stand 3–5 hours before grilling.

2. Meanwhile, in a saucepan, heat the olive oil over medium heat. Add the onion and garlic and cook until slightly brown, about 10 minutes. Add the stock, ketchup, vinegar, parsley, Worcestershire sauce, coffee, and black pepper, stirring to combine. Bring the mixture to a boil and then reduce the heat to medium-low; allow to simmer, stirring occasionally until the mixture has reduced to 1/4 cup, about 10 minutes. Allow to cool slightly and then puree the sauce in a food processor or blender until smooth. Reheat the sauce slightly before serving.

3. Heat a grill pan or gas or charcoal grill over high heat. Grill the tri-tip for about 6–8 minutes, turning occasionally until well browned on all sides and crust forms. Reduce the heat of the grill and allow the meat to cook until the internal temperature reaches 135°F/57°C for medium-rare, about 15 minutes. Allow the meat to rest for 5 minutes before slicing very thin on a bias across the grain, about 1/4-inch.

4. Cut the baguette into 4-inch pieces and cut open each side to create a sandwich. Lay out about 5–6 slices of beef onto each baguette and add a spoonful of the warmed sauce on top.

ANCHO RUBBED ROASTED BEEF CHUCK EYE ROLL

The chuck eye roll is actually an extension of the rib eye muscle. As it extends into the front of the carcass, it toughens and separates into multiple muscles. The cut is very flavorful but requires a long, slow cooking method. If slow roasted, it provides a flavor that rivals any cut on the carcass.

YIELD: 6 SERVINGS

Beef Chuck Eye Roll	3–4 lbs/1.36–1.81 kg

RUB

Freshly ground black pepper	2 Tbsp/30 mL
Ancho chile powder	1 Tbsp/15 mL
Worcestershire sauce	4 tsp/20 mL
Olive oil	1 Tbsp/15 mL
Oregano	2 tsp/10 mL
Salt	1 tsp/5 mL
Cumin, ground	1 tsp/5 mL
Red pepper flakes	1/2 tsp/2.5 mL
Garlic cloves, minced	4/4

METHOD

1. In a large bowl, combine all rub ingredients and stir to combine. Add the chuck roll, and turn to coat in the mixture, massaging the spices into the meat. Cover with plastic wrap and let stand for 1–3 hours.
2. Heat oven to 450°F/230°C. Using butcher's string, tie about 5–6 knots on roast to maintain shape (be sure not to tie roast before applying spice mix to guarantee spices get deep into meat).
3. Place the roast on a rack in a pan and cook for 20 minutes. Lower the oven's temperature to 300°F/150°C and continue to cook for 1 1/2 hours. Remove the meat and let stand 10 minutes before carving.

BEEF CHURRASCO

Beef churrasco is a traditional grilled South American dish. It can be made with any number of different flat cuts of beef. Typically reserved for skirt or flank steak, it is also possible to use the lesser-known sirloin flap. The sirloin flap is a slightly tough cut that can be ideal for churrasco. The steak-like cut is basted with a salt and garlic mixture during the cooking.

Originating from Portugal, but now found throughout South and Central America, churrasco is prepared in a number of different regional styles. Argentine churrasco is served with a chimichurri herb sauce. Brazilian churrasco is an Asado-style dish, skewered and cooked next to hot coals. In Nicaragua, the steak is marinated in the chimichurra before cooking.

Alternative cuts: Sirloin flap, tri-tip, skirt steak, hanger steak, flank steak, top round cap, flat iron steak

Beef sirloin flap, pounded thin or split flat 2–3 lbs/907g–1.1.36 kg

(Using a Jaccard knife can increase tenderness and allow for marinade to get deeper into meat).

SALT BASTE
Kosher salt	2 Tbsp/30 mL
Hot water	1 cup/240 mL
Garlic cloves, minced	2/2

CHIMICHURRI SAUCE
White vinegar	1/4 cup/60 mL
Extra-virgin olive oil	2 Tbsp/30 mL
Salt	1/2 tsp/2.5 mL
Garlic cloves, whole	6/6
Jalapeño peppers, stems removed, minced	2/2

(Continues)

Parsley, finely chopped	1 cup/240 mL
Cilantro	1/4 cup/60 mL
Oregano, finely chopped	1/4 cup/60 mL

METHOD

1. In a large bowl, dissolve the salt in the hot water. Add garlic. Heat a grill pan or a gas or charcoal grill over high heat. Grill the sirloin flap for a few minutes on each side until the meat browns and char starts to form. Brush the salt baste on the meat, allowing it to dry. Brush on the baste 2–3 more times, turning meat with each baste. Allow the meat to reheat between each basting, as this forms a type of salty crust. Do *not* marinate meat in baste before cooking. Grill the meat to medium, approximately 10–15 minutes depending on thickness.

2. In a large bowl, combine all ingredients for chimichurri sauce or combine in a food processor and pulse a few times for a finer mixture. If too spicy, reduce the amount of jalapeño or use a milder pepper, such as habañero. Serve with meat, sliced or whole as a large portion. (Some recipes allow steak to marinate in chimichurri for 2–3 hours before cooking.)

FIGURE **9.2** Beef churrasco.

GERMAN BEEF ROULADE

Beef roulade is made from the top round, which is sliced into flat cutlets, stuffed, and rolled. There are many other cuts that can be used, if cut correctly. Any of the cuts from the round, except the shank, can be cut for roulade. Butterflied cuts of sirloin and tri-tip can be used. The "chain" from a beef tenderloin works very well. Boneless short ribs, thin sliced shoulder, or flat iron cuts will work as well. Be sure to select solid cuts that do not have many collagen bands.

YIELD: 6–7 PORTIONS

Beef slices, approximately 4 × 6 in, 1/4-inch thick 3 lbs/1.36 kg (Approximately 12–14 slices)

(It is best to cut slices thin from the start as opposed to attempting to pound a thick cut. Pounding should only be done to create an even surface.)

German spicy prepared mustard	2 1/2 Tbsp/38 mL
Bacon, diced small	3 oz/85 g
Onions, chopped	1 1/2 cups
Dill pickle, chopped	2/3 cup/160 mL
Flour	1/2 cup/120 mL
Beef brown stock	2 1/2 cups/600 mL
Salt	as needed/as needed
Freshly ground black pepper	as needed/as needed

METHOD
1. Pound meat to an even thickness and spread ___ t__. of mustard on each slice.
2. In a large skillet, cook bacon and onions over medium heat until brown; pour off excess fat, reserving 1/2 cup. Add pickle and remaining mustard to skillet and cook for a minute longer

(Continues)

to combine flavors. Spread mixture over meat, and gently roll up, folding in the corners to prevent leaking. Using butcher's string, tie several knots on each roast to help keep shape.

3. Heat oven to 325°F/163°C. In a large skillet, rondeau, or Griswold, heat the reserved bacon fat over medium-high heat. Add the beef rolls and brown well on all sides, about 8–10 minutes.

4. Transfer the beef rolls into a baking dish or heavy dutch oven. Stir the flour into the remaining fat in the skillet until smooth, working to scrape up any browned bits, and then gradually stir in the beef broth. Place over medium heat, and cook until thickened, stirring occasionally. Pour the sauce over the beef rolls and bake for 1 1/2 hours or until fork tender.

5. Remove the rolls and set aside. Remove any excess fat from the sauce, strain, and season with salt and pepper as needed. Serve with meat.

Note: Beef roulade is traditionally served with spaetzle noodles or dumplings. Roulade recipes are flexible and many variations of ingredients can be included.

FIGURE **9.3** German beef roulade.

BEEF SATAY SKEWERS

Satays are an excellent way to convert moderately tender beef cuts into profitable appetizers. Recipes for satays often request cuts from the top round, flank steak, skirt steak, or top sirloin, but other tender cuts will work well. The cleaned tenderloin chain is perfect for this dish but be sure to remove all silverskin.

Tenderloin chains, cleaned, cut into 8–10 pieces, pounded to 1/4-inch even strips (tenderloin chains can vary in size, but generally weigh between 1/4 to 1/2 pound/113 to 227 g each, once cleaned) 4–5 ea

SKEWERS

MARINADE

Lemongrass, minced	1/4 cup/60 mL (peel away exterior layers, chop off bulb and dry ends)
Small onion, quartered	1/1
Garlic, coarsely chopped	2/2
Ginger, chopped	1 Tbsp/15 mL
Tumeric, ground	1/2 tsp/2.5 mL
Coriander, ground	1 Tbsp/15 mL
Cumin, ground	2 tsp/10 mL
Soy sauce, dark	3 Tbsp/45 mL
Fish sauce	3 Tbsp/45 mL
Brown sugar	3 Tbsp/45 mL
Fresh lime juice	1 Tbsp/15 mL

(Continues)

METHOD

1. In a large bowl, combine all marinade ingredients, stirring well to combine. Add meat, turn to coat, cover with plastic, and let stand under refrigeration for 4–5 hours (overnight is okay, but it can overpower the meat).
2. Skewer the meat by weaving the stick in and out of the strip.
3. Heat a grill pan or gas or charcoal grill over high heat. Grill the meat, turning often, for about 10 minutes.

Note: Satays are traditionally served with dipping sauces, such as peanut sauce.

FIGURE **9.4** Beef satay skewers.

BEEF CARBONNADE

Beef carbonnade is a very flavorful braise that can utilize a variety of beef cuts. It is best to choose cuts that have a fair amount of collagen connective tissues, which provide flavor. Using an overly lean piece can result in a "dry" texture.

Suggested cuts are beef shoulder clod steaks, top-blade steaks (cut across grain), striploin end steaks, and sectioned chuck roll steaks (eliminate large, fatty sections). Cuts from the round can be used also, but tend to be dry. If using round cuts, be sure to use highly marbled pieces, such as those from prime graded beef.

It may make sense to tie each steak to keep a uniform shape during the braise.

YIELD: 6 SERVINGS

Beef braising steaks, 8 oz/227 g each, about 11 1/2-inches thick	3 lbs/1.36 kg
Vegetable oil	4 Tbsp/60 mL, divided
All-purpose flour	as needed/as needed
Onions, large, sliced	3/3
Garlic cloves, large, sliced	3/3
Beef or veal stock	16 fl oz/480 mL
Dark beer	12 fl oz/360 mL
Dried thyme, crumbled	1/2 tsp/2.5 mL
Salt	as needed/as needed
Pepper	as needed/as needed
Buttered egg noodles (alternatives: spaetzle noodles, Czech bread dumplings)	as needed/as needed
Parsley, chopped	as needed/as needed

(Continues)

METHOD

1. Heat one tablespoon of oil (or enough to thinly coat the bottom of pan) in a large skillet or rondeau over medium-high heat. Place the flour in a shallow wide dish, and dredge the beef in the flour, shaking off any excess. Add 3–4 of the beefsteaks to the hot skillet and cook until beef is brown on both sides, turning occasionally, about 6 minutes. Transfer the meat to a large dutch oven. Repeat process until all meat is cooked, adding more oil as needed per batch.

2. Reduce heat to low and add remaining oil to skillet. Add the onions and garlic and cook, stirring occasionally, until onions are golden brown and tender, about 20 minutes. Transfer onion mixture to dutch oven.

3. Add broth, beer, and thyme to beef mixture. Cover and simmer over medium-low heat until beef is fork-tender, approximately 1 hour 45 minutes.

4. Remove the beef from the liquid and set aside. Continue to cook the liquid, uncovered, until it reduces to a sauce-like consistency. (This dish can be prepared ahead of time and re-heated. Use caution when handling tender cooked steaks; they sometimes fall apart.) Garnish with parsley.

Veal Recipes

The veal breast is generally undervalued and most purveyors are happy to sell it a reasonable price. Some products such as veal bacon or brisket are available, but veal breast is a good buy and should remain so for years to come.

YIELD: APPROXIMATELY 6 SERVINGS

Veal Breast, boned, cut with pocket	3–4 lb./1.36–1.81 kg
Bacon strips	3/3
Veal trimmings, ground	1/2 lb/227 g
Onion, medium, chopped	1/2 cup/120 mL
Soft breadcrumbs	1 cup/240 mL
Sour cream	1 cup/240 mL
Egg, beaten	1/1
Parsley, chopped	1/4 cup/60 mL
Chives	1/2 tsp/2.5 mL
Salt	1/2 tsp/2.5 mL
Tarragon, crushed	1/2 tsp/2.5 mL
Basil, crushed	1/2 tsp/2.5 mL
Pepper	**Pinch Pinch**
Vegetable oil	3 Tbsp/45 mL
Cornstarch	1 Tbsp/15 mL
Brown veal stock	6 fl oz/180 mL
Sour cream	1/4 cup/60 mL
Dill weed, dried	1 tsp/5 mL
Olive oil	2 Tbsp/30 mL

(Continues)

METHOD

1. Heat oven to 325°F/163°C. Heat a 12-inch skillet over medium-high heat. Add bacon, and brown until crisp. Remove and drain. Crumble bacon and reserve.
2. Heat the same skillet over medium-heat and cook ground veal and onion until tender. Remove from heat and drain off excess fat. Stir in crumbled bacon, breadcrumbs, 1/3 cup sour cream, egg, parsley, chives, salt, tarragon, basil, and pepper, mixing well to combine.
3. Carefully spoon the stuffing into the pocket of the veal breast. Close the meat with skewers, and then, using butcher's string, tie several knots to hold the meat securely shut.
4. In a large dutch oven, heat 2 tablespoons of oil over medium-high heat. Brown the meat well on all sides, about 8–10 minutes; drain. Transfer the meat to a roast pan, cover, and place in oven for 2–2 1/2 hours, basting occasionally with pan drippings.
5. Transfer meat to a warm platter, remove the skewers, and cover the meat.
6. If necessary, strain the drippings and return to the pan. In a separate bowl, combine the cornstarch and the brown veal stock. Stir in the remaining sour cream and then add this mixture to the pan. Place dutch oven over medium-high heat and cook, stirring occasionally, until the mixture is thickened and bubbly.
7. Untie the roast and slice the meat. Serve with the finished sauce.

FIGURE **9.5** Stuffed breast of veal.

BRAISED VEAL SHORT RIBS

Veal short ribs are cut from either the veal breast or veal chuck. They are typically sold as 4-bone short ribs weighing about 12 oz to 1 lb/340 to 454 g each section. Veal short ribs tend to be leaner than those from beef and can be cooked like Osso Buco.

Veal short ribs	12–4 bone-in 1 1/2-inch sections (about 3/4 lb/340 g each)
Salt	as needed/as needed
Freshly ground black pepper	as needed/as needed
All-purpose flour	1 cup/240 mL
Canola or olive oil	1/2 cup/120 mL
Pancetta or salt pork, chopped	1/4 cup/60 mL
Onions, diced	1 cup/240 mL
Celery, diced	1 cup/240 mL
Carrots, diced	2 cups/480 mL
Garlic cloves, chopped	6-8/6-8
Bouquet garni (1 bay leaf, pinch thyme, a few black peppercorns)	1/1
White wine	20 fl oz/600 mL
Veal stock	96 fl oz/2.88 L

(Continues)

METHOD

1. Heat the oil in a large, heavy braising pot over medium-high heat. Season the short ribs with salt and pepper and then dredge in flour, especially on the meaty side of the ribs. Brown the ribs on all sides, about 8–10 minutes. Remove the ribs and reserve. Reduce the heat to medium and add the salt pork or pancetta, diced onions, celery, carrots, and garlic and cook until light golden brown. Add the wine and stir to deglaze the pan, making sure to scrape up any browned bits. Return the short ribs to the pot, add the stock and the bouquet garni, and bring mixture to a boil. Reduce the heat to a simmer and cover. Cook for about 1–2 hours, until very tender. Season with salt and pepper. Strain the braising liquid and thicken if desired.

FIGURE **9.6** Braised veal short ribs.

GRILLED VEAL FLANK STEAK ADOBO STYLE

The veal flank steak is a flat, thin piece that is excellent grilled and sliced. It works well over salad dishes or as an inexpensive grilling café or bistro menu item. Flank steaks weigh around 8 oz/241 g each and can be used as an individual portion, but it would be advisable to slice it across the grain and on a bias to increase tenderness.

Veal flank steak, 6–10 pieces about 8 oz/241 g each

MARINADE

Orange juice	1/2 cup/120 mL
Lime juice	1/4 cup/60 mL
Garlic cloves, chopped	4/4
Chile flakes	1 tsp/5 mL
Salt	1/2 tsp/2.5 mL
Oregano	1 Tbsp/15 mL
Olive oil	2 Tbsp/30 mL

METHOD

1. In a large bowl, combine all ingredients for marinade; stir well to combine. Add veal flank steaks and turn to coat. Cover with plastic wrap and let stand for 3–6 hours.
2. Heat a grill pan or gas or charcoal grill over medium-high heat. Grill steaks until medium doneness, about 3–4 minutes on each side. (Overly rare veal tends to be unappealing.) Let stand 3–4 minutes before slicing across the grain on a bias.

Pork Recipes

BROWN PORK STOCK

Roasted pork bones	8 lbs/3.63 kg
Cold water	6 qts/5.76 L
Basic mirepoix (equal parts carrots, onions, celery, roasted until lightly brown)	1 lb/454 g
Sachet d'Espices (bundled parsley, thyme, bay leaf, peppercorns, garlic clove)	1/1
Salt	as needed/as needed

METHOD

1. Simmer the roasted bones in water for about 3–4 hours. Add in the roasted mirepoix, sachet, and salt; simmer for 1–2 hours on low.
2. Strain the stock and chill properly or use immediately.

FRESH HAM STEAMSHIP ROAST

YIELD: SERVES 20–40, DEPENDING ON THE THICKNESS OF THE SLICES

The fresh ham or uncured pork hind leg remains a very reasonable purchase. The difficulty is in marketing it. The acceptance of "roast pork ham" may not sound appealing on the menu. For catering, we often see carving stations where the meat is cut to order in front of the customer. An idea of how to sell the inexpensive fresh ham and offer a new idea for a carving station would be to sell a pork steamship roast. A steamship is traditionally a beef item where the entire round is roasted. The shank meat portion is cut away, leaving a Frenched exposed bone. The pelvic bone is also removed for easy carving. On the pork steamship, the skin is removed again for easy carving. Some chefs choose to brine the meat before roasting to ensure a moist product.

Large, fresh ham, skin removed, leaving some skin on exterior, shank end Frenched off, pelvic bone removed	13–17 lbs/5.9–7.7 kg

BASIC ENHANCEMENT BRINE

Water	1 gal/3.84 L
Salt 1 lb/454 g	
Sugar	1 lb/454 g
Garlic cloves, cut into slivers	4/4
Salt as needed/as needed	
Pepper	as needed/as needed
Caraway seeds (optional)	1 tsp/5 mL

(Continues)

BASIC MIREPOIX

Onions, chopped	2 cup/480 mL
Carrots, chopped	1 cup/240 mL
Celery, chopped	1 cup/240 mL
Bay leaves	2/2
Water or brown pork stock	16 fl oz/480 mL
Dry white wine	8 fl oz/240 mL

METHOD

1. In a container large enough to hold the ham leg, mix together all the brine ingredients until dissolved.
2. Submerge the ham and let stand under refrigeration for 24 hours. Using a brine pump may decrease the brining time or increase moisture level.
3. Rub salt, pepper, caraway seeds into exterior, poke small holes into fat and stick in garlic slivers.
4. Place the brined ham on a rack, standing up so the shank is upward. Roast for a total of 4 hours at 300°F/149°C, or until an internal temperature of 160°F/71°C is reached. At about 2 hours, add mirepoix and bay leaves into bottom of pan. Once the vegetables caramelize (half hour), add the liquids to the pan. If the liquid evaporates away, keep adding extra stock or water to make a rich brown sauce.
5. Remove roast from pan, let stand 10 minutes before carving.
6. Strain the roasted mirepoix and pan juices, or *jus,* through a chinoise; reduce if necessary. Add salt and pepper as needed.
7. Slice 1/4 inch/6 mm thick slices. Serve slices with a touch of the jus.

BARBEQUE PULLED PORK

Pulled pork is prepared a number of different ways around the country. There is no one way that is the signature. The one main goal is to start with fresh pork shoulder and end with shredded, very tender pork that can be eaten on a roll. Usually there are some sweet and sour flavors added, but again, there are many ways to prepare it. Brining the pork before cooking is typical and can enhance moisture and flavor.

INGREDIENTS

Pork Shoulder (Full shoulder, Boston butt, or picnic), bone in 10–12 lbs/4.54 kg–5.44 kg

BRINE MARINADE

Garlic cloves, chopped	4/4
Cider vinegar	12 fl oz/360 mL
Water	64 fl oz/1.92 L
Salt	10 oz/284 g
Molasses	3/4 cup/180 mL
Onions, medium, chopped	2/2
Bay leaves	2/2

BRAISING SAUCE

Canola oil	1/4 cup/60 mL
Onions, chopped	2/2
Tomato paste	1/4 cup/60 mL
Brown pork stock (can use beef also)	32 fl oz/960 mL
Salt	as needed/as needed
Pepper	as needed/as needed

(Continues)

BARBEQUE SAUCE

Cider or malt vinegar	4 fl oz/120 mL
Prepared ketchup	1/4 cup/60 mL
Molasses	1 Tbsp/15 mL
Hot sauce (More can be added if desired)	2 Tbsp/30 mL

METHOD

1. Mix the brine ingredients together thoroughly and soak meat for 24 hours under refrigeration. Remove the pork shoulder and place in a barbecue cooker/smoker. Charcoal can be used, but for the best flavor, use hickory or apple wood coals.

2. Cook over low heat for about 3–4 hours, until deep tan in color.

3. In the meantime, heat oil in a braising pan and brown the onions. Place the smoked pork in the pan with all the braising ingredients, cover, and cook on medium-low heat until meat peels easily off the bone (another 3–4 hours). Add more stock if needed.

4. Once fully cooked, remove the meat from braising liquid and add in barbecue sauce ingredients. Reduce the liquid to sauce consistency. The barbecue sauce should be tangy and sweet.

5. Shred the pork in large bowl. Add in enough barbecue sauce to make it juicy. Serve on rolls with coleslaw or re-heat in a covered pan and hold until needed. The pulled pork can be chilled in this state and re-heated the next day.

APPLEJACK CURED BRAISED PORK BELLY

Fresh raw pork belly (skinless)	5–6 lbs/2.23–2.72 kg
Applejack	2 oz/60 mL
Whole grain prepared mustard	2 Tbsp/30 mL
Fresh thyme	2 Tbsp/30 mL
Salt	2 Tbsp/30 mL
Fresh ground black pepper	1 Tbsp/15 mL
Garlic cloves, chopped fine	6/6
Brown pork stock	32 fl oz/960 mL
Carrots, medium, chopped	4/4
Onions, medium, chopped	2/2
Celery stalks, chopped	6/6

METHOD

1. Cure the pork belly by rubbing it with the applejack, mustard, thyme, salt, pepper, and gar-lic. Cover and press with a weight if possible. Let the meat cure under refrigeration for about 48 hours.

2. Place the pork belly in a flat pan and cover thoroughly with 12 ounces/360 mL of stock. Add the chopped carrots, onion, and celery. Cover and braise in the oven for 4 to 5 hours or until tender.

3. Remove the pan from the oven and chill. Remove the top layer of fat from the braising liquid. Remove the meat from the liquid, which is now a jelly-like consistency. Cut into 1 by 4 in. chunk portions.

4. Heat the oven to 450°F/232°C.

5. Warm the braising liquid and strain the sauce over the meat. Place the meat and the sauce in a pan and let cook in the oven, uncovered, periodically basting the sauce over the meat, until it develops a slightly crusty glaze. Portions can be heated individually or all together.

Note: Typically served over braised vegetables or cabbage. Also served in smaller portions as a side dish with other meats.

BULK BREAKFAST SAUSAGE

YIELD: 40 4 oz/113 g PATTIES

Making any pork sausage is a profitable way to utilize usable trim or inexpensive pork cuts. As a rule, most fresh pork sausage is made with a fat-to-lean ratio of 30% fat to 70% lean. Some cuts of pork, such as the Boston butt, achieve this ratio naturally. Any pork trim can be used, but it is always necessary to determine the fat-to-lean ratio. Breakfast sausage is a very basic variety that can easily be made in any kitchen that has a grinder attachment for a mixer. Once produced, it can be made into breakfast patties, stuffed into casings for links, or used as an ingredient in a variety of other recipes. There are literally hundreds of sausage recipes that can be derived from this basic process by adding or changing ingredients. English bangers, German bratwurst, and French strasbourger sausage are similar in techniques but different in flavor because of the spices used. Feel free to experiment and make your own signature sausage.

This recipe utilizes a brand-name product, Bells Poultry Seasoning. There are other poultry seasonings out there, and many chefs have their own seasoning that they have created. One of the key ingredients in Bell's is sage. If substituting another poultry seasoning, be sure to add some rubbed sage to the mix.

Another key to making sausage is to keep the meat cold. Chilling all the parts of the grinder and keeping the trimmings cold throughout will ensure a quality mix. Sausage is like pie dough, where it can change if mixed warm. The fat can separate from the lean, making the sausage very dry.

INGREDIENTS

Lean pork trim	7 lbs/3.18 kg
Fat pork trim cut into 1-in cubes	3 lbs/1.36 kg
(If using fat back for fat trim, reduce to 2.5 lbs/1.13 kg and increase lean to 7.5 lbs/3.4 kg)	
Salt	3 oz/85 g
White pepper	1/2 oz/14 g

(Continues)

Bells Poultry Seasoning	1/2 oz/14 g
Ice cold water (or 1 lb/454 g of crushed ice)	2 cups 480 mL

METHOD

1. Carefully weigh seasonings and mix together dry ingredients. Mix fat and lean trimmings and sprinkle spices over, mixing thoroughly. Let stand under refrigeration for 10 minutes.
2. Grind through medium coarse die, 1/4-in/6 mm, and mix lightly.
3. Grind again through 1/8–in/3mm die, making sure meat moves through grinder rapidly.
4. Mix sausage using paddle attachment for about 1 minute, adding ice cold water gradually. Mixing can be done by hand but gloves should be worn primarily due to the stickiness involved. (An alternative is to add ice during the second grind instead of cold water. This ensures the grinding process stays cold. Be sure the grinder attachment can handle grinding ice.)
5. Once mixed, perform a taste test on a small patty by pan searing. Sausage should be a little tangy with a peppery aftertaste, which goes well with pancakes and sweet syrup.
6. Form patties into circular shape about 1/2-inch/1 cm thick, weighing 4 oz/113 g. Store covered on parchment or wax paper. Yield will be about 40 4 oz/113 g portions. Will hold for about three or four days.

Note: If stuffing the sausage into casings, do so right after the grinding and mixing segment. Do not wait to stuff or meat will "set up" or stiffen in about three hours, making the process more difficult.

FIGURE **9.7** Bulk breakfast sausage.

PINCHOS MORUNOS

YIELD: 24–30 SMALL SKEWERS

This traditional spicy Spanish dish evolved when the Christian populations adapted Moorish Muslim seasonings typically used on lamb to pork. The Spanish often use the famous Iberico pork for this recipe, which is very distinct and matches the full-flavored spicing. *Pincho* translates as "little thorn" or "little pointed stick," so *pincho moruno* roughly translates as "a small skewer of pork." Today, we see the *pinchitos* or *pinchos* on tapas menus.

Pork shoulder cushion meat, completely trimmed, removing all fat and connectives, cut into 1-inch/3 cm cubes (some recipes call for tenderloin, but this can often result in a dry product) 4 lbs/1.81 kg

Olive oil	3/4 cup/180 mL
Cumin, ground	3 Tbsp/45 mL
Coriander, ground	2 Tbsp/30 mL
Sweet Spanish paprika	2 Tbsp/30 mL
Hot pepper flake	2 tsp/10 mL
Turmeric, ground	1 tsp/5 mL
Oregano, dried	1 Tbsp/15 mL
Sea salt	as needed/as needed
Freshly ground black pepper	1 tsp/5 mL
Minced garlic	1/4 cup/60 mL
Fresh flat-leaf parsley, chopped	1/4 cup/60 mL
Fresh lemon juice	1/4 cup/60 mL
Lemon wedges for garnish	

(Continues)

METHOD

1. Mix the olive oil, cumin, coriander, paprika, cayenne pepper, turmeric, oregano, salt, and black pepper together in a mixing bowl.
2. Rub the pork cubes with the spice mixture. Combine the garlic, parsley, and lemon juice in a mixing bowl and add the pork cubes. Toss well. Cover and refrigerate overnight.
3. Soak small wooden skewers. Place 4 pork cubes on each skewer. Grill over medium heat, turning skewers often until cooked through and golden brown, about 7–10 minutes.
4. Transfer the skewers to a platter and serve with lemon wedges.

FIGURE **9.8** Pinchos Morunos.

PANCETTA

Pancetta is used as a flavor agent in many dishes. This dry-cured pork belly is relatively simple to make but caution must be taken when curing any item. Be sure to follow sanitation rules and do not use as a raw product, even though pancetta is sometimes consumed "as is" in Italy. This recipe uses a nitrite product called Insta Cure. Be sure to measure this ingredient accurately and do not ingest in any raw form.

INGREDIENTS

Skinless pork belly	10–12 lbs/4.54–5.44 kg
Kosher or sea salt	8 oz/227 g
Insta Cure #1	2 tsp/10 mL
Dextrose (brown sugar can be a substitute)	1 oz/28 g
Garlic cloves, smashed	8/8
Rosemary	2 Tbsp/30 mL
Ground mace	2 tsp/10 mL
Coriander, ground	1 Tbsp/15 mL
Juniper berries, crushed	1 oz/28 g
Ground white pepper	1/2 oz/14 g
Coarse ground black pepper	1 oz/28 g

METHOD

1. Mix the ingredients together and thoroughly rub onto the belly. Place the belly in a flat pan with a heavy weight on top. Refrigerate for 3 days.
2. Remove the weight and re-massage the belly with any salt that was not absorbed. The belly will start to lose liquid. A slight sprinkle of extra salt over any off-color areas will ensure an even cure.

(Continues)

3. Replace the weight and store for another 4–5 days. Remove the belly and rinse off any exterior salt. Let the belly air dry on a rack until tacky.

4. Roll the belly into a log shape. Tie it very tightly with slipknots every inch/1 cm and hang under refrigeration in low humidity for about 20–25 days. (Ideally, pancetta should hang at around 50°F/10°C, but many health departments may not allow it.) If mold occurs during hanging, wipe the exterior with a small amount of vinegar.

5. To use, slice the pancetta thin and pan fry like bacon or cut into strips. Unused portion can remain hanging for weeks. Do not wrap in plastic or it may turn moist and develop mold.

Lamb Recipes

SYRAH BRAISED LAMB SHOULDER

Most of the value in lamb is located in the racks and loin cuts. These cuts, although very high quality and popular, present some difficulties when considering profit margins. There are thousands of recipes for the "middle meat" cuts; highlighting the shoulder cuts, leg, and breast sections are much less expensive and, therefore, this publication will focus on recipes for those cuts.

YIELD: 8 SERVINGS

The complex rich flavor of a Syrah wine is a great complement to the robust flavor of lamb. The shoulder, if boned with extra fat and sinews removed, can be a quality braise item. If purchasing a whole bone–in shoulder and boning it out, the bones are excellent for making the lamb broth needed for this recipe. A bone–in shoulder weighs about 8 lbs/3.63 kg.

INGREDIENTS

Lamb shoulder, boneless and well trimmed, tied into solid roast 1 in/1 cm spacing. (Can be divided into two roasts.)	4–5 lbs/1.81–2.27 kg
Cumin, ground	2 Tbsp/30 mL
Olive oil	2 Tbsp/30 mL
Cracked black pepper	1 Tbsp/15 mL
Thyme	2 Tbsp/30 mL
Salt	1 1/2 tsp/7.5 mL
Syrah red wine	16 fl oz/480 mL
Lamb broth (can be made from bones from shoulder if purchased that way)	32 fl oz/960 mL
Bay leaves	2/2

(Continues)

METHOD

1. Whisk together the olive oil and spices (except bay leaves) in bowl. Place the lamb roast into the spices and coat thoroughly.
2. Preheat a heavy-bottomed pot over medium-high heat and sear the roast until brown on all sides, about 10–15 minutes. Reduce the heat and add the wine, broth, and bay leaves. Cover and cook in 325°F/163°C oven for about 3 hours or until fork tender. (If using a divided shoulder, cooking time will be reduced.)
3. Remove the roast from liquid and reduce, skimming excess fat and bay leaves. Adjust with salt as needed. Slice the meat and serve with the sauce.

Note: Wild rice pilaf is a nice side dish.

MOROCCAN-STYLE LAMB STEW

YIELD: ABOUT 12 PORTIONS

Lamb recipes from many North African countries feature strong spices, such as coriander. The flavor of lamb is well suited for these flavors. If purchasing bone-in items, the bones can be utilized to make the broth in this recipe.

Boneless, trimmed lamb shoulder, shank, or tougher leg pieces cut into 1 1/2 in /4 cm cubes 5 lbs/2.27 kg

Cumin, ground	2 Tbsp/30 mL
Coriander, ground	1 Tbsp/15 mL
Salt	2 tsp/10 mL
Fennel seeds, toasted slightly	2 tsp/10 mL
Cayenne pepper	1/2 tsp/2.5 mL
Ground black pepper	1 tsp/5 mL
Olive oil, divided	6 Tbsp/90 mL
Onions, medium, finely chopped	3/3
Tomato paste	2 Tbsp/30 mL
Lamb broth	1 qt/960 mL
Chickpeas, soaked or precooked	2 cups/480 mL
Dried apricots	2 cups/480 mL
Plum tomatoes, large, chopped	3/3
Cinnamon sticks	2/2
Fresh ginger, peeled, minced	1 Tbsp/15 mL
Lemon zest, packed	2 tsp/10 mL
Fresh cilantro, chopped (optional)	3 Tbsp/45 mL

(Continues)

METHOD

1. Mix the dry spice ingredients in bowl (except cinnamon). Add the lamb and coat thoroughly.
2. Heat the oil in heavy large rondeau over medium-high heat. Add the lamb and cook until browned on all sides. It may be necessary to cook lamb cubes in smaller batches to achieve browning. Remove the lamb and reserve.
3. Reduce to medium heat. Add the onion and tomato paste and sauté for about 5 minutes, until tender.
4. Add the broth, chickpeas, apricots, tomatoes, cinnamon sticks, ginger, and lemon zest and bring to boil, scraping up any drippings from the bottom of the pan. Return the lamb to the pan.
5. Reduce heat to low, cover, and simmer until lamb is just tender, about 1 hour.
6. Uncover and simmer until sauce thickens, about 20 minutes. Season with salt and pepper as needed. Portion and sprinkle with cilantro (optional).

FIGURE **9.9** Moroccan-style lamb stew.

SPICY JERKED LAMB RIBLETS WITH RUM BARBECUE SAUCE

YIELD: 6 SERVINGS

Lamb breasts are similar to pork spare ribs. They usually have a fair amount of fat on the exterior, which needs to be trimmed away. There is also a brisket bone structure that can be trimmed away, creating what is known as the Denver-style rib. Denver ribs can be purchased pre-trimmed but are more expensive.

Lamb breasts trimmed, brisket bones removed (Denver ribs), trimmed of heavy fat cover	6 ea/6 ea

RUM BARBECUE SAUCE

Butter, unsalted	1 Tbsp 15 mL
Onion, medium, chopped	1/1
Garlic, chopped	1 Tbsp/15 mL
Chili powder	2 Tbsp/30 mL
Jalapeño pepper, chopped	1 Tbsp/15 mL
Dark rum	2 fl oz/60 mL
Worcestershire sauce	3 fl oz/90 mL
Tomato paste	4 oz/113 g
Cider vinegar	2 fl oz/60 mL

JERK SEASONING RUB

Garlic cloves, mashed to paste	4/4
Kosher salt	2 Tbsp/30 mL
Brown sugar	2 Tbsp/30 mL
Curry powder	1 Tbsp/15 mL
Thyme	1 Tbsp/15 mL
Fresh ginger, grated	1 Tbsp/15 mL
Crushed red pepper	1 Tbsp/15 mL

(Continues)

Dry ground mustard	2 tsp/10 mL
Black pepper	1 Tbsp/15 mL
Allspice	1 tsp/5 mL
Cinnamon	1 tsp/5 mL
Cayenne pepper	1 tsp/5 mL

METHOD

1. To make the Rum Barbecue Sauce, heat the butter in a pan, add the onions and garlic, and sauté until slightly browned.
2. Add the chili powder and jalapeño peppers and sauté until slightly soft. Add in Worcestershire sauce, tomato paste, vinegar, brown sugar, and rum. Cook over low heat and reduce until thickened.
3. Mix together all seasonings for the Jerk Seasoning Rub.
4. Rub the spice mix thoroughly into the lamb. Cook over charcoal or char-grill on medium-high heat for about 10 minutes, turning often until thoroughly browned. Be cautious not to allow too much flaring, as lamb fat will ignite easier than other fats.
5. Remove from the grill and place on rack in a pan. Brush the ribs with barbecue sauce and place in 325°F/163°C oven for about 2 hours or until meat pulls away from bones easily. Brush the ribs with the barbecue sauce as needed to develop a nice glaze. The ribs can be served whole as a single portion or cut into individual ribs.
6. Offal Recipes

Offal Recipes

SMOKED BEEF TONGUE REUBEN SANDWICH

This recipe uses the concept that beef tongue, smoked and cooked, can be sliced like any cold cut. Smoked beef tongue requires a long, slow cooking time, but then can be stored cold for days, similar to a ham or corned beef.

Smoked beef tongue, large (about 3–4 lbs/1.36 kg–1.81 kg)	1/1
Bay leaves	1/1
Garlic cloves	4/4
Black peppercorns	8–10/8–10
Sauerkraut	1 lb/454 g
Emmenthaler Swiss cheese, sliced thinly	1 lb/454 g
Large crusty rye bread (with or without seeds)	12 slices/12 slices
Salted butter, slightly softened	1/4 cup/60 mL

RUSSIAN DRESSING

Ketchup	1/2 cup/120 mL
Mayonnaise	1/2 cup/120 mL
Dill pickle, finely chopped	1 1/2 Tbsp/23 mL
Worcestershire sauce	1/4 tsp/1.25 mL
Mixed together well	

METHOD

1. In a large pot, place the tongue, bay leaves, garlic, and peppercorns. Cover with water until tongue is submerged. Place on lid and bring to a boil; reduce heat and simmer for 2 1/2 to 3 hours. Tongue should become fork tender and exterior skin should peel easily.

(Continues)

2. Remove tongue and let stand until cool enough to handle. Peel away the exterior skin and any fat or tough sections on the underside. Tongue can now be sliced or stored cold until needed.

3. For slicing, use a sharp slicer or scimitar and slice thinly, starting from the thick end. Ideally, if the tongue is chilled, it can be sliced thin on an electric slicer. If slices are too thick, sandwich may be tough.

4. Lay out bread and butter one side of each piece. For each sandwich, place two slices of buttered bread down on clean surface; spread a small amount of Russian dressing evenly over each slice. On one slice, lay out about 4–8 oz/113–227 g of sliced tongue, top with sauerkraut, and then a few slices of Swiss cheese. Top with the other slice of buttered bread with the buttered side facing up.

5. Place the sandwich on a medium-high heated flat griddle and grill until the cheese starts to melt and the bread is a deep golden brown on both sides, about 10–12 minutes. Starting with warm meat and sauerkraut will speed the process. Cut the sandwich and serve with salads or BEER!

VARIATIONS
Use horseradish mustard instead of Russian dressing.
Leave the sandwich open face and grill the bottom; then place under broiler to crisp the Swiss.
Use Gruyere cheese instead of the milder Swiss.

FIGURE **9.11** Smoked Beef Tongue Reuben Sandwich.

VEAL SWEETBREADS SAUTÉED WITH WILD MUSHROOMS

YIELD: 6 SERVINGS

FOR SWEETBREADS

Canola oil	2 Tbsp/30 mL
Veal sweetbreads, blanched, peeled, and pressed overnight	6 3-oz pieces/85-g pieces
Plain breadcrumbs	1 cup/240 mL
Salt	as needed/as needed
Pepper	as needed/as needed

FOR MUSHROOMS

Brown veal stock	8 fl oz/240 mL
Sherry vinegar	1/4 tsp/1.25 mL
Shallot, peeled and minced	1/1
Chanterelle mushrooms, sliced	1/4 cup/60 mL
Maitake mushrooms, sliced	1/4 cup/60 mL
Black trumpet mushrooms, sliced	1/4 cup/60 mL
Olive oil (can use truffle-infused oil for more flavor)	2 Tbsp/30 mL
Parsley, chopped	2 Tbsp/30 mL
Butter	2 Tbsp/30 mL
Salt	as needed/as needed
Pepper	as needed/as needed

(Continues)

PREPARATIONS

1. For the sweetbreads, heat the canola oil over medium-high heat. Coat the sweetbreads with breadcrumbs. Season and sear the sweetbreads on both sides until golden brown. Remove from the heat, lightly pat dry with paper towel, and set aside in warm oven.

2. For the mushrooms, heat the olive oil in a sauté pan and sauté the shallots until softened. Add the mushrooms and sauté for 1–2 minutes. Add the veal stock and sherry vinegar, salt, and pepper. Simmer for 3–4 minutes.

3. Using a slotted spoon, remove the mushrooms and reserve in bowl. Reduce the stock for about 15–20 minutes until thickened. Reduce heat, add butter, and reintroduce the mushrooms. Stir lightly.

4. Position the sweetbreads on plate with sauce.

Note: Can be served as entrée or appetizer.

READINGS AND RESOURCES

The Meat Buyer's Guide: Meat, Beef, Pork,
Lamb and Veal
by North American Meat Processors Association,
Wiley, 2006

The Art of the Cold Kitchen,
Garde Manger, CIA, Wiley

Field Guide to Meat,
Aliza Green, Quirk Books, Philadelphia, PA
Copyright 2005

The History of Meat Trading,
Derrick Rixson, Nottingham University Press,
Copyright 2000

Meat Cuts and Muscle Foods,
Howard J. Swatland, Nottingham University Press,
Copyright 2004

The Meat We Eat, 14th Edition,
John R. R. Romans, William J. Costello,
Wendell C. Carlson
Prentice Hall, 2000

The Complete Meat Cookbook: A Juicy and
Authoritative Guide to Selecting, Seasoning, and
Cooking Today's Beef, Pork, Lamb, and Veal,
Bruce Aidells, Denis Kelly
Houghton Mifflin Company, 2001

Web Sites:

United States Department of Agriculture
http://www.fsis.usda.gov

Oklahoma State breeds site
http://www.ansi.okstate.edu/breeds/cattle//

National Pork Producer's Council
http://www.nppc.org/index.php

University of Nebraska, beef and pork sites
http://bovine.unl.edu/
http://porcine.unl.edu/porcine2005/pages/index.jsp

National Cattlemen's Beef Association
http://www.beefusa.org/

American Sheep Industry Association
http://www.sheepusa.org/

Broken Arrow Ranch, Game Purveyor
http://www.brokenarrowranch.com

Meat–Poultry Magazine
http://www.meatpoultry.com

GLOSSARY

aging—The holding of meat under controlled temperature and atmospheric conditions to improve palatability. Natural enzymes, called proteases, degrade the muscle fibers from within, increasing tenderness.

aerobic bacteria—Bacteria that need oxygen to live and reproduce.

aitch bone—Curved, exposed section of the pelvic bone that is attached to the top round.

anaerobic bacteria—Bacteria that can live and grow without oxygen.

antelope—Animal in the Cervidae family used for meat. Sometimes sold as *venison*.

antemortem—Before slaughter. First inspection done at this time.

A.P—(as purchased) Items of meat as received from the vendor, typically uncut or untrimmed. Refers to the raw material cost in a butcher's yield test.

aspic—Clear, edible jelly made from highly clarified and reduced stock. Used as a coating.

baby back ribs—Ribs from the loin section of the market hog. Smaller and more tender than spare ribs.

backstrap—Yellow elastin strip that is found along the spine and into the neck. Should be removed before cooking. Also refers to the loin eye muscle of venison.

bacon—Cured and smoked pork belly. Can be made from other cuts, such as jowl.

ball tip—Small steak cut from the bottom sirloin section of beef. Actually, an extension of the knuckle.

baron of beef—Whole round of beef with the shank Frenched and the aitch bone removed. Same as *steamship round*.

baseball steak—Center cut section of the top sirloin butt. Used for medallions.

baste—To add moisture while cooking. Deep basting is a term used for solution-injected meats.

belly—Wide, boneless area of the side of a hog; typically used for bacon or pancetta.

Berkshire—Heirloom English breed of hog known for superior-quality flavor and marbling.

binder—Products used to stabilize and texture processed meat items.

bison—American breed of buffalo; large bovine processed like beef.

blade bone—Scapula found in the shoulder.

blade meat—Meat lying over the rib eye muscle. Also known as the *deckle*.

block ready—Partially trimmed and ready to cut into portions, usually a bone-in item; also known as *chop ready*.

blown bag—Vacuum-pack bag that has lost its seal, minimizing shelf life.

bob veal—Veal from very young calves, less than one month old.

boning knife—Small (six inch or less) knife with a stout handle used for boning meat. May be flexible, semi flexible, or stiff. Has curved or straight blade.

Boston butt—Skinless top section of the pork shoulder.

boucher—French, butcher.

bouillon—Hearty broth made from meat and bones.

braise—Cooking method where meat is seared and then cooked in liquid to tenderize.

branded beef—Beef that has the name brand of the packing company attached. May indicate in-house grading beyond the USDA grade.

brochette—Meat cut into cubes and used for grilling on a skewer. Also known as *kabob* or *shashlik*.

broil—To cook with direct heat above or below the meat item.

B.R.T—(bone, rolled, and tied). Term used when ordering roasts.

buffalo—Large bovine animal; typically refers to American bison, but can be a variety of other species.

butterfly—To split open a roast, steak, chop, or cutlet and flatten to double its surface area.

butcher—1. A person with knowledge of all aspects of meat processing, from animal to finished portions. 2. In a kitchen, the person responsible for meat fabrication and all aspects of *mis en place* for meat items. 3. The act of slaughtering for meat.

calf—1. Young bovine offspring. 2. Classification of meat, differentiating from veal, being older, having a redder color, and larger in size.

Canadian bacon—Boneless, sliced, smoked pork loin.

cap meat—Meat off the top of the rib eye, blade meat, deckle.

caramelization—The result of browning meat, creating flavors by altering the proteins.

carcass—A slaughtered "dressed," eviscerated animal, unsplit.

casings—Cleaned intestines used for sausage stuffing.

center cut—The removal of the undesirable end pieces of a meat item to achieve a higher quality. Example: center cut pork loin.

chain—The long side muscle on the edge of the beef tenderloin.

charcuterie—1. The preservation of pork meat. 2. The curing of pork for ham, bacon, sausages, terrines, and other forcemeats.

chateaubriand—A center cut, trimmed piece of beef tenderloin, usually served for two.

chef's knife—An eight- to fourteen-inch long knife with a wide, thick blade, used for chopping, slicing, and mincing.

chicken steak—Steak cut by cross-cutting the top blade chuck. Contains a thick collagen band.

chine bone—The inside section of the backbone vertebrae along the loin and rib sections, often removed for easier cutting.

chop—An individual cut from the loin section of pork, veal, lamb, venison.

chop ready—Trimmed and ready to cut into chops with little effort.

collagen—Meat connective tissues, sinews, and cartilages that break down in a moist cooking method.

conformation—The amount of meat to bone on a carcass, evaluated when grading carcass.

coppa—Italian-style ham, dry cured from pork shoulder.

corned beef—Brisket or round cuts, salt cured and slow simmered.

country ham—Dry-cured southern-style smoked ham.

cowboy steak—A Frenched beef rib eye steak.

crown roast—The circular-shaped roast formed by frenching a rack section and tying it into shape. Typically, the center is stuffed.

Cryovac—Brand name of vacuum-packaging bags.

culotte muscle—Top cap on a beef top sirloin butt.

cure—To preserve by salting.

curing salt—A mixture of sodium chloride and sodium nitrite, used to accelerate curing, usually tinted pink to differentiate from regular salt.

deckle—Cap meat over the rib eye muscle.

delmonico steak—Typically a trimmed boneless rib eye steak; also a boneless striploin steak.

denuded—Meats completely trimmed and free of fat and connective tissues.

Denver ribs—Trimmed spare ribs of lamb.

diaphragm—Skirt steak, breathing support muscle on the inside of a carcass.

dressed—A cleaned carcass, without hide, hooves, or viscera.

dry aged—The process of aging meat, primarily beef and lamb, outside of a vacuum packaging bag, Primarily done to larger meat cuts with bone and fat coverage. Increases tenderness and flavor.

dry cured—The process of packing meat in salt to cure as opposed to brine curing. Increases the required time to cure the meat.

edible byproducts—Any edible organ meats, glands, fats, skin, or connectives.

elastin—Strong, yellow band of connective tissue that is located along the back and into the neck. Should be removed before cooking.

end steak—The tougher steak located on the sirloin end of a striploin, also known as "vein" steak.

enhanced—Term used to describe a water-based solution added to meat to increase moisture. Can include sodium phosphate.

evisceration—The process of removing the viscera or internal organs during the slaughter process.

export-style rib—Bone-in rib eye, trimmed with a measured lip of fat on its edge. Also known as *bone-in, lip on*. Purchased for fabricating bone-in steaks or standing rib roasts.

fabrication—The act of cutting meat; butchering.

fatback—The dense subcutaneous fat found along the back of a hog above the loin eye muscle.

feather bones—Part of the vertebrae structure, connected to chine bone, thin and flat.

feed lot—Contained animal feeding facility, used to fatten animals for market; feed yard.

fillets—Thin cut portions of meat, boneless.

filet mignon—A thick-cut portion of the beef tenderloin, denuded and ready to cook.

finished cattle—Cattle fattened for market, typically USDA graded after slaughter.

finger bones—Part of the lumbar vertebrae bone structure; connects to the chine bone.

finger meat—Meat found between the rib bones; intercostal meat.

FIFO—(first in, first out) Mantra used for rotating stock and product.

flanken—Portion cut beef short ribs about two inches in length.

flap—Sirloin flap steak.

flat iron—Steaks created from the top blade chuck cut after trimming all connective tissues.

flank steak—Flat steak found off the bottom of the beef loin.

foodservice cut—Any item produced by the meat industry that is cut and packaged for the intended use in a foodservice operation, as opposed to "retail" cut.

forequarter—Front quarter of a beef side from the twelfth rib on.

foresaddle—Front half of the lamb, veal, or venison carcass.

formula-/special-fed veal—Veal animals raised on a controlled diet, typically containing some milk byproducts.

free range—Animals that are allowed access to the outdoors while growing. Individual name brands may influence meaning.

Frenched—Exposing the end of the rib bone for presentation.

fresh—Purchasing terminology that describes meats that have never been cooked, cured, smoked, or canned.

fryer rabbit—Classification for young rabbit, typically weighing around three pounds.

FSIS—Food Safety and Inspection Service, a sector of the USDA.

gooseneck—Cut of meat containing the eye round, bottom round flat, and the heel.

gelatin—The result of cooking bones and skin in water and reducing to a highly thickened state. Becomes solid when chilled.

grain—The directional pattern in which muscle fibers are aligned; used when determining direction for cutting.

grass-fed—Animal finished on grass only; may be fed stored hay or silage in winter.

gross weight—The weight of the purchased item and its packaging.

HACCP—Hazard Analysis Critical Control Points, a system used in the meat industry to identify hazards and monitor food safety; mandatory for USDA-inspected facilities.

halal—Meat slaughtered and processed in accordance to Islamic law.

ham—Back leg of a hog; sold fresh, cured, or smoked.

haunch—Back leg of venison, from the sirloin on.

hanger steak—Section of the diaphragm where the two skirt steaks meet; only one per animal.

heel—Tough section of the gooseneck; also horseshoe.

hindquarter—Back section of a beef side, from the thirteenth rib on.

hind saddle—Back half of the lamb, veal, or venison carcass.

hip—Sirloin section, also beef round if in Canada.

hot carcass weight—Weight of the carcass directly after slaughter; used in evaluation and grading.

hotel rack—Primal rack, unsplit; from lamb or veal.

HRI (hotel, restaurant, and institution) cuts—Foodservice cuts; any cut typically purchased for a restaurant etc.; typically requires some minor fabrication.

in-house grading—The processor assesses quality and assigns labeling in accordance to its own standards; not USDA grading, which is a separate process.

inter-muscular fat—Fat between muscle groups, divides muscle sections.

intra-muscular fat—Marbling; fat within the lean muscle fibers, creating moisture and tenderness.

IQF (individually quick frozen)—Individually quick frozen; rapidly frozen portion-cut meat items.

Jaccard—Name brand of a popular meat tenderizing tool; uses multiple knives to break muscle fibers.

kabob—Cubes of meat for skewer, grilling, and broiling.

Kansas City strip steak—Bone-in striploin steak, sometimes boneless also.

kosher—Meats slaughtered and processed in accordance to Jewish law.

kurobuta—Japanese Berkshire-style hog, known for high marbling scores and darker color.

lamb—Young ovine animal; market term.

lard—Rendered fat from a hog; the act of wrapping fat over a roast.

leaf lard—Fat from the inside of a hog carcass; lumbar fat, very dry and good for rendering.

London broil—Any variety of thick cut steaks grilled or broiled and sliced thinly.

lumbar fat—The hard, crumbly fat from the lumbar region over the tenderloin; also known as *kidney fat*.

meat cutter—Assembly-line fabricator in the meat-processing industry. May be skilled in several aspects of meat cutting.

meat processor—Large or small meat fabrication facility; primarily a wholesale meat producer that cuts and packages a variety of meat items.

meat purveyor—A vendor of meat products; may or may not process meat in house.

marbling—Intramuscular fat, fat within the lean muscle; evaluated when grading; adds moisture and tenderness.

marinate—The process of tenderizing, adding moisture and flavor to a meat item by soaking, tumbling, or injecting. A form of enhancement.

market hog—Hog finished to market weight, 170 to 200 pounds, on average.

marrow—The soft, fat-laden interior of bones, used for flavoring and classic sauces.

medallion—Small, circular, even, meat portion cuts used for sauté or grill.

middle meat—Cuts from the loin or rib sections of beef, veal, lamb, or pork; usually high in value.

milk–fed veal—Fed a milk byproduct; same as *formula-fed veal*.

moist cooking method—Slow cooking meats with moisture; braising, stewing, slow poaching, steaming.

muscle profiling—Isolating individual muscles and evaluating them for palatability, taste, and tenderness.

mutton—Older, mature ovine animal, not suitable as lamb.

NAMP (North American Meat Processors)—An association of meat processor responsible for the meat buyers guide, which categorizes commercially produced meat cuts.

nature-fed veal—Same as *formula-fed veal*.

needled—Mechanical tenderization of meat item, pinned, Jaccard.

net weight—Weight of the purchased meat item, without packaging.

niche-market meats—Meat items that differ from the standard commercially produced meat items; may refer to breed, feeding style, cutting style, producers size, locality, or any other factor that may be considered "niche." Typically implies small-market item.

noisette—Veal or lamb medallions cut from the loin section.

pack date—Date the meat item was placed in the vacuum bag. Important spec when ordering.

pancetta—Italian style of curing the pork belly without smoking; used as flavor agent, typically rolled into tight spiral shape.

pasture–raised—Animals grown outdoors with access to pasture and forage.

papain—Enzyme found in papaya; used to tenderize meat.

peeled—Fat cover removed, sometimes denuded.

picnic—Bottom section of the pork shoulder, sold skin on unless specified.

petite tender—Small muscle found in the beef shoulder clod.

porterhouse—Cut created from the short loin, includes the tenderloin and strip loin together; typically the tenderloin must be at least one third of the entire steak.

postmortem—After slaughter; condition considered during meat inspection.

portion control/portion cuts—Individual, uniform, cut portions, ready to cook, requiring no fabrication.

primal cut—First, major cuts of a carcass, untrimmed and requiring further fabrication.

prime—Highest grade given to meat by the USDA.

prime rib—Refers to a cut of the beef rib eye. Does not indicate quality grading.

prosciutto—Italian dry cured ham allowed to age for months, developing unique flavors.

PSE (pale, soft, exudating)—Condition afflicting pork, making it watery, jello-like, and resulting in a dry product. Caused by stress and improper handling and also genetic susceptibility.

PSMO (peeled, side muscle on)—Beef tenderloin spec referring to the trim level and the long side muscle known as the "chain."

PSO (purchaser-specified options)—Refers to any number of available trim specs for items, including fat depth, length, bone length, etc.

purge—Meat juices that leak from meat while in vacuum packaging. Looks like blood in the bag; can indicate age of the product.

quality grade—The grade applied by the USDA that determines the palatability of a meat item; can assign value. Not a mandatory grade and is paid for by the purveyor.

roast ready—Trimmed rib eye with some fat on to aid in roasting.

RTE (ready to eat)—Precooked.

saddle—Unsplit loin section of lamb, veal, or venison.

sausage—Ground meat seasoned, mixed, and formed into casing or patty.

salumi—Any number of Italian cured meat items, including hams, pancetta, salami, and more.

sauté—Dry cooking method of pan searing thin cuts of meat in a shallow amount of oil or butter.

scotch tender—Cut from the chuck section of beef, resembles the tenderloin but not very tender; also known as the *mock tender*.

seasonality—The availability of meat items in certain seasons. Modern meat farming has eliminated most seasonality, but there are some items that increase in quality at certain times of the year. Can also refer to seasonal pricing of items.

sedentary muscle—Muscles that are not used frequently, resulting in tenderness. The tenderloin is a sedentary muscle.

serrano ham—Spanish-style dry cured ham, similar to the Italian prosciutto.

shell—A bone in striploin.

shortloin—The section of beef or veal containing the striploin and the tail section of the tenderloin, purchased to make porterhouse and t-bone steaks.

shoulder tender—Teres Major muscle in the shoulder clod, very tender.

sirloin—The hip section of the loin containing the top sirloin butt, tri-tip, sirloin flap, and ball tip; known also as *rump*.

smoked meat—Adding smoke to flavor and preserve meat items; there are three types: hot smoke, cold smoke, and smoke roasting.

sodium nitrate/nitrite—Caustic salt isolate used to rapidly cure meat by denaturing proteins; used mostly in diluted forms.

sodium phosphate—Used to help retain water in meats; ingredient found in many enhanced and cured products.

spring lamb—Young lamb, thirty to forty pounds on average; less than one year old.

SRM (specified risk material)—Parts of the animal considered dangerous for use, due to its ability to carry rogue prion proteins that can cause bovine spongiform encephalopathy.

steamship round—Whole primal leg with the pelvic bone removed and the shank bone frenched. Used for roasting whole and carving on a buffet.

St. Louis ribs—Trimmed spare ribs, missing the brisket bone section.

stifle joint—Knee joint.

subcutaneous fat—Fat directly under the skin; solid fat used for barding.

subprimal—Cuts created by dividing the primal; often sold as HRI cuts.

t-bone steak—Steak cut from the short loin, containing the striploin and a small section of the tenderloin.

TBS (top, bottom, sirloin) leg—Leg boned and divided into subprimals.

tournedos—Center cut tenderloin medallions.

tri-tip—Smallish cut from the sirloin, typically grilled whole and sliced.

USDA—United States Department of Agriculture, responsible for inspecting and grading meat.

vacuum packaging—A system for packaging meat in plastic and removing the air, minimizing spoilage.

value-added product—Meats that have been trimmed, seasoned, or pre-cooked to add extra value.

vein steak—End steak; the last one or two steaks from the sirloin side of the striploin, tougher, and with a collagen band that intersects in the middle.

venison—Meat from any animal in the Cervidae family; deer meat.

Warner Bratzler Shear Force Test—System for testing tenderness by cutting through a piece of meat and measuring the force required.

wet cured—Cured in a salt brine.

wet aged—Meat aged in a vacuum package; increases tenderness but does not affect flavor dramatically.

yield grade—Identifies the amount of salable meat or cutability in a carcass.

APPENDIX

MEAT PURCHASING

Once a foodservice operation decides on a meat menu item it has to purchase the cuts to create that dish. It is up to the purchaser to determine how the meat should be purchased depending on the ability of the kitchen staff. Some restaurants decide to forego all fabrication and buy pre-cut or even pre-cooked portions. These eliminate the labor and yield loss involved in producing the cut. The downside of this is that it limits the purchaser to those exacting cuts and does not allow for any flexibility on the menu. An example would be a restaurant that purchases an eight-ounce striploin steak. That chef is stuck with the eight ounces whereas a chef that purchases a full striploin can trim it to specs and cut an eight-, ten- or twelve-ounce steak from the same piece.

The goal of the purchaser, whether it's a chef, owner, purchasing agent or anyone responsible for buying, is to produce the least expensive portion with the highest quality product and stay within the proper food cost for the establishment. Being able to analyze the fabrication skills of the kitchen staff and also the general quantity that will be used will be crucial when deciding how to buy. What may work for one establishment may not for another.

Developing proper meat specs for purchasing, even if for pre-cut portions, is very important to the success of the establishment. The meat purveyor/vendor must understand clearly what is required by the restaurant so they can fill the order correctly. Also, the restaurant must have a clear understanding of what is acceptable and what must be rejected. The purchaser and the meat purveyor must have a good understanding about all the products that might be ordered. Most meat purveyors will provide a list of all the products they can provide. A foodservice establishment should also create a list of everything they might be ordering.

When buying meat first an establishment must decide who to buy from. The buyer may be purchasing for a variety of businesses. Most typical would be the restaurant. Also, hotels, resorts, cruise ships, casinos, catering services, retail stores, schools, institutions, military operations, and others all buy meat to be produced into portions. Restaurants can vary in size, cuisine, seasonality, and all sorts of restraints that may help dictate how the restaurant will buy its meat. A small establishment with a passionate highly trained chef may be able to buy large primal cuts and fabricate all portions in-house and utilize everything that comes with the cut. This place may even include this fact on its menu stating "all meats butchered on the premises" and use it in advertising.

On the other hand, a chef may choose to buy pre-cut portions to free up time to do more complicated foods such as desserts.

A high volume restaurant that has a minimally trained crew such as a chain type restaurant might not be able to fabricate in house and would need all the meat cutting to be done off site by the purveyor. These establishments will establish strict specs for their portions. Managers will need to check products to be sure specs are adhered to.

Many high volume restaurants will have contracted agreements to ensure a steady flow of product arrives consistently to the restaurant.

VENDOR TYPES

GENERAL FOODSERVICE PURVEYOR

This type of purveyor sells a huge variety of goods of which meat is just one part. Often the large purveyor has a large assortment of meat specs and quality grades. They feature most national brand name items and sell a large variety of pre-trimmed HRI and portion cuts. They often have a knowledgeable sales staff that can be helpful in ordering products. Often the general food purveyor is regionally or nationally owned and is part of a larger corporation. This enables the large purveyor to purchase products in huge quantity, therefore offering the best prices.

There are a few drawbacks of purchasing from a large purveyor. It may be that they have a minimum order. In other words, the restaurant would need to buy a minimum dollar amount that might be difficult for a smaller establishment to meet, especially in slower times of the year.

Also a delivery surcharge may be included. Many companies now charge a fuel surcharge. If your establishment is off the beaten path this charge may be substantial. Typically delivery will be once or twice a week by a large semi-trailer truck. Proper forecasting of usage is very important.

Large distributors use a catalog of items. It is very important for the purchaser to understand purchasing specs and check over orders as they delivered. There may be a charge for returned items.

MEAT PURVEYOR

The meat purveyor is more regional than the large foodservice distributor. They are typically long established smaller corporations, often second or third generation family owned. They may still fabricate some meat from whole primals and might be able to provide dry aged products. Often these establishments are USDA inspected and have their own brand names and labels that are not available anywhere else.

The true meat purveyor is focused on customer service. They will often deliver multiple times per week and will custom cut meat items outside the norm.

INDEX

PHOTO CREDITS